Regulatory Stewardship of Health Research

ELGAR STUDIES IN LAW AND REGULATION

Series Editor: Roger Brownsword, *Professor of Law, King's College London, UK*

Regulation is a ubiquitous concept in today's world. The proliferation of new technologies necessitates continual re-appraisal of the rules that govern them, whilst globalization increases the complexity of interaction between governance systems on a national, regional and international level. As a field of study, regulation continues to grow and evolve, both in consideration of specific sectors, and at a conceptual level, as the rationale and motivation for regulation are scrutinized.

This new and exciting series is an important forum for original works of scholarship that explore regulation and its interaction with the law. It favours work that has a critical, innovative or analytical perspective and, whilst having a primary focus on legal writing, welcomes approaches that draw on other disciplines. The scope of the series encompasses a wide range of regulatory fields, from biotechnology and ICT to machine learning and AI, from security, food, and environment to health, leisure, and employment. At the same time the series plays host to broader discussions on the nature of risk, governance models, the role of democracy, regulatory theory and many others.

The primary mission of the series is to stimulate the development of original thinking across law and regulation and to foster the best theoretical and empirical scholarship in the field.

Titles in the series include:

Regulatory Stewardship of Health Research

Navigating Participant Protection and Research Promotion

Edward S. Dove

School of Law, The University of Edinburgh, UK

ELGAR STUDIES IN LAW AND REGULATION

Cheltenham, UK • Northampton, MA, USA

Published by
Edward Elgar Publishing Limited
The Lypiatts
15 Lansdown Road
Cheltenham
Glos GL50 2JA
UK

Edward Elgar Publishing, Inc.
William Pratt House
9 Dewey Court
Northampton
Massachusetts 01060
USA

A catalogue record for this book
is available from the British Library

Library of Congress Control Number: 2019952431

This book is available electronically in the **Elgar**online
Law subject collection
DOI 10.4337/9781788975353

ISBN 978 1 78897 534 6 (cased)
ISBN 978 1 78897 535 3 (eBook)

Typeset by Columns Design XML Ltd, Reading

Printed and bound by CPI Group (UK) Ltd, Croydon, CR0 4YY

Contents

Acknowledgements

This research was conducted with the funding support of the Wellcome Trust, connected with a five-year Wellcome Senior Investigator Award entitled 'Confronting the Liminal Spaces of Health Research Regulation' (Award No: WT103360MA). I am grateful to Wellcome for their generosity and enthusiasm in supporting both my research and the research of the Liminal Spaces Project team, including its global dissemination through open access.

This book would not have been possible without the cooperation and gracious hospitality of the people whom I interviewed and observed over the course of a year. I thank each of them for their patience and forthrightness in sharing their insights and experiences with me. Undoubtedly, not all of the participants in my research will share the interpretation I place on my findings. Nonetheless, I trust that they are defensible and contribute to the debate about what research ethics committees (RECs) do in practice, and how to improve the regulatory framework for health research involving human participants.

I owe my gratitude to the authorities and individuals who helped assist in bringing my empirical investigation to fruition. This includes the Health Research Authority; Jo-Anne Robertson at the Research Governance and Quality Assurance Office of the University of Edinburgh; the staff at the Wellcome Library; the staff at the Archive and Museum Services of the Royal College of Physicians of London; and the transcription team at 1st Class Secretarial Services.

I would also like to acknowledge the excellent support I received from Edward Elgar Publishing in the preparation and completion of the book, in particular from Iram Satti, Saffron Watts, Stephanie Tytherleigh, Claire Greenwell, and Conor Byrne, and from Roger Brownsword, series editor of Elgar Studies in Law and Regulation. It has been much appreciated.

Heartfelt thanks go to my fellow Liminal Spaces Project team members (Nayha Sethi, Agomoni Ganguli-Mitra, Catriona McMillan, Annie Sorbie, Emily Postan) for their friendship and ongoing academic support. There are many mentors who have guided me before and during the writing of this book. In particular, I am deeply grateful for the mentorship and friendship of Bartha Knoppers, Barbara Prainsack, Mark Taylor, and David Townend. I am also grateful to Emma Cave, Emilie Cloatre, Sharon Cowan, and Shawn Harmon for their comments on an earlier draft of this book.

My principal 'academic steward', Graeme Laurie, deserves special thanks. A paragon among mentors, his dedication, guidance, patience, and good cheer sustained me throughout the research and writing of this book. Truly, I cannot ask for a better mentor, nor can I ask for a better friend.

Finally, and most importantly, I thank my sister, Sarah, and my parents, Ed and Jody, for their abiding love and invaluable support. As always, they helped me at every turn. It is to them that this book is dedicated.

Abbreviations

AMS	=	Academy of Medical Sciences
AWI	=	Adults with Incapacity (Scotland) Act 2000
BMJ	=	British Medical Journal
CIOMS	=	Council for International Organizations of Medical Sciences
COREC	=	Central Office for Research Ethics Committees
CSO	=	Chief Scientist Office (Scotland)
CTIMP	=	Clinical Trial of an Investigational Medicinal Product
GAfREC	=	Governance Arrangements for Research Ethics Committees
GMC	=	General Medical Council
HARP	=	HRA Assessment Review Portal
HCRW	=	Health and Care Research Wales
HFEA	=	Human Fertilisation and Embryology Authority
HRA	=	Health Research Authority
HSC	=	Health and Social Care in Northern Ireland
HTA	=	Human Tissue Authority
IRAS	=	Integrated Research Application System
IRB	=	Institutional Review Board
LREC	=	Local Research Ethics Committee
MHRA	=	Medicines and Healthcare products Regulatory Agency
MRC	=	Medical Research Council
MREC	=	Multi-site Research Ethics Committee
NHS	=	National Health Service
NIH	=	National Institutes of Health
NIHR	=	National Institute for Health Research
NPSA	=	National Patient Safety Agency

NREAP	=	National Research and Ethics Advisors' Panel
NRES	=	National Research Ethics Service
NRS	=	NHS Research Scotland
OECD	=	Organisation for Economic Co-operation and Development
OREC	=	Office for Research Ethics Committees
ORECNI	=	Office for Research Ethics Committees Northern Ireland
PIS	=	Participant Information Sheet
PRS	=	Proportionate Review Service
QA/QI	=	Quality Assurance/Quality Improvement
RCP	=	Royal College of Physicians of London
REB	=	Research Ethics Board
REC	=	Research Ethics Committee
REC SOPs	=	Standard Operating Procedures for Research Ethics Committees
RED	=	Research Ethics Database
RES	=	Research Ethics Service
RGF	=	Research Governance Framework for Health and Social Care
R&D	=	Research and Development
ShED	=	Shared Ethical Debate
SOP	=	Standard Operating Procedures
SSA	=	Site-Specific Assessment
UKECA	=	United Kingdom Ethics Committee Authority
WHO	=	World Health Organization

1. Introduction

I. THE AIMS OF THIS BOOK

Research ethics committees (RECs) occupy a critical position in health research governance. In the United Kingdom (UK), 86 National Health Service (NHS) RECs review approximately 6000 research applications each year[1] that seek to involve potential research participants who are in the NHS system. One of the tasks of NHS RECs is to ensure 'that any anticipated risks, burdens or intrusions will be minimized for the people taking part in the research and are justified by the expected benefits for the participants or for science and society'.[2] Through their discretionary power to modify or reject an applicant's research design, RECs can impact what knowledge is produced and can significantly affect the relationship between researchers and research participants.

In this book, I am interested in the roles and practices of RECs in light of recently implemented health research regulation in the UK that explicitly seeks to promote health research in the country, in part by streamlining regulation itself. It is unclear how these recent regulatory changes, stressing efficiency and maximization of UK competitiveness for health research as well as maximization of return from investment in the UK, may affect the substantive and procedural workings of RECs. It is also unknown whether the modification of research regulation at the level of legal architecture to promote research—seen, for example, in the Care Act 2014 and in the mandate of the Health Research Authority (HRA)—'trickles down' to the day-to-day practices of RECs, which the HRA is responsible for managing directly in England and indirectly across the UK.

---

[1] Health Research Authority, 'Research Ethics Committee Members Area' <www.hra.nhs.uk/about-us/committees-and-services/res-and-recs/research-ethics-committee-members-area/> accessed 11 October 2019.

[2] Health Research Authority, *Governance Arrangements for Research Ethics Committees: 2018 Edition* (Health Research Authority 2018) [colloquially known as and cited hereinafter as GAfREC] para 1.2.2.

More granularly, we lack good empirical understanding about how and why RECs make the decisions they do, and how the dynamics of RECs and central 'managing' regulators play into decisions in this evolving regulatory backdrop.[3] This book fills this lacuna by: (1) going inside RECs to ask and examine how they, as individual members and as a collective body, see themselves in a changing regulatory environment; and (2) going inside a managing regulator (the HRA) to gather perspectives on the roles of RECs and the relationship between the HRA and RECs, which in turn provides deeper understanding of the meta-level contributions of these entities as regulatory agents, both in their own right and in an interconnected way.

Thus, this book offers an original, empirical investigation of health research regulation and RECs, examining how these entities, designed to essentially give an ethical 'licence' to researchers, undertake ethics deliberation and work under the umbrella of regulation that is becoming more streamlined and research-promoting. The primary aim of this book is to provide both an original, critical understanding of what RECs and regulators actually do (and see themselves doing), and also to explain and understand the nature of health research regulation. The objective is to provide my intended audience of students, academics, lawyers, regulators, and policymakers a crucial contribution to understanding the roles RECs and members within them (and connected to them) play in regulating health research.

The research findings further offer normative assessments of RECs and health research regulation, thereby informing policy decisions. As I will argue, *regulatory stewardship* is a crucial concept that emerges from the empirical investigation and warrants consideration beyond the health research regulatory landscape. Indeed, a secondary aim of this book is to encourage a reimagining of 'regulatory spaces' if they are seen to be under-delivering in what they set out to achieve. Through theoretical insight and empirical investigation, I will suggest what regulation and regulators across a range of ecosystems—health and non-health—can do to stimulate meaningful research oversight without adding to any burden of pre-existing regulatory measures.

As we go to press, an example of this wider potential influence on regulation is provided by the UK Government in its white paper,

---

[3]   On this point, see e.g. Wellcome Trust, 'A Blueprint for Dynamic Oversight: How the UK Can Take a Global Lead in Emerging Science and Technologies' (2019) <https://wellcome.ac.uk/sites/default/files/blueprint-for-dynamic-oversight.pdf> accessed 11 October 2019.

Regulation for the Fourth Industrial Revolution.[4] In it, the Government sets out plans to transform the UK's regulatory system to support innovation, while protecting citizens and the environment. As part of this plan, it calls for the establishment of a 'digital Regulation Navigator' to help businesses 'find their way through the regulatory landscape and engage with the right regulators at the right time on their proposals'.[5] The concept of regulatory stewardship, as elucidated in this book, can help put platforms such as the Regulation Navigator on firmer policy footing.

In this book, I distinguish law from regulation. Both law and regulation are notoriously tricky to define, not the least because of cultural variation in ascribing meaning to phenomena that are 'legal' or 'regulatory'. I take law to mean a system of rules, codes, and pronouncements promulgated by state or state-like actors within a particular community (e.g. sub-national, national, international) with the aim of regulating the actions of its members and which it may enforce by the imposition of penalties. Examples of law include a statute and statutory instrument or a judgment from a court of law. By contrast, 'regulation is a broader category and includes much more flexible and innovative forms of social control'.[6] I define regulation as a set of rules, principles, mechanisms, strategies, or activities promulgated by state or non-state actors that either affect behaviour as an incidental effect or are designed to steer behaviour in a socially, politically, and/or economically desirable way. It may involve self-regulation, persuasion, and co-regulation. Thus, regulation is broader than law and can encompass anything from codes of practice of professional bodies to traffic lights and signs in a neighbourhood. My definition of regulation does *not* privilege the state; the state is simply one node among many actors sharing control of resources. In turn, law and regulation are components of governance, which refers to the constellation of actors and mechanisms that promulgate, implement, or enforce norms across sites of authority.

---

[4] UK Government, 'Regulation for the Fourth Industrial Revolution: White Paper' (2019) <www.gov.uk/government/publications/regulation-for-the-fourth-industrial-revolution> accessed 11 October 2019.

[5] ibid 24.

[6] Neil Gunningham and Cameron Holley, 'Next-Generation Environmental Regulation: Law, Regulation, and Governance' (2016) 12 Annual Review of Law and Social Science 273, 274.

II. ANTHROPOLOGY OF REGULATION

In my investigation, I employ an 'anthropology of regulation' methodology, influenced by regulatory theory and the anthropological concept of liminality. Liminality refers to a threshold phase in social transitions characterized by processual (temporal and spatial) dynamics.[7] Harnessing liminality as a sensitizing concept in an anthropology of health research regulation enables one to examine the ways in which practices, people, and entities are structured in and by regulation, and vice versa. The reasons for this choice of liminality—drawing our attention to processes and experiences of change in human dynamics—are explained more fully below and in Chapter 4.

As I argue in a later chapter, anthropology of regulation transcends the confines of a law-based approach by focusing on what happens within the regulatory spaces and under the layers of regulation across time. In health research, we find that regulation plays as much a crucial role as law. My research explores and explains—through documentary research comprised of historical tracing and present-day regulatory analysis that explicates the internal constitution of regulation, as well as through observation and interviews—the experiences and behaviours of specific individual actors in the health research regulatory space who govern the ethics of health research involving participants, namely RECs and their managing regulators. Anthropology of regulation allows me to investigate both the nature of regulation as a social form (an ontological concern), as well as what regulation does to actors and what actors do to regulation (a functional and experiential concern). Regulatory theory is necessary to help provide potential explanatory background; empirical research is equally necessary to help provide understanding of everyday practice. In essence, anthropology of regulation allows us to bring theory and practice meaningfully together by focusing on capturing the experiences of regulators in their multiple contexts.

III. STRUCTURE OF THE BOOK

This book comprises seven chapters. Following this introductory chapter, in Chapter 2, I offer an overview of the NHS REC system. I raise the question of whether the roles and practices of RECs are shifting in

---

[7]   Samuel Taylor-Alexander and others, 'Beyond Regulatory Compression: Confronting the Liminal Spaces of Health Research Regulation' (2016) 8 Law, Innovation and Technology 149, 150.

response to 'next-generation' regulation (particularly regarding research promotion), and whether modifications to the health research regulatory space at the levels of statutory law and central regulatory authorities 'trickle down' to the day-to-day practices of RECs. At the end of the chapter, I pose several questions that drive the empirical investigation.

Chapter 3 traces the regulatory development of RECs and health research regulation within the UK, with a view to demonstrating both the growth of health research regulation and the increasingly central role that RECs play in regulating health research. While, to a certain degree, research promotion has always been embedded in the regulatory techniques of RECs, it has not until now been instantiated in law with the creation of the HRA and rules promulgated under the Care Act 2014. The subsequent and fundamental research question to explore is whether this instantiation of research promotion in law has a (hitherto absent) trickle-down effect that impacts the day-to-day practices of RECs, and if so, how, or indeed, whether the law is only now coming to reflect an everyday practice that has long existed.

In Chapter 4, I explain the research approach, theoretical under-pinnings, and analytical concepts that drive the empirical investigation. I show how regulatory theory provides a solid but ultimately insufficient foundation on its own for the empirical investigation that informs this book. I argue that there is a need for an empirically grounded discussion of regulatory practice. I propose an anthropology of regulation that contributes to socio-legal studies by drawing explicit attention to pro-cesses, passages, and change. I further draw on the anthropological concept of liminality, which serves as a sensitizing concept in addition to concepts provided by regulatory theory. Together with regulatory theory, liminality helps us to better understand the nature of transformations of actors within the regulatory space, the form of regulation in this space, as well as the behaviours and experiences of actors as they go through processes of change. Those interested in the research methods undertaken for my empirical work and which define an anthropology of regulation may consult Appendix 1.

In Chapter 5, I engage with the empirical data collected from the interviews and observations and, coupled with the findings from the docu-ment analysis, make sense of them through an anthropology of regulation approach. Through investigation of three main themes (the 'black boxes' of ethics review; regulatory connectivity; and regulators as stewards), I explore what happens in REC meetings, consider the operationalization of 'next-generation' health research regulation (particularly in light of the twin aims of protection and promotion), and investigate the procedures and substance behind risk-based regulation. I do this by querying whether risk-based regulation is being practised by RECs and the HRA, and more fundamentally, by querying the nature and function of the interactions among RECs, researchers, and the HRA. Throughout, I draw on the implications of space and time in ethics review, signifying the contribution of liminality to the normative discussion to come in Chapter 6.

Chapter 6 then further unpacks the significance of liminality of RECs and the ability of actors within the health research regulatory space to serve as 'regulatory stewards'. I do so by suggesting a normative model of what a new regulatory framework for health research oversight ought to look like if it were to explicitly endorse regulatory stewardship. I also chart how participant protection and research promotion can and should work together. I conclude that a reformulated regulatory framework could work to improve regulatory conversations between actors, provide on-going opportunities for 'regulatory play' to emerge, and shift the burden and emphasis away from more procedural work and towards flexibility and experimentation in ethics review. What I suggest, in other words, is a refinement of the extant regulatory framework, not wholesale change.

The final Chapter 7 reflects on the data, discussion, and regulatory framework presented, and proposes future directions for research. In particular, I suggest the need to further develop and test a regulatory model for health research oversight in the UK that integrates regulatory stewardship and improves regulatory interactions between different stakeholders in health research.

Having laid out the aims of this book and mapped the structure, I now turn to provide a conceptual framework of RECs, setting the scene for 'protection' and 'promotion'.

2. Conceptual framework—setting the scene for 'protection' and 'promotion'

I. INTRODUCTION

Human health research, which can be defined as research into matters relating to people's physical or mental health, is a formalized, institutionalized, and regulated activity, replete with actors, rules, tools, policies, and diffuse sets of social constraints. Researchers who wish to gather data, investigate questions, test hypotheses, and build new generalizable knowledge on topics that involve human participants confront at the earliest stages of their project design the application of abstract ethical principles such as respect for persons, social value, beneficence, and justice, not to mention rules regarding informed consent and confidentiality. Additionally, researchers confront a panoply of law and regulation. When it comes to health research involving humans, determination of its ethical acceptability has taken a particularly regulated, technocratic, and structured form, with specific groups of individuals wielding power to decide whether a research project may proceed on ethical grounds. This group is known as a research ethics committee (REC), which is also known as an institutional review board (IRB) and research ethics board (REB).

This book will explore the mandate and operation of one particular type of REC in the UK, the NHS REC, drawing on both governance instruments and policies and original empirical research. This chapter begins the process by querying whether the practices of these RECs align with their recently established regulatory mandate—as set out in instruments promulgated by the UK government, devolved administrations, and regulatory bodies—which has modified the regulatory environment involving human health research. In particular, it explores a shift from a protectionist model that has been seen by some as paternalistic, with regulators disproportionately focusing on research risks in comparison to research benefits and inexplicably road-blocking otherwise ethical research, to a more broadly facilitative model, undergirded by law, that could be called 'next-generation' in that it seeks to foster an environment that both protects research participants *and also facilitates* responsible health research through proportionate risk-based regulation and coordinated alignment of ethics review and other regulatory processes. Seemingly invigorating a public interest aim of health research oversight—to promote valuable research that advances human health for the benefit of the public—this next-generation regulation has emerged most clearly in the last decade (through policies and guidelines) and is reflected most overtly in the statutory Care Act 2014 and in the body that exemplifies this new way of regulating health research—the HRA.

This chapter raises the question of whether the roles and practices of RECs are shifting in compliance with this next-generation regulation, which was driven foremost by persistent criticism from research communities (e.g. academic, industry) regarding the perceived clogged regulatory space of 'human subjects research'. As such, I query whether modifications to statutory law and central regulatory authorities 'trickle down' to the day-to-day practices of RECs.

To begin this exploration, I first provide an overview of the UK REC system.

II. AN OVERVIEW OF THE UK REC SYSTEM

RECs serve as gatekeepers of research involving humans. While the characterization of RECs as 'gatekeepers' is not uncontroversial,[1] I contend that they are gatekeepers in that they serve to control access to the potentiality of research involving humans, and as such occupy a central position in research governance. Governments around the world have delegated to RECs the authority to decide, through a regulatory 'event licensing'[2] system and in some cases on the pain of sanction,[3] whether or not any given proposed research project involving humans (or their data or tissue) is ethical and consequently appropriate to undertake or to continue. RECs are, therefore, 'discretionary bodies with the power to apply the principles of research ethics, and the rules relating to particular fields of experimentation on human subjects, to research

---

[1] See e.g. Nathan Emmerich, 'When Is a REC not a REC? When it Is a Gatekeeper' (2016) 12 Research Ethics 234.

[2] Carl Schneider, *The Censor's Hand: The Misregulation of Human-Subject Research* (MIT Press 2015) 33.

[3] See e.g. The Medicines for Human Use (Clinical Trials) Regulations 2004, regs 49, 52.

proposals and research in progress'.[4] Largely self-regulatory creations that first arose in the United States (US) in the mid-20th century in response to both research scandals and concerns about institutional liability (as explored in the next chapter), RECs have evolved from ad hoc, unstructured committees of peer reviewers in a few hospitals— fellow physicians or biomedical researchers assessing the ethical accept- ability of a proposed project—to institutionalized, regulated bodies of diverse members existing worldwide, prospectively reviewing, deciding upon, and, to a limited degree, monitoring the 'ethical acceptability'[5] of all types of research involving humans, from epidemiological or obser- vational studies to clinical trials. As the leading international ethics guideline on health research, the Declaration of Helsinki, states: 'The research protocol must be submitted for consideration, comment, guid- ance and approval to the concerned research ethics committee before the study begins.'[6] RECs regulate not just the ethical acceptability of health research, then. Because of their gatekeeping and monitoring role, they regulate very much the production and use of health research knowledge itself through *ex ante* control of which research is approved, which research questions can be asked, and how they may be answered.

The UK has a hybrid, and one might say uncoordinated, system of RECs. Some are institution-based. Others are location or region-based, and some are centralized, covering the whole country. Several different types of RECs exist. They can be split into two main categories of non-NHS RECs (e.g. higher education institution RECs) and NHS RECs. In this book, I address only the latter.

2.1 NHS RECs

NHS RECs, also known more formally as 'RECs within the UK Health Departments' Research Ethics Service' (RES), are region-based commit- tees. Officially overseeing a local health area within the NHS system, in

---

[4] Paul McNeill, *The Ethics and Politics of Human Experimentation* (CUP 1993) 205.

[5] See e.g. Council for International Organizations of Medical Sciences, *International Ethical Guidelines for Health-Related Research Involving Humans* (Council for International Organizations of Medical Sciences 2016), Guideline 23: 'All proposals to conduct health-related research involving humans must be submitted to a research ethics committee to determine whether they qualify for ethical review and to assess their ethical acceptability [...]' [hereinafter CIOMS Guidelines].

[6] World Medical Association, *Declaration of Helsinki* (World Medical Association 2013), para 23.

practice they operate within a centrally administered system that enables them to review research applications and provide an ethics opinion on health research involving humans in the NHS taking place anywhere in the UK. The Care Act 2014 defines an NHS REC as:

> *a group of persons which assesses the ethics of research involving individuals*; and the ways in which health or social care research might involve individuals include, for example—(a) by obtaining information from them; (b) by obtaining bodily tissue or fluid from them; (c) by using information, tissue or fluid obtained from them on a previous occasion; (d) by requiring them to undergo a test or other process (including xenotransplantation).[7]

Across the UK, 86 NHS RECs review approximately 6000 research applications each year that seek to involve potential research participants (including patients) who are in the NHS system.[8] There are 2 RECs in Northern Ireland; 7 in Wales; 11 in Scotland; and 66 in England (including the National Social Care REC in London). Formally existing since 1991 (but as will be discussed in Chapter 3, informally existing prior to this), they are committees of between 7 and 18 individuals (one-third of whom must be 'lay'[9]) who are independent of research sponsors,[10] funders, and investigators, and serve to opine on the ethical acceptability of research involving NHS staff, or patients and/or their tissue and data, among other kinds of health-related research.[11] Currently,

---

[7]   Care Act 2014, s 112(2) (emphasis added).

[8]   Health Research Authority, 'Performance Report 2018/19' <www.hra.nhs.uk/about-us/what-we-do/annual-report/annual-report-and-accounts-201819/performance-report/> accessed 15 October 2019.

[9]   The UK classifies REC members as either 'expert' or 'lay', the latter category meaning 'a mixture of people who reflect the currency of public opinion', and the former category meaning people who 'have relevant formal qualifications or professional experience that can help the REC understand particular aspects of research proposals' (i.e. physicians and other health care professionals). Lay members 'are people who are independent of care services, either as employees or in a non-executive role'. See GAfREC paras 1.2.2, 4.2.3. The HRA has decreed that half of the lay members must be 'lay plus' members, who are people who have never been care professionals, researchers in a care field, or chairs, members, or directors of care service bodies or organizations providing care.

[10]   Research sponsors are the organizations responsible for the management and conduct of the research.

[11]   GAfREC para 2.3.

there are over 150 staff members (e.g. REC Managers, HRA Regional Managers) and over 1000 volunteer members of NHS RECs across the UK.

Depending on where their REC is situated, NHS REC members are appointed by the HRA in England, the Business Services Organisation through the Office for Research Ethics Committees Northern Ireland (ORECNI) in Northern Ireland,[12] and the local Health Boards in Scotland and Wales.[13] Each REC has a Chair, a Vice Chair, and an Alternate Vice Chair, and is coordinated by a Manager (as well as an Assistant, who, along with REC Managers in England, may be responsible for several RECs).[14] Unlike in other countries, there is no requirement that a REC specifically include a lawyer, theologian, ethicist, patient advocate, or 'community member'.

Though only some kinds of health research must obtain prior REC approval under the law, institutional, journal, and regulatory policies confirm that few health research projects may proceed without an NHS REC receiving and reviewing the research protocol and attendant documents, and providing a positive (i.e. favourable) opinion. As the standard operating procedures (SOPs) for NHS RECs state: 'The policy of the UK Health Departments is that the operating procedures required by the EU Directive and the Clinical Trials Regulations should also apply in general to the review by RECs in the UK of all other health and social care research reviewed under GAfREC.'[15] A 2011 Academy of Medical Sciences (AMS) report also notes the wide reach of these RECs: 'Because positive opinion from a REC is required for all studies that take

---

[12] Office for Research Ethics Committees Northern Ireland <www.hsc business.hscni.net/orecni.htm> accessed 15 October 2019.

[13] Even though RECs in Scotland and Wales may cover more than one Health Board, or so-called 'regions' (e.g. the two RECs based in Edinburgh, known as South East Scotland REC 1 and 2, officially cover both NHS Lothian and NHS Borders, together known as the South East Scotland region in the NHS Research Scotland node), generally the bigger Health Board (in terms of resources) will make the appointment. As the GAfREC state, 'Where an NHS Scotland Health Board is not a REC appointing authority, they must contribute proportionately to the running costs of their NHS Research Scotland nodal research ethics service' (GAfREC 37).

[14] GAfREC para 4.2.13.

[15] Health Research Authority, *Standard Operating Procedures for Research Ethics Committees* (Version 7.4, Health Research Authority 2019) [hereinafter REC SOPs], Introduction.

place in the NHS, this review forms a core component of the regulation and governance pathway.'[16]

Common categories of NHS REC review include:

- Clinical Trials of an Investigational Medicinal Product (CTIMP), including NHS Phase 1 CTIMPs in healthy volunteers;
- research involving medical devices;
- qualitative health research involving participants identified in the context of, or in connection with, their past or present use of the NHS or social care services;
- health-related research involving children, adults lacking capacity, or prisoners; and
- the establishment of research tissue banks and research databases.

The research applicants who must submit a REC application would therefore include, for example, pharmaceutical and medical device companies; health care professionals in the NHS; academic researchers at higher education institutions (including postdocs and students); and prison health researchers. Thus, whether a researcher is conducting clinical, epidemiological, or even law and social science-driven health research, if the proposed project involves NHS patients or service users as participants, the researcher must apply for NHS ethics approval through application to a REC. A favourable opinion from a REC is not a licence to immediately begin research. Researchers must also obtain research governance permission (i.e. assessment of governance and legal compliance) from each relevant NHS management authority. In England and Wales, this is done centrally through HRA and Health and Care Research Wales (HCRW) Approval and applies to all project-based research taking place in the NHS in England and Wales. Projects led from Scotland or Northern Ireland must apply through the appropriate NHS/HSC permission process for the relevant lead nation.

As noted, a centralized attitude is taken to managing RECs in the UK, compared to a more 'devolved' institution-based approach seen in other jurisdictions such as Canada or the US. NHS RECs are overseen by central regulators, including the United Kingdom Ethics Committee Authority (UKECA) for those RECs 'recognized' to give an ethics opinion on a CTIMP. In England, RECs are overseen by the RES, a service under the auspices of the HRA, which itself is an arm's-length

---

[16] Academy of Medical Sciences, *A New Pathway for the Regulation and Governance of Health Research* (Academy of Medical Sciences 2011) 76.

body situated in England's Department of Health and Social Care. The HRA's RES operates five offices across England (London, Bristol, Nottingham, Manchester, and Newcastle), which in turn manage RECs more or less within their region. Each office is led by a RES Regional Manager.

There are equivalent RESs in the three other nations. In Scotland, the Health Boards function as the HRA equivalent, while four Scientific Officers and the Chief Scientist Office (CSO) function as the equivalent for the RES for RECs within NHS Scotland. (Much more will be said about these Scientific Officers in later chapters.) There are equivalent bodies in Northern Ireland (ORECNI) and Wales (Health and Care Research Wales Ethics Service), but as will be seen, in practice, the HRA through its RES has taken a leading (and coordinating) role for managing RECs throughout the UK, albeit to varying degrees and with varying degrees of success.

NHS RECs tend to convene once per month, up to 10 or 11 times per year, for a 'full committee' meeting that can run anywhere from two-and-a-half to five hours. The majority of the meeting time is spent reviewing new applications, which generally are capped at six per meeting (the norm is between four and six per meeting). In-between the monthly meetings, a smaller group of REC members discuss up to four new applications submitted for 'Proportionate Review', that is, applications submitted for a quicker review because they are said to raise 'no material ethical issues'). These discussions usually take place via emails or teleconference. A smaller group of REC members (usually led by the Chair) also meet each month outside the formal monthly meeting to discuss 'substantial amendments' submitted by researchers concerning their applications already approved by the REC. For full review, RECs are required to provide a final opinion within 60 calendar days of receipt of a valid application, and a provisional opinion within ten working days of the application's review at the meeting.[17] RECs are required to provide an opinion on a Proportionate Review application within 21 calendar days of receipt of a valid application.[18] Summaries of research and the

---

[17] GAfREC para 3.2.9. If the REC renders a 'provisional' opinion requesting further information, the 60-day (for a non-Proportionate Review application) or 21-day (for a Proportionate Review application) clock is suspended until the information is received.

[18] REC SOPS para 4.1.

REC opinion (including those that are unfavourable) are available on the HRA website approximately 90 days after the REC opinion.[19]

While NHS RECs handle a range of health research studies, there are in fact two broad categories of committees. First, some of these RECs are so-called 'recognized' RECs, that is, legally recognized by UKECA to give an ethics opinion on a CTIMP to be undertaken anywhere in the UK. These RECs may review CTIMPs of either 'Type 1' (healthy volunteers anywhere in the UK) or 'Type 3' (patients anywhere in the UK), or both. The second category of RECs are so-called 'authorized' RECs, which means that they are established under the Governance Arrangements for Research Ethics Committees (GAfREC), but are not recognized by UKECA, and therefore cannot review CTIMP applications. Since 2007, all NHS RECs are subject to an accreditation scheme now managed by the HRA. Some RECs also have specialist expertise (known as 'committee flags') in areas such as research involving children, research involving prisoners, the establishment of research tissue banks, qualitative research, or research involving adults lacking mental capacity. A smaller category of RECs has been recognized by UKECA for the review of gene therapy studies or stem cell clinical trials (currently four RECs have such recognition). Proposed research falling within any of these areas is steered towards RECs that are 'flagged' to review such research.

Having provided a brief overview of NHS RECs, I now turn to explore their roles.

III. THE ROLES OF RECs

As will be further explained in Chapter 3, RECs are not, by and large, creatures of statute. Rather, they were created informally by the UK health research community in the 1960s, foremost to ensure British researchers could continue to receive funding from the US federal government following that country's newly enacted policy of institutionalized IRB review.[20] RECs were also created, however, in response to private and public concerns about participants' safety in health research,

---

[19] Health Research Authority, 'Research Summaries' <www.hra.nhs.uk/planning-and-improving-research/application-summaries/research-summaries/> accessed 15 October 2019.

[20] Adam Hedgecoe, '"A Form of Practical Machinery": The Origins of Research Ethics Committees in the UK, 1967–1972' (2009) 53 Medical History 331.

and in response to general guidance from both the Royal College of Physicians of London and the Ministry (later Department) of Health encouraging their formation in every hospital.[21] Thus, RECs have developed through varying forms of non-statutory regulation, namely policy, guidelines, and custom. Even today, no UK law clearly defines the roles of RECs (other than a high-level statement found in, for example, the Clinical Trials Regulations 2004 or the Care Act 2014), nor their procedural and substantive aspects, nor their legal status. Instead, the roles must be inferred through statutes as well as through interpretation of policies and guidelines.

3.1 Primary Role: Participant Protection

RECs, and arguably some of their individual members as well, perform several roles. The primary role is to protect the health, welfare, and dignity of research participants. A REC does this by issuing a single, independent opinion of a research application, set within a regulatory framework and, more broadly, a legal architecture. To quote the GAfREC, RECs aim to ensure 'that any anticipated risks, burdens or intrusions will be minimised for the people taking part in the research and are justified by the expected benefits for the participants or for science and society'.[22] As the GAfREC further state emphatically: 'Whatever the research context, the interests of participants come first. Their dignity, rights, safety and well-being must be the primary consideration in any research proposal, as well as in REC review.'[23] In other words, a REC must act to safeguard research participants and minimize risk of harm to them. They do this by means of anticipatory avoidance— serving as independent watchdogs of projects and as gatekeepers of ethical conduct in research, rendering an opinion that seeks to avoid or at least mitigate any harm to participants.

This primary 'risk minimizing' or 'participant safeguarding' role is crucial to understanding the linkages between RECs, other health research regulators, researchers, participants, science, and society. RECs ostensibly engage in a variety of prospective inquiries, tests, and decision-making processes to determine whether a research project is 'ethical' and whether potential research participants are sufficiently

---

[21] McNeill, *Human Experimentation* (n 4) 66–7. See also Julia Neuberger, *Ethics and Health Care: The Role of Research Ethics Committees in the United Kingdom* (King's Fund Institute 1992) 9.

[22] GAfREC para 1.2.2.

[23] ibid para 3.2.1.

protected. This role has been constant, to varying degrees, in RECs since their creation and serves to assuage society that science will proceed in a responsible manner. This, then, can be seen as a variation of a public interest aim: the public has an interest in seeing its constituent members (specifically research participants, be they volunteering healthy individuals or patients) sufficiently safeguarded against harm from research endeavours. Undertaking this primary role also suggests that the process effectively results in an 'ethical covenant', whereby the REC must trust that, following their approval and the research that eventually gets underway, the researchers will proceed as they have promised to do. Indeed, as we will see, beyond the expectation of a filing by a researcher of the completion of an annual progress report and submitting any substantial amendments to the project, there is limited power for a REC to monitor researchers following initial approval of the project.[24] This suggests an unmet need by regulatory actors—be they RECs or others—to steward researchers as they move past the approval stage and through the research lifecycle.

3.2 Secondary Role(s): Research Promotion

Protection of research participants may be RECs' primary role, but crucially, they have also always performed secondary roles. One such role is a variation of the public interest aim: RECs have an obligation to society to facilitate ethical and socially valuable research. Similarly, RECs also have an obligation to researchers, namely through treating researchers' proposals with respect and due consideration and enabling their ethical research. If most forms of research are seen as a public good and a morally valuable activity that pursues knowledge and innovation serving humanity, RECs serve not just to protect research participants from being exploited, exposed to excessive risks, or injured; they also serve to evaluate research for its putative societal benefit alongside participant protection. So, in some sense—and as will be explored empirically in later chapters—RECs engage in a value weighting system of protection and promotion. This said, the GAfREC indicate that these roles are not equal, but rather secondary, even placing 'science and society' under a separate heading and below the heading 'protection of research participants':

---

[24] GAfREC paras 3.2.15–3.2.17.

Science and society

RECs act primarily in the interests of research participants. The interests of researchers and research *are always secondary* to the dignity, rights, safety and well-being of people taking part in research. RECs take into account the interests and safety of the researchers, as well as the public interest in reliable evidence affecting health and social care, and enable ethical and worthwhile research of benefit to participants or to science and society.[25]

Such a 'role hierarchy' or 'principle hierarchy', as it were, aligns with international statements on research ethics, including the European Union's (EU's) Good Practice Directive,[26] the Council of Europe's Convention for the Protection of Human Rights and Dignity of the Human Being (Oviedo Convention),[27] and the Declaration of Helsinki. This does not foreclose a proportionate or other kind of approach to account for the value of participant protection and the value of research. Indeed, no guidelines or regulations for RECs exhort them to have regard *solely* for the rights, interests, and welfare of participants. What it does suggest, though, is that the goals of research and the researcher, while important, should always be secondary to the dignity, rights, and well-being of the research participant.

IV. AMBIGUITY IN THE ROLE HIERARCHY

Despite the GAfREC's text, the role hierarchy of RECs in the UK has long been ambiguous. In 1984, for example, the Royal College of Physicians of London (RCP) issued a highly cited document, *Guidelines on the Practice of Ethics Committees in Medical Research* ('RCP Guidelines'), which served as a much-needed source of information and opinion on a range of matters concerning the procedures of RECs, with the aim of standardizing them. The objectives of RECs, according to the Guidelines, were 'to facilitate medical research in the interest of society,

---

25 GAfREC para 3.2.2 (emphasis added).

26 See Commission Directive 2005/28/EC of 8 April 2005 laying down principles and detailed guidelines for good clinical practice as regards investigational medicinal products for human use, as well as the requirements for authorization of the manufacturing or importation of such products [2005] OJ L91/13, ch 2, s 1, art 2 ('The rights, safety and well being of the trial subjects shall prevail over the interests of society').

27 Convention for the Protection of Human Rights and Dignity of the Human Being with Regard to the Application of Biology and Medicine: Convention on Human Rights and Biomedicine (1997), art 2.

to protect subjects of research from possible harm, to preserve their rights, and to provide reassurance to the public that this is being done. Committees also protect research workers from unjustified attack.'[28] Elsewhere, the RCP Guidelines stated that 'it is important [for RECs] to be continuously aware of the need to avoid impeding good medical research. The Committee should indeed seek to facilitate good research'.[29] This statement was retained in future editions and arguably strengthened: the latest edition of the RCP Guidelines from 2007 states emphatically that 'RECs have a duty to encourage important ethical research'.[30]

Similarly, informal guidance for REC members stresses a dual role that involves some kind of balancing. For example, the sixth edition of the *Manual for Research Ethics Committees*, last published in 2003, states that:

> Members of Research Ethics Committees have the responsibility of ensuring that medical research on humans is conducted in an ethical manner. In order to fulfil this function, Research Ethics Committees must engage in reasonable discussion and consideration of the ethical issues in each of the research proposals they have to review. This is demanding and time-consuming work, and the responsibilities entailed are considerable. *On the one hand* there is the need to contribute to the evidence base upon which modern medicine is based, *on the other* is the need to protect those who participate in the research process.[31]

As discussed more fully in the next chapter, the language of 'protection and promotion' has been instantiated in statutory regulation such as the Care Act 2014 and operationalized in the mandates of the HRA and in the mandates of RES offices across the four nations. For instance, HRA guidance for potential REC members states: 'The key duty of a REC is to protect the interests of research participants whilst at the same time facilitating ethical research.'[32] The claim that RECs equally serve to

[28] Royal College of Physicians, *Guidelines on the Practice of Ethics Committees in Medical Research* (1st edn, Royal College of Physicians 1984) 1.

[29] ibid 2.

[30] Royal College of Physicians, *Guidelines on the Practice of Ethics Committees in Medical Research with Human Participants* (4th edn, Royal College of Physicians 2007) 4.

[31] Sue Eckstein (ed), *Manual for Research Ethics Committees* (6th edn, CUP 2003) xvii.

[32] Health Research Authority, 'Information for Potential Research Ethics Service Committee Members' <www.hra.nhs.uk/documents/1025/standard-application-pack-rec-members.pdf> accessed 16 October 2019.

facilitate ethical research—perhaps even as a duty if we interpret the 2007 RCP Guidelines suggesting such—establishes a different message regarding the regulatory role of RECs in health research, as seen in both the literature and in documents such as the GAfREC, and arguably a message that is more pronounced than in other countries.

4.1 To Protect *and* (Equally) Promote?

It could be said that regulation is by its nature designed to affect behaviour of some kind (whether to restrict or to enable it), and therefore in some sense RECs have always, even if indirectly, been implicated in the facilitation of *ethical* health research. By considering, commenting on, guiding, and approving research studies that are well-designed scientifically and in accordance with law and established rules and principles of ethical conduct, RECs do promote a certain desired kind of behaviour, and this is what makes them regulators. Yet, even if regulation is, at its essence, about steering and therefore affecting social behaviour, critical questions still remain regarding: (1) how the interplaying roles of participant protection and research promotion might influence REC performance and decision-making, and (2) whether there might be regulatory misalignment between some of the instruments specifically for RECs—emphasizing participant protection—and regulatory instruments governing central regulators of health research and RECs themselves—imposing ethical research promotion—that impacts the overall quality and effectiveness of health research regulation.

As I have noted, that the UK emphasizes both protection and promotion is not new. For years, the country has held in some of its regulations and policies that RECs aim to facilitate (ethical) health research. The guidelines for RECs first emanated from the health research-promoting Royal College of Physicians in 1984. Then, as now, there was scholarly concern that 'the British guidelines have tipped the balance too far in the direction of the interests of researchers and have not given sufficient emphasis to the protection of subjects'.[33] Then, as now, there was a concern that 'committee members are confused by a perceived conflict between the requirement to facilitate research and their need to be critical of research'.[34]

---

[33] Paul McNeill, 'Research Ethics Review in Australia, Europe, and North America' (1989) 11 IRB: Ethics and Human Research 4, 5.

[34] McNeill, *Human Experimentation* (n 4) 67, citing the study of REC members conducted by Julia Neuberger. See Neuberger (n 21) 44 ('There is ambivalence arising from the sense that REC members should be supporting and

Moreover, several international (non-legal) policy instruments also suggest a dual role of protection and promotion for RECs.[35] For example, Canada's Tri-Council Policy Statement for ethical conduct for research involving humans states: 'The importance of research and the need to ensure the ethical conduct of research requires both researchers and [REC] members to navigate a sometimes difficult course between the two main goals of providing the necessary protection of participants and serving the legitimate requirements of research.'[36] Similarly, New Zealand's National Ethics Advisory Committee states that the ethics review system should '[f]acilitate research and innovative practice that contributes to knowledge and improved health outcomes' and '[p]rotect participants in health and disability research and innovative treatment'.[37]

So, what is different? In short, I argue it is the legal embeddedness of research promotion. The research promotion role has moved 'up the ladder' in the regulatory framework for RECs and in the regulation of health research, to implementation in law, most pointedly in the Health and Social Care Act 2012 and Care Act 2014. What was once guidance has now become legal rule. To date, we do not really know the practical impact, if any, of this explicit legal shift, especially on RECs. At this preliminary, scene-setting stage, however, we can speculate that several different processes are at play in this shift.

4.2 Ethical, Political, and Regulatory Processes

Determining the ethical acceptability of research is not just a complex and amorphous ethical process; it is also a political process. REC members may employ discursive strategies to convince other members of

---

facilitating research rather than criticising it, and from the knowledge that RECs have inadequate powers, and often insufficient status, within their [District Health Authorities]').

[35] Holly Fernandez Lynch and others, 'Of Parachutes and Participant Protection: Moving Beyond Quality to Advance Effective Research Ethics Oversight' (2019) 14 Journal of Empirical Research on Human Research Ethics 190.

[36] Canadian Institutes of Health Research, Natural Sciences and Engineering Research Council of Canada, and Social Sciences and Humanities Research Council of Canada, *Tri-Council Policy Statement: Ethical Conduct for Research Involving Humans – TCPS 2* (Government of Canada 2018).

[37] National Ethics Advisory Committee (New Zealand), 'Cross-Sectoral Ethics Arrangements for Health and Disability Research: Discussion Document' (2014) <https://neac.health.govt.nz/system/files/documents/publications/consultation-cross-sectoral-ethics-arrangements-health-disability-research.docx> accessed 16 October 2019.

their position on an issue; power dynamics may arise between 'expert' and 'lay' members, not to mention between the REC Chair and the other members. The REC Manager and Scientific Officer themselves may play a crucial stewardship role that involves managing expectations and relationships across a network of actors. As a committee, RECs may be drawn further into power dynamics with their 'managing' regulatory authorities. As further chapters will demonstrate, hortatory guidelines and self-regulation have given way to legal regulation and centralized regulatory bodies to coordinate and manage RECs. RECs must navigate the complexities of modern health research and the challenging cross-cutting demands from their managing regulators that encourage both protection of research participant interests and also promotion of health research. This entails a *working through* of the interests of researchers and research participants, and of science and society as well—which suggests that the process of determining whether research is ethically acceptable is also a regulatory process.

The legal scholar William Curran observed many years ago that '[t]he use of review committees is a common law approach. These committees will be building the law as they go along.'[38] Curran's comment was more aspiration than observation; nevertheless, the regulatory process is observed both in statutory regulations that RECs follow or apply to research proposals (e.g. research involving adults with incapacity), as well as in the regulatory techniques they employ to govern research. Indeed, as regulators themselves, RECs can look not only to what laws and regulations may (or may not) say about a proposal, they can also issue researchers many self-generated regulatory commands in their opinion letter, concerning, for example, whether a research design is flawed; whether a researcher may use human tissue; whether a participant has mental capacity to consent; whether different groups of participants should be included in the project; and not uncommonly, whether the information sheet says too little about burdens or risks or misrepresents what may happen in the project. Such commands, it seems, reflect a hybrid blend of legal and ethical reflection that *in toto* signify a pervasive power to render a regulatory judgement of 'yes', 'maybe', or 'no'. In effect, the REC's opinion is a regulatory event licence: without a positive opinion, research simply cannot proceed, either by way of law (in the case of clinical trials, for instance), policy, or practice (in most

---

[38] William Curran, 'Governmental Regulation of the Use of Human Subjects in Medical Research: The Approach of Two Federal Agencies' (1969) 98 Daedalus 542, 585.

other instances of health research, where it likely would not be published in any reputable journal).

Since the millennium, and especially as NHS RECs are now under the direct or indirect management of the HRA through the Care Act 2014, the role hierarchy of participant protection and research promotion has flattened. To some, this is concerning. Years ago, legal scholar Emma Cave and bioethicist Søren Holm expressed concern that the EU Clinical Trials Directive 2001/20/EC 'led to a subtle change of emphasis from the protection of research participants to the facilitation of research'.[39] In the same time period, Deryck Beyleveld, a legal scholar, expressed concern about a conflict of interest the dual roles could create:

> The root of the problem is that, despite the World Medical Association Declaration of Helsinki, the management of the REC system believes that the role of RECs is not just to protect the rights of research subjects, but also to facilitate good quality research. [...] [T]his just highlights a conflict of interest. A dog cannot serve two masters, and the role of RECs, in fact, is solely to try to prevent unethical research. The facilitation of research is the role of other bodies.[40]

It must be said that the ethical, political, and regulatory processes by which RECs render an opinion may well manifest quite differently under the research-transformative HRA compared to when these above statements were made in the early years of the millennium. The HRA's centralizing command may resolve some or most of the problems that critics (mainly health researchers) have levelled against RECs for years, but it may also lead to collateral, even unintended changes in how RECs review research proposals. If changes do emerge in this next-generation regulatory environment, it is an as-yet unknown answer what impact they may have on participants, researchers, and society. Phrased both empirically and normatively, can and should RECs both protect and promote? And if this is indeed how they operate, what model of health research regulation might be best suited to deliver these roles effectively?

A secondary question arises regarding the mechanism of working through protection and promotion. The roles may work together, but they are not necessarily balanced, nor might 'balance' be the appropriate mechanism. 'Balance' is ubiquitous in the legal and regulatory literature,

---

[39]   Emma Cave and Søren Holm, 'New Governance Arrangements for Research Ethics Committees: Is Facilitating Research Achieved at the Cost of Participants' Interest' (2002) 28 Journal of Medical Ethics 318.

[40]   Deryck Beyleveld, 'Law, Ethics and Research Ethics Committees' (2002) 21 Medicine and Law 57, 72–3.

alongside terms such as 'reasonable' and 'public interest', but can serve as a rhetorical ploy in regulation to mask lax reasoning or other mechanisms that might be in play to render judgement. Robert Veatch has observed that IRBs in the US may employ different techniques to interpret and apply the 'fundamental' biomedical ethics principles of respect for persons, beneficence, and justice. These include: (1) a 'single principle view', where one principle takes precedence over the others; (2) a 'simultaneity view', where all principles must be satisfied simultaneously for a research protocol to be deemed acceptable; (3) a 'balancing view', where the principles taken together must be satisfied on balance; and (4) a 'ranking view', where principles can be rank-ordered such that the highest ranking principle must be fully satisfied before the next rank is considered. Veatch further observes that regulation in the US fails to offer a theory of what should happen when a proposed research project involves a conflict of principles.[41] In the subsequent chapters, I take up this important observation, arguing that it may apply equally to the objectives of protection and promotion, and that, in the absence of an expressed theory of how these two objectives should be achieved, a regulatory framework should be crafted to help actors in health research move through these critical questions in the research lifecycle.

If, as a secondary question, we investigate the rhetorical use of or under-theorized reference to 'balance', we may further wonder if RECs evaluate research proposals implicitly in stages and act as gatekeepers or stewards at several thresholds. For example, do they first assess a proposal to see if it satisfies a 'tolerable (risk of) harm' (i.e. participant protection) threshold, and if so, then move on to consider whether it satisfies a subsequent 'social value' or public benefit (i.e. research promotion) threshold? If so, what happens in these stages of dual commitment—of accommodating potential harms to participants as well as potential benefits to society, not to mention other considerations? In this realm of possibility, might a REC take a lead in maximizing outcomes such as suggesting 'improvements' to the research questions, methods, proposed uses of findings, and so on? If so, this would suggest less a concern with adjudicating 'balance' and more a concern with stewarding research optimization.

This question of balance versus optimization (or something else) regarding protection and promotion remains open. It also raises several

---

[41] Robert Veatch, 'Ranking, Balancing, or Simultaneity: Resolving Conflicts among the Belmont Principles' in James Childress and others (eds), *Belmont Revisited: Ethical Principles for Research with Human Subjects* (Georgetown University Press 2005).

additional questions about the impact this next-generation regulatory environment may have on RECs—whether RECs encounter these potentially competing roles of protection and promotion in their work, and if so, how it is operationalized in their practices.

V. CONCLUSION

RECs have been a backbone in regulating the ethical acceptability of health research for half a century. They serve as gatekeepers that determine whether a proposed research project is ethically acceptable and therefore may proceed. RECs not only play a central role in health research regulation, they also hold tremendous power over what knowledge is produced, and from knowledge production across the translational divide, what medico-scientific innovations are created. While many support the underlying idea of *ex ante* ethics review by a committee as a means of protecting and promoting the rights, interests, and welfare of participants, many also have expressed dissatisfaction with the structure of the ethics review system and the individual processes of RECs. As later chapters will explain, multiple regulatory techniques and instruments have been employed over the years in the hopes of remedying the many problems attributed to RECs, foremost the concerns of inefficiency and ineffectiveness. Many researchers found the regulatory techniques and instruments of yore, particularly through the 1990s and in the form of 'guidance', to offer a weak remedy.

Recent changes may bode differently. Since its formation in late 2011, the HRA has been tasked with both protecting research participants from harm and facilitating a productive research environment by streamlining health research regulation. The HRA is a central regulatory body that is seen to help make the UK once again an attractive place to conduct health research such as clinical trials. Money, jobs, and international pharmaceutical and regulatory competition are all at stake. One pathway to make the country more attractive for conducting health research, and to provide national economic benefit, is to remove perceived regulatory thickets. Ethics review has been viewed as part of this thicket.

The HRA, particularly through its RES and equivalent bodies across the UK, are working to make REC processes more effective and efficient. As the HRA's RES website states: 'We have a duty to provide an efficient and robust ethics review service that maximises UK competitiveness for health research and maximises the return from investment in the UK, while protecting participants and researchers.'[42] What is unclear, however, is how this stress on *duties* of efficiency and maximization of 'UK competitiveness for health research' and maximization of 'return from investment in the UK' may affect the substantive and procedural workings of RECs. Can or should efficiency, as well as competition and investment maximization, be accomplished while simultaneously protecting participants? The UK is seen by many as a leader in health research and its regulation, and many have taken an interest in the country's recent reforms. As one author notes in a review of health research regulation across four countries:

> The current regulatory complexity [across the globe] appear[s] to be largely irrational, probably arising from piecemeal reactions to specific problems and scandals in the past. Thus, the new [...] HRA is of great interest in terms of future developments. If successful, it may have an impact outside [the UK].[43]

Empirical evidence is needed to investigate the questions posed in this chapter. Through document analysis, in-depth interviews, and observation—and guided by anthropological and regulatory theory—we should endeavour to build a knowledge base from which we can investigate the nature of health research regulation, pinpoint weaknesses, and recommend improvements—in other words, we should embark on an anthropology of regulation and build an evidence-based regulatory framework. There is a need for qualitative research, asking how and why RECs make the decisions they do, and how the nested dynamics of RECs and central 'managing' regulators play into decisions. By gaining a critical understanding of what RECs actually do and exploring the nature of health research regulation, such research could offer a crucial contribution to understanding the roles actors play in health research and how these roles transform over time and across stages in research.

The next chapter traces the regulatory development of RECs and health research regulation within the UK, with a view to demonstrating both the growth of health research regulation and the increasingly central role that RECs play in regulating health research. For many years, there were repeated calls for reform to how RECs were structured and operated, particularly from the research community—a community, of course, that

---

[42]   Health Research Authority, 'Research Ethics Service and Research Ethics Committees' <www.hra.nhs.uk/about-us/committees-and-services/res-and-recs/> accessed 16 October 2019.

[43]   Elina Hemminki, 'Research Ethics Committees in the Regulation of Clinical Research: Comparison of Finland to England, Canada, and the United States' (2016) 14 Health Research Policy and Systems 5, 9.

always has participated in and been directly affected by RECs. The REC system in the UK has indeed recently undergone structural reform, partly due to ongoing macro-regulatory changes occurring at the EU level that impact Member States' national regulations. Overall, these reforms appear to have been to the satisfaction of the research community. What we will see is that, while to a certain degree, research promotion has always been embedded in the regulatory techniques of RECs, it has not until now been instantiated in law with the creation of the HRA and rules promulgated under the Care Act 2014. The subsequent and fundamental question to explore is whether this instantiation of research promotion in law has a (hitherto absent) trickle-down effect that impacts the day-to-day practices of RECs, and if so, how, or indeed, whether the law is only now coming to reflect an everyday practice that has long existed, or whether a more robust regulatory model—specifically a model built around regulatory stewardship—is needed to make sense of how protection and promotion are to work together.

3. The making of RECs as health research regulators

I. INTRODUCTION

The previous chapter provided a conceptual framework of RECs and their roles in regulating health research. I claimed that while research promotion—acting to advance knowledge and discovery in the interests of science and society—has been a long-standing role of RECs in the UK, that role traditionally has been situated as secondary in many (but not all) regulatory instruments and, somewhat less clearly, in practice. I claimed further that research promotion is now embedded as a twinned objective of health research regulators in law, which signals a 'flattening' of the role hierarchy of participant protection and research promotion in RECs. I use the term 'signals' because ultimately this is a claim that warrants empirical investigation. Chapters 2 and 3 provide a space to query, based on regulatory and historical analysis rather than empirical investigation, the 'trickle-down' effect this next-generation, streamline-emphasizing regulatory environment has on RECs—that is, whether RECs can be expected to encounter this twin role of protection and promotion in their work today (or before), and if so, how it is felt and operationalized in their practices. Through conceptual overview and deep historical tracing, I highlight the uneasy tension between protection and promotion, which consequently demands certain further, empirically based research that reciprocally, also helps make better sense of the historical context provided here.

This chapter steps back in time to better understand the present context, and to further set the stage for the empirical investigation and analysis presented in later chapters. I present a historical tracing of the development of RECs as health research regulators within the UK. The aim in this chapter is not to provide simply more background to the current environment, but rather to argue that there has been growth in the volume and complexity of health research regulation since the mid-20th century, with a consequent backlash against the perceived negative repercussions for research, health, and the economy. I further argue that

RECs are a critical node in health research regulation, which is comprised of a variety of actors who may at times hold cross-cutting resources and motives. To properly examine the development of RECs and the responses by various actors to mitigate their many perceived problems (most significantly, as a bureaucratic bulwark against otherwise ethical research), we would be better served to examine the health research regulatory environment itself. This chapter claims that through significant reforms, RECs and their managing regulators have come to serve as a focal point for not only the protection of research participants, but also the sustainability and promotion of health research.

Tracing history over the past half-century, we will see that as health research gained prominence in the UK as both a driver of scientific knowledge and economic development, self-regulation of health research—ad hoc peer review by fellow scientists based on professional norms and local customs—gradually gave way to stricter, stronger, more centralized forms of regulation, particularly through policies and guidelines set by the UK's constituent governments. This was done in an effort to steer health research in an ethical manner and provide coordination and coherence for researchers, research sponsors, and the general public. In the course of this regulatory evolution, RECs became institutionalized within the NHS system (albeit haphazardly) and proliferated in number. Pressure was placed on RECs by different stakeholders to review research applications for 'consideration, comment, guidance and approval'[1] as this was seen as conforming to emerging good international practice. But this pressure led to RECs facing increased scrutiny and opprobrium from members of the research community, many of whom argued that RECs were performing the reviews poorly. The accusation was that RECs were too numerous in number, duplicative in their reviews of the same application for a multi-site project, and overly complex, opaque, and inconsistent in their functions. By the late 1990s, the picture painted by some was one of regulatory chaos rather than order. Despite a degree of reforms in the early 2000s, there remained concern about the future of health research in the UK due to ostensibly obstructive and economically destructive regulation.

Largely, these calls appear to have been answered. RECs and other parts of the research ethics oversight system have undergone substantial reform in the past decade. Partly this is due to ongoing macro-regulatory and macro-political changes occurring at the EU level that impact

---

[1] World Medical Association, *Declaration of Helsinki* (World Medical Association 2013) para 23.

Member States' national regulations. This next-generation health research regulatory reform is designed to be 'streamlined'—attuned and proportionate, calibrated to the 'scale and complexity of the research proposed'.[2]

The tone of the current regulatory era is reflected in the HRA's RES, which, as noted in the previous chapter, states on its website: 'We have a duty to provide an efficient and robust ethics review service that maximises UK competitiveness for health research and maximises the return from investment in the UK, while protecting participants and researchers.'[3] This appeal to efficiency and a 'duty' to maximize UK competitiveness for health research and maximize the return from investment in the UK reflects an increasingly neoliberal discourse in government policy grounded in regulatory speed and considers economic optimization the central aim of governance.

The research community largely seems satisfied with the most recent reforms. The number of academic articles lamenting the state of ethics review in the UK has dwindled and transformed into praise; many look at the UK's ethics review system today with envy, viewing it as comparatively highly coordinated, efficient, and robust.[4] But what do these regulatory reforms tell us about the nature of next-generation health research regulation and what its impact might be on RECs, to say nothing of its impact on research participants and publics? With the creation of the HRA in late 2011, the statutory rules promulgated under the Care Act 2014, and ensuing changes in regulatory instruments governing RECs, a key question arises: does instantiation of research promotion in law and at the governmental level of health research regulatory bodies have a trickle-down effect that impacts the day-to-day practices of individual, 'independent' RECs? Or, is law now merely reflecting a long-standing everyday practice of RECs? More broadly, has anything *really* changed in how ethics 'is done' by RECs, or have the changes only been at a higher, more overtly political level of legal and regulatory architecture?

---

[2]   GAfREC para 3.2.4.

[3]   Health Research Authority, 'Research Ethics Service and Research Ethics Committees' <www.hra.nhs.uk/about-us/committees-and-services/res-and-recs/> accessed 16 October 2019.

[4]   Elina Hemminki, 'Research Ethics Committees in the Regulation of Clinical Research: Comparison of Finland to England, Canada, and the United States' (2016) 14 Health Research Policy and Systems 5, 11 ('Certain features of REC work in individual countries could serve as a model for others. Streamlining of the ethics committee system in England […] [is an example]').

I begin to answer these questions through a historical tracing, with the development of RECs in the UK in the late 1960s and their scattered, at times haphazard entrenchment as health research regulators in the 1970s and 1980s. Following this, I explore the formal establishment of local research ethics committees (so-called LRECs) in 1991, multi-site research ethics committees (so-called MRECs) in 1997, and the earlier incarnation of the central regulatory bodies (Central Office for Research Ethics Committees (COREC) and National Research Ethics Service (NRES)) that sought to manage them, particularly in England. I then discuss the creation of three important regulatory instruments in the early 2000s—the Research Governance Frameworks from each of the four nations, the GAfREC originally issued separately in England and Scotland, and the UK-wide Standard Operating Procedures for Research Ethics Committees (REC SOPs)—all set within the backdrop of the controversial 2001 EU Clinical Trials Directive[5] and the UK's national transposition of the Directive as the Medicines for Human Use (Clinical Trials) Regulations 2004,[6] which ended the bifurcated and much-maligned LREC/MREC system and brought RECs, for the first time, within a legislative framework with imposed statutory duties.

Throughout this deep historical tracing of regulatory reform in the UK across the decades, I weave in critical commentary proffered by the research community that lobbied repeatedly for regulatory reform, particularly in the 1990s and through the first decade of the 2000s. I then discuss more recent regulatory reforms such as the introduction of the online, centralized Integrated Research Application System (IRAS) in 2004; the regulatory streamlining-oriented HRA in 2011; the Health and Social Care Act 2012; the Care Act 2014; the Central Booking Service and the online HRA Assessment Review Portal (HARP) in May 2014; the harmonized UK Policy Framework for Health and Social Care Research released in 2017 that replaces the four nations' Research Governance Frameworks; and recent government white papers and policy papers encouraging further streamlined health research regulation. I

---

[5]   European Parliament and Council Directive 2001/20/EC of 4 April 2001 on the approximation of the laws, regulations and administrative provisions of the Member States relating to implementation of good clinical practice in the conduct of clinical trials on medicinal products for human use [2001] OJ L121/34 (EU Clinical Trials Directive).

[6]   The Medicines for Human Use (Clinical Trials) Regulations 2004, as amended by the Medicines for Human Use (Clinical Trials) Amendment Regulations 2006, SI 2006/1928.

reflect on the sometimes-troubled interaction between different stake-holders and RECs, which in turn, enables me to conclude with a reflection on the potential changing regulatory nature of RECs.

What I aim to show in this chapter is that while research promotion has emerged as a recent *statutory* phenomenon in health research regulation, it has existed, somewhat ambiguously, as a critical value throughout the history of RECs, appearing in various disguises. Similarly, participant protection has always been a driving value of, and role for, RECs; however, this has never been the sole, as opposed to primary, concern of RECs. Indeed, RECs were created as much out of pragmatic response and political necessity, driven by concerns of organizational liability and financial harm, as they were out of concern for participant protection. Participant protection and research promotion have had an uneasy, unequal, but sustained marriage across the RECs' lifespan. And along the way, REC members have faced the challenging task of working in a space that demands that they liaise with various regulatory actors and that they not only operate within the (shifting) space's confines, but also help shape its contours.

II. REC DEVELOPMENT IN THE UK

The notion of *ethical evaluation* of a *proposed* research project by a *committee* of qualified people has long been viewed by many scholars as necessary, but not necessarily sufficient, for the successful functioning of, and public trust in, health research. RECs, it is said, reflect a well-designed and pragmatic system of 'social control' by researchers' peers and the lay public. As bioethicist William May opined in 1975: 'The primary guarantee of protection of subjects against needless risk and abuse is in the review before the work is undertaken. [...] [I]t is the only stage at which the subject can be protected against needless risk of injury, discomfort, or inconvenience.'[7] Legal scholar and bioethicist John Robertson similarly concluded in 1979: 'The [REC] is an important structural innovation in the social control of science, and similar forms are likely to be developed for other such controversial areas.'[8] By regulating research in an event licensing capacity—that is, by offering opinion on and ethics

---

[7]   William May, 'The Composition and Function of Ethical Committees' (1975) 1 Journal of Medical Ethics 23, 24.

[8]   John Robertson, 'Ten Ways to Improve IRBs' (1979) 9 Hastings Center Report 29.

approval of a research project before it commences—RECs are seen to mitigate risks to researchers, participants, and society.

At the same time, with sustained stakeholder support and growing institutionalization through stronger forms of regulation, RECs have come to hold tremendous power over how research is shaped—and thus, what knowledge is produced—and how the relationship between a researcher and a research participant is circumscribed. As historian Laura Stark observes, ethics committees 'are empowered to turn a hypothetical situation (this study *may be* acceptable) into shared reality (this study *is* acceptable). [...] [T]hey change what is knowable.'[9]

How did RECs come to hold such power? As we will see, the institutionalization of RECs was a gradual, deliberate endeavour by the government to hold researchers to account, but it was devised in a way that attempted to balance government oversight with research community self-regulation. Achieving this balance was not always successful.

2.1 Pragmatic Creation in the 1960s

Some of the first RECs in the UK were constituted following recommendations in the 'Responsibility in Investigations on Human Subjects' policy statement, published in the Report of the Medical Research Council (MRC) for 1962–63,[10] which was presented to Parliament in July 1964. However, in his ground-breaking historical study of RECs, sociologist Adam Hedgecoe carefully details how, as a whole, RECs were born not out of any particular research scandal, but rather out of the practical and economically driven necessity of British researchers to maintain funding from the well-endowed US Public Health Service. Hence, many RECs arose only after the US Surgeon General's policy from 8 February 1966, announcing that all research institutions in the US *and overseas* receiving Public Health Service funds for health research would have to receive prior approval from an ethics committee—a committee of the principal investigator's 'institutional associates'—based at each institution, and with each committee determining what would constitute ethical research.[11] RECs were thus created as a pragmatic

---

[9] Laura Stark, *Behind Closed Doors: IRBs and the Making of Ethical Research* (University of Chicago Press 2012) 5.

[10] Medical Research Council, 'Responsibility in Investigations on Human Subjects' in Medical Research Council, *MRC Annual Report, 1962-63* (Cmnd 2382 1963).

[11] US Public Health Service, 'Memo to the Heads of Institutions Conducting Research with Public Health Service Grants from the Surgeon General',

compromise to events unfolding in different locales and to concerns by different actors about the smooth operation of medical research and maintaining (or increasing) funding for it. Interestingly, the Thalidomide scandal of 1962 and the pioneering English whistle-blower doctor Maurice Pappworth's exposés (discussed below) had little impact on regulatory development.[12] Instead, as will be seen, the defining feature of REC creation in the UK was the maintenance of the medical profession's self-regulation.

Many more RECs were created after a July 1967 report from a committee of the Royal College of Physicians of London (RCP), which recommended that each competent authority (e.g. Board of Governors, Medical School Council, Hospital Management Authority) in medical institutions across the country should ensure 'that all projects involving experimentation on humans' be approved by 'a group of doctors including those experienced in clinical investigation'.[13] The RCP report was careful to warn that:

> [I]t is of great importance that clinical investigation should be free to *proceed without unnecessary interference and delay*. Imposition of rigid or central bureaucratic controls would be likely to deter doctors from undertaking investigations, and if this were to happen, the rate of growth of medical knowledge would inevitably diminish with resultant delay in advances in medical care.[14]

At the same time, the RCP recognized that 'it has now become necessary for a procedure to be available for the ethical guidance of clinical investigators. The provision of such guidance would not only serve to allay understandable anxiety in the public, but would be appreciated by clinical investigators, themselves, when faced with ethical problems.'[15] The then Ministry of Health widely circulated the RCP report, providing it a form of regulatory approbation, albeit indirect. These early RECs

---

8 February 1966 (Department of Health, Education and Welfare 1966); Adam Hedgecoe, '"A Form of Practical Machinery": The Origins of Research Ethics Committees in the UK, 1967–1972' (2009) 53 Medical History 331.

[12] Duncan Wilson, *The Making of British Bioethics* (University of Manchester Press 2014) 44–51.

[13] Max Rosenheim, 'Supervision of the Ethics of Clinical Investigations in Institutions: Report of the Committee Appointed by the Royal College of Physicians of London' (1967) 3 BMJ 429, 430.

[14] Royal College of Physicians of London, *Committee on the Supervision of the Ethics of Clinical Investigation in Institutions* (Royal College of Physicians of London 1967) [hereinafter 1967 RCP Report] 3 (emphasis added).

[15] ibid 3–4.

were constituted only to give guidance to staff in hospitals or similar institutions. The RCP report 'deliberately' did not give specific guidance on the structure or functioning of such committees since it considered that what might be appropriate in one institution might be inappropriate elsewhere:[16] according to the RCP committee, 'the way in which this could best be organised must vary with different institutions'.[17] A green light was given in regulatory instruments for local ways of operating RECs—as determined by the medical profession.

Pappworth's book, *Human Guinea Pigs*, was published in 1967, which, similar to the US whistle-blower doctor Henry Beecher's ground-breaking article a year prior,[18] laid out damning evidence of unethical research carried out in the UK and other jurisdictions.[19] Pappworth advocated that clinical research studies undergo prospective ethics committee review by physician-researchers' peers, with committees at each hospital board being responsible to the General Medical Council (GMC), which in turn would be answerable to Parliament. His book meant to ensure those policy recommendations were robust and implemented, but few in government read his book or bothered to take notice. As the bioethics historian Duncan Wilson notes, while Pappworth's work 'alerted the public to the ethical issues associated with clinical experiments, and contributed to a broader critique of professional expertise, it had little impact on the governance of medical research or treatment'.[20] Change would eventually come, but only when the self-regulating medical profession deemed it necessary in light of political and economic interest.

Still, these exposés have some importance. The value of Pappworth's and Beecher's exposés is that they augmented public dissatisfaction with research oversight on both sides of the Atlantic. As the US and UK were both undergoing rapid economic expansion in the post-war era, health research and science were seen as key drivers of progress and prosperity. But progress and prosperity could only be sustained by a robust

---

[16] Michael Denham and others, 'Work of a District Ethical Committee' (1979) 2 BMJ 1042.

[17] 1967 RCP Report (n 14) 4.

[18] Henry Beecher, 'Ethics and Clinical Research' (1966) 274 New England Journal of Medicine 1354.

[19] Maurice Pappworth, *Human Guinea Pigs: Experimentation on Man* (Routledge & Kegan Paul 1967). Pappworth had earlier published a damning article on the same subject. See Maurice Pappworth, 'Human Guinea Pigs: A Warning' (1962) 171 Twentieth Century 66.

[20] Wilson (n 12) 50.

regulatory system that garnered public trust and avoided scandal. In response—and when the profession felt it had to act to retain its power—the era between the late 1960s and early 1970s was marked by revolutionary regulatory enactments.

The Ministry of Health issued its first circular on RECs—HM(68)33: 'Supervision of the Ethics of Clinical Investigations'—in May 1968 to Regional Hospital Boards, Hospital Management Committees, and Boards of Governors, referring to the earlier reports of the MRC and RCP. HM(68)33 recommended that hospitals should establish ethics committees, tellingly termed 'informal advisory bodies'. As Claire Gilbert and colleagues observe of this development, hospital 'authorities were not legally required to establish ethics committees, and the committees were offered no formal legal status. No specific guidelines on practices and methods were given because it was thought that strict rules of conduct would not be adaptable to local needs.'[21] And as Hedgecoe observes, the Ministry of Health seemed content to rely on the RCP as a form of regulatory 'proxy' to ensure the spread of RECs. But, the RCP's powers were limited, not least in compelling REC creation at each hospital and ensuring that hospitals (and hence the NHS and its Ministers) took legal responsibility for RECs' decisions:

> It is not that RECs were not a form of self-regulation, but rather that this informal status was less the result of *laissez-faire* 'drift' on the part of the policy makers than a deliberate, *active* decision to dissociate these committees from NHS bodies and thus help preserve the idea of clinical autonomy.[22]

Following the request of the Chief Medical Officer in 1971 for analysis of the supervision of the ethics of clinical research in hospitals and other institutions,[23] in July 1973, a further report was published by the RCP that provided details of the recommended composition and scope

---

[21]   Claire Gilbert and others, 'Diversity in the Practice of District Ethics Committees' (1989) 299 BMJ 1437.

[22]   Hedgecoe, '"A Form of Practical Machinery"' (n 11) 350.

[23]   Apparently, the Chief Medical Officer, Sir George Godber, was responding to external pressure, foremost from the Patients Association, to inquire into allegations of unethical research practices in teaching hospitals. See Jenny Hazelgrove, 'British Research Ethics after the Second World War: The Controversy at the British Postgraduate Medical School, Hammersmith Hospital' in Volker Roelcke and Giovanni Maio (eds), *Twentieth Century Ethics of Human Subjects Research: Historical Perspectives on Values, Practices, and Regulations* (Franz Steiner Verlag 2004) 193.

of ethics committees,[24] including a call for 'experienced clinicians with a knowledge of clinical research investigation' and a recommendation that 'there should be a lay member'.[25] The report stated that 'supervision' of research ethics in an advisory role should normally be the sole function of the committee rather than as a police watchdog, and that applications should be made to an ethics committee for all proposed clinical research investigations, including trials of drugs approved under the Medicines Act 1968 and teaching demonstrations on students.[26] The report stated that the object of ethics committees was 'to safeguard patients, healthy volunteers and the reputation of the profession and its institutions in matters of clinical research investigation'.[27] Further, it recommended that ethics committees 'be small and they must not be so constituted as to cause an unreasonable hindrance to the advancement of medical knowledge'.[28]

This was the first clear regulatory statement in the UK of the role of RECs in protecting participants, but one notices that the aim of protecting participants and 'public safety' is considered *as important* as that of protecting researchers and institutions and 'improving rather than blocking' research. What is unclear is how exactly these two concerns of protecting participants and not unduly hindering the advancement of medical knowledge were to be reconciled by committee members. Regardless, this view towards safeguarding the medical profession's reputation and improving research while protecting participants seems to have aligned well with what REC members considered their aims to be: protecting participants but also not stifling research. In a 1979 article, members of one REC stated:

> The ethical committee decided it had three main aims: firstly, to ensure that the highest ethical standards are maintained during research investigation on man *while ensuring that, at the same time, research is not stifled*; secondly, to ensure the protection, safety, and well being of the patient or volunteer, whether or not the procedure is to be of benefit to him; and, thirdly, to ensure

---

[24]   Royal College of Physicians of London, *Committee on the Supervision of the Ethics of Clinical Research Investigations in Institutions* (Royal College of Physicians of London 1973) [hereinafter 1973 RCP Report]. See also Editorial, 'Guardians of Ethics' (1973) 4 BMJ 502.

[25]   Editorial, 'Guardians of Ethics' (n 24).

[26]   Editorial, 'Local Ethical Committees: Council Approves Revised Report' (1981) 282 BMJ 1010.

[27]   1973 RCP Report (n 24) 3.

[28]   ibid.

that subjects are fully informed about any research that affects them and also that consent is properly obtained.[29]

The RCP's 1973 report was evidently endorsed and promoted by the government. In June 1975, HM(68)33 was replaced by HSC(IS)153: 'Supervision of the Ethics of Clinical Research Investigations and Fetal Research', which emphasized that 'all proposed clinical investigations should be referred to an ethical committee'.[30] That same year, a new version of the Declaration of Helsinki was released and for the first time mentioned RECs in its guidance for ethical biomedical research: 'The design and performance of each experimental procedure involving human subjects should be clearly formulated in an experimental protocol which should be transmitted to a specially appointed independent committee for consideration, comment and guidance.'[31]

By the late 1970s, RECs were a well-established feature at hospitals, but it became apparent that their remit should expand to cover much of the health research occurring outside of hospitals as well, given the growth of research in universities and stand-alone research sites. In 1974, the NHS was reorganized such that local area health authorities became responsible for clinical research conducted in all premises under their control, so many RECs began to consider research projects in the wider community and not just in a hospital. Some changed their name to reflect the larger district area and independence from any specific hospital.[32] As a 1981 editorial in the BMJ reported: 'It is now apparent that the ethical committees, which were set up to review hospital-based research, should have a wider composition and cover research in all fields of medical practice.'[33] Taking a cue from these regulatory developments, research funders such as the MRC began to make it a condition of funding that researchers have local ethics committee approval for research involving clinical trials and for investigations involving human subjects, whether conducted within or outwith a hospital.[34] These local RECs that sprang

---

[29] MJ Denham and others, 'Work of a District Ethical Committee' (1979) 2 BMJ 1043 (emphasis added).

[30] Department of Health and Social Security, 'Supervision of the Ethics of Clinical Research Investigations and Fetal Research', HSC(IS)153 (Department of Health and Social Security 1975).

[31] World Medical Association, Declaration of Helsinki (World Medical Association 1975) Principle I.2.

[32] Denham and others (n 29) 1043.

[33] Editorial, 'Local Ethical Committees' (n 26) 1010.

[34] Ian Thompson and others, 'Research Ethical Committees in Scotland' (1981) 282 BMJ 718.

up across the country continued to have wide latitude to interpret whether a research project was ethically acceptable.

The meta-regulatory question that would soon arise was whether the institutionalization of RECs should be spearheaded by the government or by the medical profession. As we will see, the response in the 1980s reflected the same tone as the previous decades, if not more so: strong self-regulation by the medical profession and the absence of centralizing, state-led regulatory control.

2.2   Limited Regulation of RECs through the 1980s

By the early 1980s, RECs were established as 'satellite regulators' of health research in multiple countries, as recommended by international guidance such as the Declaration of Helsinki and the 1982 International Ethical Guidelines for Biomedical Research Involving Human Subjects, published by the Council for International Organizations of Medical Sciences (CIOMS) in collaboration with the World Health Organization (WHO). The RCP's report from 1973 was superseded in 1984 with its now well-known Guidelines on the Practice of Ethics Committees in Medical Research (RCP Guidelines).[35] As already noted in Chapter 2, the RCP Guidelines stated that RECs were 'to facilitate medical research in the interest of society' and (equally) 'to protect subjects of research from possible harm'.[36] The RCP Guidelines were seen as the best 'effective standard for RECs in the UK,[37] and, apparently, they were needed. As early as the late 1970s—little more than ten years after many RECs were created—the research community maligned both the rapid growth and complexity of RECs, as well as the inconsistency in their operations in part due to reorganizations of the NHS.[38] One commentator lamented:

---

[35]   Royal College of Physicians, *Guidelines on the Practice of Ethics Committees in Medical Research* (1st edn, Royal College of Physicians 1984).

[36]   ibid 1.

[37]   Paul McNeill, *The Ethics and Politics of Human Experimentation* (CUP 1993) 67.

[38]   Denham and others (n 29); Thompson and others (n 34). See also BT Williams, 'NHS Locally Organised Research Scheme: Regional Research Committees and the Way They Work' (1978) 1 BMJ 85; Ethical Committee, University College Hospital, 'Experience at a Clinical Research Ethical Review Committee' (1981) 283 BMJ 1312; Pauline Allen and others, 'Research Ethical Committees in 1981' (1982) 17 Journal of the Royal College of Physicians 96.

Decentralisation of the management of the NHS locally organised research scheme was intended to enable regional health authorities to develop arrangements best suited to their local circumstances [but] [t]he variations in the structure and practice of regional research committees suggest [...] that differing standards of adjudication and review may also have resulted.[39]

Similarly, Ian Thompson and colleagues' survey of 34 RECs in Scotland in 1980 found that:

In their present form research ethical committees do not satisfy fully the interests of the public or the research worker. There is inadequate representation of lay interests at all levels, and with most committees maintaining strict confidentiality over their proceedings there is little other scope for public accountability. The limited use of expert assessors and capricious monitoring leave the research worker in a state of uncertainty. [...] The committees provide only limited safeguards for patients and research workers, and more effective, standardised procedures are [needed].[40]

In 1982, Peter Lewis remarked that while the establishment of RECs was 'in many ways [...] an excellent thing' because it 'restrains the over-enthusiastic researcher and provides protection to those who take part in research both as subjects and investigators', there were a 'number of negative aspects of the present system'.[41] Among his system-level concerns was the 'institutionalization of ethics' in medical research whereby in approving a project the REC agrees 'to shoulder a portion of the investigator's responsibility', meaning the researcher 'has a measure of responsibility lifted from him and begins to act as if his actions were directed by a higher authority': 'In the state of devolved responsibility between the committee and the investigator, each can push its ethical responsibilities off onto the other.'[42] Lewis also voiced concern about the procedural nature of RECs, commenting that they were 'by nature bureaucratic and process applications using guidelines which tend to become stereotyped'.[43]

Concerns were also raised about the inconsistency and randomness of RECs, in part a symptom of the self-regulatory, clinical autonomy paradigm supported by the government. By the late 1980s, Gilbert and colleagues noted that RECs seemed to spring up haphazardly and

---

[39]   Williams (n 38) 87.

[40]   Thompson and others (n 34) 718, 720.

[41]   Peter Lewis, 'The Drawbacks of Research Ethics Committees' (1982) 8 *Journal of Medical Ethics* 61.

[42]   ibid 61–2.

[43]   ibid 62.

idiosyncratically across the country: some within hospitals, others independently but with responsibility to a district health authority or management team that appointed them, and others within pharmaceutical companies for Phase 1 clinical trial studies.[44] RECs were, in other words, operating in a hybrid regulatory space where they were seen as under-regulated regulators but themselves over-regulating health research. In part, this was due to the government's explicit position of deferring regulatory authority to the medical profession and, in line with the 1980s neoliberal ethos, even removing regulation where they could. Hedgecoe and others have noted that in the early 1980s (and until the coming into force of the Clinical Trials Regulations 2004), the government deregulated areas of biomedical research such as Phase 1 clinical trials to encourage more clinical trials (and thus investment) in the country, all but removing regulatory oversight from the Medicines Division of the Department of Health and Social Security and later the Medicines Control Agency (the predecessors of the Medicines and Healthcare products Regulatory Agency, or MHRA), and placing both ethics and scientific review within RECs alone.[45] While RECs could be a thorn in the sides of researchers, RECs typically were less stringent than drug regulators, especially from a methodological and scientific standpoint, and were one less regulatory authority from which researchers and sponsors would need to secure approval.

But all the same, many commentators found the REC system Byzantine. RECs were public, private, institutional, and regional. The prevailing opinion was that the only common approach of RECs was to bewilder researchers and stifle research. Few were clear as to the remit and scope of their review, much less the standards by which they undertook evaluation of a research proposal. The RCP Guidelines were revised in 1990, but it had become apparent to many in the research community that under-regulated, inconsistent RECs were too damaging to research, despite the fact that most REC members were researchers or clinicians themselves, and guidance from the RCP encouraged them to facilitate research. Guidelines were not enough, many felt; it was time for the government to step in and attempt to achieve some marked level consistency in how these committees were structured and how they functioned. As an editorial in the BMJ in 1990 opined, citing articles recently published by researchers in its own journal and a report

---

44   Gilbert and others (n 21).
45   Adam Hedgecoe, 'A Deviation from Standard Design? Clinical Trials, Research Ethics Committees, and the Regulatory Co-Construction of Organizational Deviance' (2014) 44 Social Studies of Science 59, 63.

published by the Institute of Medical Ethics in 1986:[46] 'evidence suggests that the ethical control of medical research remains inconsistent and ineffective', 'sensible suggestions about the structure and process of ethics committees have been widely ignored', and '[t]hirty years should have been adequate for ethics committees to get their act together, yet there are still wide discrepancies in their constitution and working'.[47]

The problem was that no regulatory network or central health research regulatory authority existed for distributing guidelines and standards to achieve procedural and substantive consistency,[48] and many RECs seemed to ignore the RCP Guidelines and operate as they pleased, revelling in what was little more than self-regulation and local control within a health district. Julia Neuberger's in-depth empirical investigation of RECs across the UK in the early 1990s found that it was lack of statutory regulation of RECs that caused the most serious problems, including researchers not taking RECs seriously. In short, Neuberger found that RECs were fundamentally disempowered regulators of research. 'RECs have not hitherto followed guidelines particularly closely', she reported; they 'lack power, being advisory to [district health authorities] and other appointing authorities, and have no policing or monitoring role'.[49] Her stark conclusion was that RECs were neutered regulators:

> However hard they work, however thorough their examination of research protocols on a case-by-case basis, however much better constituted and trained, and however well supported they may be administratively, *unless they have the power to ensure that all research is submitted to them and to stop research that they regard as unethical, they will not be taken sufficiently seriously.* For these reasons and others, this report, whilst making detailed recommendations for improvements to present practice, recommends that *there should be proper legislation.*[50]

---

[46] Institute of Medical Ethics, *Research Ethics Committees in England and Wales: The Institute's Survey* (Institute of Medical Ethics 1986, Supplement No 2).

[47] Stephen Lock, 'Monitoring Research Ethical Committees' (1990) 300 BMJ 61.

[48] Michael Gelder, 'A National Committee for the Ethics of Research' (1990) 16 Journal of Medical Ethics 146.

[49] Julia Neuberger, *Ethics and Health Care: The Role of Research Ethics Committees in the United Kingdom* (King's Fund Institute 1992) 8.

[50] ibid (emphasis added).

2.3 Formal LREC/MREC Establishment and Further Criticism in the 1990s

On the heels of Neuberger's investigation, a degree of regulatory clarity came in August 1991 when the Department of Health issued Health Service Guideline (91)5: 'Local Research Ethics Committees', which replaced HSC(IS)153 from 1975 and formally introduced LRECs in England. (Wales and Scotland passed their own guidelines to establish LRECs in 1991 and 1992, respectively.[51]) Hedgecoe observes that this 'marked the point where power over the shape of ethics review shifted from the medical profession (in the form of the RCP) to central government.'[52] The Health Service Guideline, colloquially referred to as 'the Red Book', stated that 'every [NHS] health district should have a local research ethics committee to advise NHS bodies on the ethical acceptability of research proposals involving human subjects'.[53] LRECs would scrutinize research projects involving patients from within the specific health authority. Thus, each LREC acted on behalf of and for the local health authority in an advisory capacity, so it was ultimately the NHS body (e.g. NHS Trust, Special Health Authority) that would decide whether a project should go ahead. However, no sanctions for non-compliance were mentioned in the Red Book and thus NHS institutions were not compelled to adopt the guidelines and institute LRECs.

This regulatory guidance and the Department of Health taking responsibility for RECs failed to quell the research community's criticism of RECs. And, arguably because the guidance was not statutory regulation as advocated by commentators such as Neuberger, RECs were still not taken 'sufficiently seriously' by many researchers.[54] Neuberger's report was written just after the Red Book's release; analysing the new guidance, she concluded that 'whilst their tone is tougher than that of previous versions, they lack the detailed discussion of the RCP guidelines'.[55] Neuberger also observed that the Red Book differed somewhat

---

[51]   See Welsh Government, Welsh Health Circular WHC(91)75; Scottish Office, Department of Health, NHS Circular 1992(GEN)3.

[52]   Adam Hedgecoe, 'Scandals, Ethics, and Regulatory Change in Biomedical Research' (2017) 42 Science, Technology, & Human Values 577, 585.

[53]   Department of Health, 'Local Research Ethics Committees', HSG(91)5.

[54]   See also Hedgecoe, 'Scandals' (n 52), who argues that the Red Book was a reflection of two strands of thinking common in the 1980s: the need to standardize RECs to protect the interests of researchers and to reduce the influence of the medical profession.

[55]   Neuberger (n 49) 13.

in substance from the 1990 RCP Guidelines (having superseded the original 1984 version). The Red Book suggested that multi-centre research could be approved by a single LREC, whose decision would then be accepted by other committees, but the details were not specified and so, unsurprisingly, this never happened. Each LREC sought to approve research conducted in its health district, regardless of the outcome of reviews conducted by LRECs elsewhere. Though some RECs voluntarily entered into local arrangements to recognize other local REC decisions, this was by no means universal and rarely extended beyond a single health authority boundary.[56] The light-touch regulatory approach from the Department of Health only served to exacerbate REC differentiation across the country. By this time, there were over 200 RECs across the UK. Studies from the mid-1990s indicated that large variations in application requirements, review procedures, and opinions occurred in practice among different LRECs.[57] The level of support and accountability of RECs to their appointing authorities were equally variable.[58] Calls for a common, standardized research application form were widespread in medical and science journals. Despite the introduction of SOPs for LRECs in 1994,[59] members of the research community continued to express discontent with stifled health research due to RECs.

The REC structure was partially modified in 1997 when new Department of Health guidelines sought to simplify the procedure for ethics review of multi-centre studies. HSG(97)23[60] required research studies

---

[56] Clive Collett, 'Setting the Strategic Landscape for the HRA: Ethics Governance' (2013) (unpublished internal HRA paper provided to the author).

[57] George Alberti, 'Local Research Ethics Committees: Time to Grab Several Bulls by the Horns' (1995) 311 BMJ 639; Paul Garfield, 'Cross District Comparison of Applications to Research Ethics Committees' (1995) 311 BMJ 660; Claire Middle and others, 'Ethics Approval for a National Postal Survey: Recent Experience' (1995) 311 BMJ 659; Alison While, 'Ethics Committees: Impediment to Research or Guardian of Ethical Standards?' (1995) 311 BMJ 661.

[58] Collett (n 56).

[59] See Christine Bendall, *Standard Operating Procedures for Local Research Ethics Committees: Comments and Examples* (McKenna and Company 1994); Christine Bendall and J Riddell, *Using Standards for Local Research Ethics Committees: A Guide to Using the Framework of Standards and the Standard Operating Procedures* (NHS Training Division 1994); Leigh and Baron Consulting Limited and Christie Associates, *Standards for Local Research Ethics Committees: A Framework for Ethical Review* (Department of Health 1994).

[60] Equivalent guidance was published in Wales and Scotland: DGM 98/25 and MEL 97/8, respectively. According to the original GAfREC, MRECs

conducted in the UK that involved four or more LREC geographic localities (i.e. four or more health authority boundaries) to have approval from both a single 'MREC' in the country (out of 13 that eventually existed), and the LREC for each participating site. As a Department of Health document noted, the rationale for the MREC creation was to streamline research governance processes to improve the environment for clinical trials:

> [the] reasons for streamlining the system for LREC review of multi centre trials [...] [are] [...]. To contribute to improved clinical outcomes by approving potentially beneficial research more efficiently [...]. To reduce delays to good research [...] [and] [...]. To avoid a large number of LRECs all devoting time to the same aspects of identical protocols.[61]

The MREC system was overseen by the NHS Research and Development Directorate (and was directly accountable to the Department of Health), whereas LRECs were overseen by regional health authorities. Research could not proceed until each LREC informed the approving MREC of its lack of objection with respect to 'locality issues', which were later specified in the first edition of the GAfREC released in 2001. This meant that LRECs could provide advice about the local acceptability of a protocol and could reject the research protocol for 'locality issues', but could not amend the study protocol or the study instruments. One MREC approval would be valid throughout the UK; if the MREC declined to give a favourable opinion on the application, any existing approval by LRECs still stood, but those LRECs had to be informed of the MREC's decision.

Despite this regulatory change that was intended to smooth approvals for multi-site research, many researchers found that, in practice, MREC

'undertake the review of the ethics of the research protocol, including the content of the patient information sheet and consent form. No further ethical review of these items shall be undertaken by other RECs (except in the process of a "second review" [...]).' See Department of Health, *Governance Arrangements for NHS Research Ethics Committees* (Department of Health 2001) para 8.7. Locality issues undertaken by LRECs were 'limited to': 'the suitability of the local researcher; the appropriateness of the local research environment and facilities; specific issues relating to the local community, including the need for provision of information in languages other than English'. ibid para 8.8.

[61] Department of Health, 'Review of Ethics of Multi-Centre Trials', February 1995, CMO's Consultative Group on Research Ethics, RE/95/1, NPA, as quoted in Hedgecoe, 'Scandals' (n 52) 586.

approval did not necessarily lead to more efficient and cost-effective LREC approval.[62] As Collett notes:

> Many local RECs did not trust these newly-formed MRECs and were unhappy to relinquish their perceived responsibility for the *ethical* review of research projects taking place within their patch. This often resulted in lengthy delays whilst LRECs and the MREC disagreed over *ethical* issues occasionally resulting in the local REC refusing to approve the study for their local site.[63]

In summary, though RECs in the NHS system have existed sporadically and informally since the late 1960s, they had no formal standing until guidance was put forth by the Department of Health in 1991, and it must be emphasized that this was only guidance. Through the 20th century, then, RECs in the UK were simply ungoverned by statutory regulation. Until the 21st century, when statutory regulations were introduced that legally required REC review and approval for certain types of health research, there was no legal requirement for health researchers to obtain prior REC approval, and there was no statutory regulation that governed the practices of RECs. This is not to say that the impact of REC practices was unfelt by researchers. On the contrary, as we have seen, their impact on controlling research was profound. RECs' informal and extra-legal authority was acute, and for many researchers, deeply troubling. Clinical autonomy and self-regulation would have to be reined in.

III. CENTRALIZATION AND LEGISLATION IN THE NEW MILLENNIUM

By the late 1990s, RECs had become an established if maligned feature in health research regulation. In response to (1) criticisms that the functions and standards of RECs were imprecise and harmful to valuable research; (2) the coming into force of the EU Clinical Trials Directive; and (3) the North Staffordshire research scandal that erupted in the

---

62   Rustam Al-Shahi and Charles Warlow, 'Ethical Review of a Multicentre Study in Scotland: A Weighty Problem' (1999) 33 Journal of the Royal College of Physicians of London 549; Isobel Larcombe and Martin Mott, 'Multicentre Research Ethics Committees: Have They Helped?' (1999) 92 Journal of the Royal Society of Medicine 500; Nicholas Dunn and others, 'Costs of Seeking Ethics Approval Before and After the Introduction of Multicentre Research Ethics Committees' (2000) 93 Journal of the Royal Society of Medicine 511.

63   Collett (n 56) 4 (emphasis in original).

1990s, RECs underwent significant changes in the new millennium. They became governed by a variety of governance mechanisms—including top-down, state-led commands and controls—that sought to make them work efficiently and harmoniously, and in so doing, impacted more directly how they worked. In the early 2000s, a flurry of guidance, tools, and processes from the UK's Health Departments emerged to 'update' RECs to make the process smoother for researchers and more robust for the public interest, including the establishment of the COREC in 2000; a Research Governance Framework in 2001; GAfREC in 2001; the requirement for a single UK-wide REC opinion in 2004 that replaced the LREC/MREC system; formalized UK-wide SOPs for RECs in 2004; an online Research Ethics Database (RED) to enable REC administrators to import application data and documentation and to process and control research applications through to the approvals stage and to record and track post-approval activity; and the creation of an online portal to submit research applications (today known as IRAS) in 2004.

Yet the sharp growth of health research regulation through guidelines and frameworks that sought to make RECs more efficient, consistent, and robust in their processes—coupled with the passage of three major Parliamentary statutory instruments on clinical trials, human tissue, and mental capacity—led to a perception that research was getting further buried in paperwork and bureaucratic acronyms, and that RECs were getting papered over but not fundamentally reformed. As RECs were created before there was any national legal requirement for their use or adherence to a governing framework, consistency, effectiveness, and cooperation were long-standing challenges. Regulatory add-ons did not remedy the problems identified by many, or if they managed to plug the hole on one issue, others would appear. Deeper regulatory solutions were called for to solve the problems created in part by misaligned, siloed regulation itself.

Researchers were frustrated with the growing amount of bureaucracy in the system.[64] Some felt that the process of acquiring ethics approval

---

[64]   Hilary Hearnshaw, 'Comparison of Requirements of Research Ethics Committees in Eleven European Countries for a Non-Invasive, Interventional Study' (2004) 328 BMJ 140; Glyn Elwyn and others, 'Ethics and Research Governance in a Multicentre Study: Add 150 Days to Your Study Protocol' (2005) 330 BMJ 847; Nina Fudge and others, 'Streamlined Research Governance: Are We There Yet?' (2010) 341 BMJ c4625; Andrew Thompson and Emma France, 'One Stop or Full Stop? The Continuing Challenges for Researchers Despite the New Streamlined NHS Research Governance Process' (2010) 10

was 'so onerous that it is compromising clinical research',[65] and that the system had become a 'rather prescriptive, bureaucratic and rigid process', with 'a fairly standardized review procedure and application form, leading to standardised research procedures'.[66] Researchers were particularly unhappy with having to obtain both REC approval and 'R&D permission' (i.e. research governance permission) from each of the NHS service providers (e.g. NHS Trusts) involved in their research project, as established in the second editions of the Research Governance Framework.

Over-regulation and a disproportionate approach to research presenting low risk were seen as the main problems. As one group of researchers intoned: 'In a risk-benefit arena that is now heavily stacked towards perceived risk, the instigators of over-regulation must bear responsibility for the real and emerging risks of a failure to deliver the potential lifesaving benefits of clinical research promptly.'[67]

Coupled with their criticisms, clinicians and researchers invoked the rhetoric of research 'promotion'. For example, in a BMJ editorial in 2000, the then President of the RCP insisted the REC system needed to be improved as it was obstructing 'research that will in the long run improve health care and health'—which was one of the 'two major functions' of a REC, along with protecting participants and the public from possible harm.[68] This positioning was strategically important, as continuing to frame RECs as carrying two equally important roles would enable the research community, including the powerful and politically connected RCP and AMS, to lobby the UK government for favourable changes to the research regulatory and governance structure.

In the following sections, I trace the steps of deep regulatory reform in the new millennium with a view to demonstrating that the reform was in direct response to criticisms made by the research community (and its

---

BMC Health Services Research 124; Helen Snooks and others, 'Bureaucracy Stifles Medical Research in Britain: A Tale of Three Trials' (2012) 12 BMC Medical Research Methodology 122; John Barry, 'Improvements to the Ethical Review Process are Good News for Psychologists and Health Researchers in Europe, Especially in the UK' (2012) 8 Europe's Journal of Psychology 1.

[65]   Louise Robinson and others, 'NHS Research Ethics Committees' (2007) 335 BMJ 6.

[66]   Sue Richardson and Miriam McMullan, 'Research Ethics in the UK: What Can Sociology Learn from Health?' (2007) 41 Sociology 1115, 1119.

[67]   Paul Stewart and others, 'Regulation: The Real Threat to Clinical Research' (2008) 337 BMJ a1732.

[68]   George Alberti, 'Multicentre Research Ethics Committees: Has the Cure Been Worse Than the Disease?' (2000) 320 BMJ 1157, 1158.

representative bodies), and that the reform was to be led by the central government, which instantiated the dual roles of participant promotion and research promotion at the level of legal architecture.

3.1   2000–10: A Series of Fundamental Reforms

To address the continuing concerns about the processes around ethics review, and to help RECs prepare for future implementation (in May 2004) of the EU's Clinical Trials Directive 2001/20/EC, England's Department of Health established COREC in 2000. COREC's mission was to improve the system of operation of RECs and to advise the Department of Health on necessary policy requirements concerning their operation.[69] COREC took on the administrative functions for MRECs and provided management support for LRECs, including through local Offices for Research Ethics Committees (ORECs) situated across ten sites in England, with each led by an OREC Manager. The local health authorities (Health Boards and Strategic Health Authorities) remained the appointing authorities for the LRECs. While COREC acted for the Department of Health in England, it 'also provided a focus for discussion and collaboration with the relevant bodies and individuals in Wales, Scotland and Northern Ireland. It undertook most of the development work to create a common UK system' for RECs.[70] Among the procedural changes instituted by COREC early in the new millennium was the creation of a Central Allocation System in 2004, a common UK-wide ethics application form, and standard opinion letters issued by RECs. Even so, some researchers criticized the application form for being too long and cumbersome.[71]

In March 2001, the Department of Health published the first edition of the Research Governance Framework for Health and Social Care (RGF), which set forth a quality and accountability framework within which research was to be undertaken in the NHS.[72] Both the RGF and GAfREC were created partly in response to a report published in May 2000 that looked into the North Staffordshire scandal, where from 1990 until 1993, it was alleged that premature infants in North Staffordshire Hospital had been put into a controlled trial of an alternative type of ventilator without

---

[69]   Collett (n 56).

[70]   ibid 4.

[71]   Konrad Jamrozik, 'Research Ethics Paperwork: What is the Plot We Seem to Have Lost?' (2004) 329 BMJ 286.

[72]   Scotland and Wales published a similar RGF that same year. Northern Ireland did not publish its first RGF until 2006.

their parents' knowledge or consent.[73] Allegations of lack of informed consent were first raised by a group of parents in the late 1990s, when apparently they first became aware that their infants had been enrolled in the controlled trial. The subsequent report, led by Professor Rod Griffiths, recommended a major overhaul of the way in which all clinical research was to be conducted in the NHS, including establishing 'formal guidance on research governance within the NHS' in the form of a national research governance framework,[74] as well as clear governance arrangements for RECs. The government accepted the key recommendation and began crafting a research governance framework in 2000.[75]

Notably, the RGF reinforced the language from previous guidance documents in the UK (especially the RCP Guidelines) that emphasized RECs should also facilitate research:

> Their primary responsibility is to ensure that the research respects the dignity, rights, safety and well-being of individual research participants. They should also work efficiently to facilitate the good conduct of high quality research that offers benefits to participants, services and society at large. Unjustified delay to such research is itself unethical.[76]

Elsewhere, the RGF also identified RECs as holding two 'key responsibilities', namely: 'ensuring that the proposed research is ethical and respects the dignity, rights, safety and well-being of participants'; and 'assuring the scientific quality of proposed research'.[77]

Working with COREC, the Department of Health also released in July 2001 its GAfREC, which replaced the previous guidance issued under

---

[73] The RGF also built on several documents published to support the government's modernization agenda of the NHS. See e.g. Department of Health, *The New NHS: Modern, Dependable* (Department of Health 1997).

[74] NHS Executive West Midlands Regional Office, *Report of the Review into the Research Framework in North Staffordshire Hospital NHS Trust* (NHS Executive 2000) para 4.1.2.

[75] Hedgecoe observes, however, that: 'The [Griffiths] panel's recommendation for the revision of research governance in the NHS was *not* an original consequence of the [North Staffordshire] scandal, but rather fed into changes that were already underway, and indeed were in part shaped by broader regulatory changes at a European level [...], rather than a national research scandal.' See Hedgecoe, 'Scandals' (n 52) 589. In other words, the Department of Health was already beginning to develop a research governance framework; the Griffiths report simply provided further impetus for regulatory reform.

[76] Department of Health, *Research Governance Framework for Health and Social Care* (Department of Health 2001) para 3.12.2.

[77] ibid 20.

cover of HSG(91)5 (which established LRECs) and HSG(97)23 (which established MRECs). Scotland published an equivalent GAfREC in October that same year.[78] Sensing that MRECs and LRECs were not operating efficiently, the GAfREC were drafted as guidance to provide 'a standards framework for the process of review of the ethics of all proposals for research in the NHS and Social Care which is efficient, effective and timely, and which will command public confidence.'[79] Meant to be read in conjunction with the RGF, the 34-page GAfREC (and its subsequently longer versions published in 2011 and 2018) set out 'general standards and principles for an accountable system of RECs'.[80] In line with prevailing international ethics guidelines such as the Declaration of Helsinki and the Council of Europe's Convention for the Protection of Human Rights and Dignity of the Human Being (known as the Oviedo Convention),[81] and more clearly stated than in the RGF, the GAfREC declared RECs as having 'primary' and 'secondary' responsibilities:

> RECs are responsible for acting primarily in the interest of potential research participants and concerned communities, but they should also take into account the interests, needs and safety of researchers who are trying to undertake research of good quality. However, the goals of research and researchers, while important, should always be secondary to the dignity, rights, safety, and well-being of the research participants.[82]

Together, both the RGF and the GAfREC signalled a subtle shift in the evolutionary development that was emerging in the UK. These regulatory instruments certainly did not jettison research promotion as a responsibility of RECs; rather, they clarified that the UK's RECs would be mandated with a primary role shared with RECs in other countries, and which heeded the message of international ethics guidelines, namely that in assessing the ethical acceptability of research, participant protection must always take precedence over the interests of research and researchers.

---

[78] Scottish Government Health and Wellbeing Directorate, *Governance Arrangements for NHS Research Ethics Committees in Scotland* (Scottish Government Health and Wellbeing Directorate 2001).

[79] GAfREC Preface.

[80] ibid.

[81] Convention for the Protection of Human Rights and Dignity of the Human Being with Regard to the Application of Biology and Medicine: Convention on Human Rights and Biomedicine (1997), art 2.

[82] GAfREC para 2.3.

To comply with and give domestic effect to the EU Clinical Trials Directive (2001/20/EC), the UK passed the Medicines for Human Use (Clinical Trials) Regulations 2004,[83] operative from 1 May 2004. Ushering in 'root and branch reform' and arguably marking 'the end of the self-regulation of research ethics',[84] the Clinical Trials Regulations 2004 established NHS RECs on a legal basis for the first time, providing detailed provisions on their composition and what RECs must, as a statutory duty, consider in preparing their ethics opinion.[85] The EU Clinical Trials Directive, under Article 6 in particular, required Member States to establish RECs and to have RECs approve clinical trial protocols. According to Article 7, for multi-centre clinical trials limited to the territory of a single Member State, Member States had to establish a procedure providing, notwithstanding the number of RECs in its territory, for the adoption of a *single opinion* for that Member State. In the case of multi-centre clinical trials carried out in more than one Member State simultaneously, a single opinion would be required for each Member State concerned by the clinical trial. Thus, the Clinical Trials Regulations 2004 provided for a single UK-wide opinion for multi-centre studies. They also set a defined time period (60 days) for issuing an ethics opinion. To avoid the confusion that would result from having parallel but different operating ethics review systems, the four UK Health Departments agreed to make it a policy to apply this approach of single REC review also to *all* health research within the NHS involving individuals, their organs, tissue, or data—not just clinical trials.

Also in 2004, version 1.0 of the UK-wide REC SOPs was produced to meet the obligations of the EU Clinical Trials Directive for the operation of ethics committees in relation to CTIMPs. As previously mentioned, the SOPs included provision for a single UK-wide ethics opinion on all types of health research, thus reducing if not eliminating the duplication

---

[83] The Medicines for Human Use (Clinical Trials) Regulations 2004, as amended by the Medicines for Human Use (Clinical Trials) Amendment 2006, SI 2006/1928. The amended Regulations were intended to give domestic effect to the EU's Good Practice Directive (2005/28/EC).

[84] Susan Kerrison and Allyson Pollock, 'The Reform of UK Research Ethics Committees: Throwing the Baby out with the Bath Water?' (2005) 31 Journal of Medical Ethics 487.

[85] See e.g. the Medicines for Human Use (Clinical Trials) Regulations 2004 reg 15(5). This said, the first statutory regulation to establish a REC was the Adults with Incapacity (Ethics Committee) (Scotland) Regulations 2002 (2002 No 190), which established a REC as per section 51 of the Adults with Incapacity (Scotland) Act 2000 (AWI Act). This REC is today referred to as the Scotland A REC.

and inconsistency in opinions rendered by RECs for multi-site studies. The SOPs obligated RECs to render a decision on any individual application within 60 days, unless the REC asked for more information (in which case the 'clock' stopped until that information was received).

New statutory and regulatory developments required RECs to consider the ethical implications of research in areas previously not considered or minimally considered. The Human Tissue Act 2004 was passed to govern the collection and use of human tissue (or 'relevant material' as the Act states), including for research purposes, in England, Wales, and Northern Ireland.[86] The Mental Capacity Act 2005 followed thereafter, again imposing greater responsibilities for RECs, this time for research involving adults lacking mental capacity. Organizational changes also occurred; following the Department of Health's Arm's Length Body Review,[87] the National Patient Safety Agency (NPSA) took over responsibility for COREC in April 2005.[88]

In April 2005, largely in response to the EU Clinical Trials Directive, the second edition of the RGF was published by the Department of Health; the three other UK nations also published their own shortly thereafter.[89] As noted by the Scottish RGF (and in language used verbatim in the Welsh and Northern Irish RGFs), and in contradistinction to the first edition of the RGF and the GAfREC, the goal of the document was to set out a 'balance' between participant protection and research promotion:

> The change in the law stimulated wide debate on good practice and regulatory process in collaborative trials. The lessons drawn are visible throughout this edition [of the RGF] and recognise the need to achieve a proper balance by

---

[86] Scotland passed its own Human Tissue (Scotland) Act 2006, with different governance arrangements. The UK's Human Tissue Authority performs certain tasks on behalf of the Scottish Government, however. All NHS RECs in Scotland are recognized by the other three UK Health Departments for the purposes of the Human Tissue Act 2004, which means that a Scottish REC can give UK-wide approval for research involving human tissue.

[87] Department of Health, *Reconfiguring the Department of Health's Arm's Length Bodies* (Department of Health 2004).

[88] Existing since July 2001, the NPSA was a special health authority covering England and Wales and coordinated system-wide NHS patient safety functions. It was abolished in 2012.

[89] Scotland published the second edition of its Research Governance Framework in 2006; Wales followed suit in 2009 (Northern Ireland published its first edition in 2006).

safeguarding the rights of patients involved in clinical trials while avoiding a disproportionate impact on those who carry them out.[90]

The English RGF, however, phrased its preface to the second edition differently, emphasizing a risk-based regulatory approach and the need to still primarily protect participants:

> Regulations on clinical trials involving medicines took effect in 2004. The change in the law stimulated wide debate on good practice and risk-based regulatory process. We have drawn lessons throughout this edition. [...] There has been new legislation on human tissue and on mental capacity, with provisions to protect those who participate in research. Whatever the context, the interests of research participants come first. Those responsible must be satisfied they have taken all reasonable steps to protect the dignity, rights, safety and wellbeing of participants. We have to be frank about risks, and businesslike about managing them.[91]

As clinical researchers continued to express publicly concerns that RECs were burdensome and 'impeded, delayed, and sometimes distorted research',[92] in late 2004, the UK government appointed an advisory group led by the then Minister of Health Lord (Norman) Warner to review the operation of RECs regulating research in the NHS in England. The review had explicit economic and regulation-streamlining aims. It was to consider 'regulatory blocks impeding research';[93] 'developments and trends affecting the remit, administration, operation and workload of NHS RECs in England';[94] and 'options for investment and measures to contain recurrent costs'.[95] The review was to recommend, among other things, 'how to reduce the time required of researchers starting high quality research'; 'provide for a single point of entry, consistent process,

---

[90]   Scottish Executive Health Department, *Research Governance Framework for Health and Community Care* (Scottish Executive Health Department 2006) Preface.

[91]   Department of Health, *Research Governance Framework for Health and Social Care* (Department of Health 2005) Foreword.

[92]   Susan Mayor, 'Advisory Group to Review NHS Research Ethics Committees' (2004) 329 BMJ 1258.

[93]   Department of Health, *Report of the Ad Hoc Advisory Group on the Operation of NHS Research Ethics Committees* (Department of Health 2004) [hereinafter Lord Warner Report] 17.

[94]   ibid. This said, observers included representatives from Scotland, Northern Ireland, and Wales in recognition of the UK Health Departments' aim to maintain a UK-wide system for ethics review.

[95]   ibid.

and single decision appropriate for all the types of research requiring a NHS REC's opinion'; and 'strengthen the systems, structures and processes supporting NHS RECs to make their business process as efficient as possible and improve users' and committee members' experience of it'. The ad hoc advisory group published their report in June 2005.

Critically, this Lord Warner Report at times stressed a dual role of RECs to protect participants and promote research: '[T]he role of Research Ethics Committees is both to protect the interests of human participants in research and to promote research that is of real value.'[96] Yet elsewhere, the report suggested that the roles were not twinned, but rather, as stated in the GAfREC, primary and secondary:

> It should remain the role of research ethical review to safeguard the rights, dignity, safety and welfare of potential human research participants by providing an independent opinion on the ethical implications of a research proposal. [...] Research of relevance and good quality is essential to underpin further developments in health and social care. This gives Research Ethics Committees a secondary role – to facilitate ethical research.[97]

The Lord Warner Report noted that 'many of the criticisms' they heard from researchers 'reflect pent-up frustration with the operation of the REC system over a number of years, and do not always take account of improvements that COREC has introduced more recently'.[98] Thus, 'major improvement in the efficiency of the process of ethical review in the very recent past [...] has not yet been fully appreciated'.[99] Nonetheless, the report acknowledged that some criticisms were valid, including unexplainable inconsistencies among RECs and overcapacity in the number of RECs (i.e. too many RECs 'with very small workloads'[100]). Systemic reform was urged: 'The achievements of the ethical review system attained so far, whilst impressive, have been largely incremental. The time has now come for a step change in the system of RECs, to address perceived weaknesses in the system, and provide better support for Chairs, members and administrative staff.'[101] Among the report's nine recommendations were further rationalizations of the number of RECs in

---

96   Lord Warner Report (n 93) para 2.6.
97   ibid Conclusions, paras 1–2.
98   ibid para 2.5.
99   ibid Conclusions, para 4.
100   ibid para 3.6.
101   ibid 15.

England, 'with more intense operation for the smaller number result-ing';[102] the creation of 'Scientific Officers' in COREC to support the work of RECs; improvements to the national application form and application process; improvements to quality assurance and training; substantial improvement to local R&D procedures and their interaction with REC review; and a more proportionate review process, that is, excluding from REC review 'surveys or other non-research activity if they present no material ethical issues for human participants'.[103]

Following the Lord Warner Report, in August 2006 COREC released its response publication, *Building on Improvement*, based on consultation with stakeholders. COREC highlighted its role both to facilitate research and help RECs protect participants.[104] The report supported pilot screen-ing studies through early provision of advice, reviews proportionate to the level of risk presented by a project, the establishment of REC centres within certain geographic areas of England, and a reduction in the number of RECs in England to 120 by 2006, with further rationalization thereafter. The COREC report also recommended removing the nominal distinction between MRECs and LRECs, and that MREC appointing authorities be transferred to be in line with those for LRECs.[105] Though the COREC report did not take up the Lord Warner Report's recom-mendation to establish Scientific Officers, it did recommend the creation of a 'new independent group of national research ethics advisers' who would:

> ensure that full committees consider only those studies needing intensive scrutiny. They will be able rapidly to review studies with minimal ethical dimensions as an executive research ethics sub-committee. In England, one or more of these sub-committees will specialise in streamlined review. National research ethics advisers will also be able to support the development of the service by providing training, advice and feedback to RECs and applicants.[106]

---

[102] ibid para 11.

[103] ibid Recommendation, para 1.

[104] Central Office for Research Ethics Committees, *Building on Improve-ment: Implementing the Recommendations of the Report of the Ad Hoc Advisory Group on the Operation of NHS Research Ethics Committees* (National Patient Safety Agency 2006) [hereinafter COREC Report].

[105] In practice, the distinction between MRECs and LRECs ended in 2004, but many RECs still maintained the nominal titles for a number of years thereafter.

[106] COREC Report (n 104) 8. Crucially, as discussed later, this recommenda-tion was never implemented.

The COREC report, like the Lord Warner Report, signalled an explicit governmental effort to streamline regulations and make the regulatory approvals and governance process smoother for researchers to promote high-quality research and national economic benefit.

Several substantial operational and procedural developments occurred within and outwith RECs following COREC's 2006 report to improve the research landscape and ethics review service, and respond to concerns outlined above that RECs were under-regulated but, ironically, also burdensome from a regulatory perspective.

In April 2006, the UK government established the National Institute for Health Research (NIHR) to better fund and support clinical and applied health and social care research, as well as research infrastructure in the NHS. While not directly impactful on RECs, the creation of NIHR signalled the government's intention to position health research as a key driver of the UK's economy. This, in turn, necessitated reforming other aspects in health research regulation to facilitate the realization of research findings into innovations. In April 2007, NRES was established, incorporating both COREC and NHS RECs in England as a means of maintaining a UK-wide regulatory framework for ethics review of research within the NHS.

That same year, the Shared Ethical Debate (ShED)[107] scheme was piloted; it became operational in 2008. The scheme works whereby selected RECs are provided with a real research application (for which consent has been given for its use in the scheme by the investigator) to review as part of their full REC meeting. These RECs review the application as a normal application, recording the discussion and decision in the minutes. The resultant minutes are analysed and the results fed back to the participating RECs, HRA operational teams, the National Research Ethics and Advisors' Panel (NREAP), and the HRA training department in order to develop HRA policies and guidance. ShED has more recently been supplemented with a 'Single Issue Debate', whereby individual RECs are given a short series of questions to respond to concerning a topic (e.g. consent in observational studies), and the responses from the REC are sent back to the HRA for evaluation. ShED's main aim over the years has been to address consistency among RECs and develop standards in ethics review.[108] Other aims are to identify and

---

[107]   Health Research Authority, 'Quality Assurance' <www.hra.nhs.uk/about-the-hra/governance/quality-assurance/> accessed 23 October 2019.

[108]   Hugh Davies, 'Standards for Research Ethics Committees: Purpose, Problems and Possibilities' (2008) 4 Research Ethics Review 152; Peter Heasman and others, 'Helping Research Ethics Committees Share Their Experience,

build consensus on an ethics issue (and the need for possible guidance to applicants and REC members); identify issues in REC processes (i.e. problems regarding minutes); and identify training needs for REC Chairs and members.[109]

Along the same lines, NRES established in 2007 a three-year rolling accreditation programme to audit RECs against agreed standards as detailed in the SOPs and GAfREC. Still ongoing, as with ShED, RECs are issued with an audit decision (now by the HRA) that is either full accreditation, accreditation with conditions (low risk non-compliance identified requiring an action plan), or provisional accreditation (high and low risk issues requiring an action plan). More recently, this has been coupled with 'quality control' checks by HRA Operational Managers, who undertake six-monthly quality control checks on RECs against agreed standards. This includes an annual observation of a REC meeting.

In 2009, NREAP was established. NRES was originally asked by the four UK Health Departments, through the UKECA, to establish a central advisory panel to help with the strategy, quality assurance, and service development of RECs and improve the research environment in the UK.[110] NREAP remains an independent body, but is hosted within the HRA (previously NRES). It serves as a resource to provide advice and support to all RECs funded by the UK Health Departments,[111] as well as appointing authorities in exercising their responsibilities under the GAfREC and SOPs.

In 2010, following the earlier pilot study from 2009 based on the recommendation from the Lord Warner Report, the Proportionate Review Service (PRS) was introduced across the UK. This PRS allows research-ers whose studies present 'no material ethical issues'[112]—previously determined initially by the researcher (who requested to book their application for Proportionate Review), now determined by RES staff,[113]

Learn from Review and Develop Consensus: An Observational Study of the UK Shared Ethical Debate' (2011) 7 Research Ethics 13.

[109]   Collett (n 56) 6.

[110]   ibid.

[111]   Health Research Authority, 'The National Research and Ethics Advisors' Panel (NREAP)' <www.hra.nhs.uk/about-us/committees-and-services/nreap/> accessed 23 October 2019.

[112]   The HRA defines 'no material ethical issues' as having 'minimal risk, burden or intrusion for research participants'. See Health Research Authority, 'Proportionate Review: Information and Guidance for Applicants' <www.hra.nhs.uk/documents/2017/01/proportionate-review-information-guidance-document.pdf> accessed 17 October 2019.

[113]   Health Research Authority, 'Proportionate Review' (n 112).

followed by REC members via a Proportionate Review sub-committee rather than at a full meeting of a REC—to not have to wait as long for a REC opinion as researchers with more 'ethically complex' studies. Indeed, the aim of Proportionate Review is to deliver the final opinion letter to the applicant within 21 calendar days of receipt of a valid application.

Finally, a key infrastructural change in the first decade of the millennium was the move in 2008 of the NRES online form to IRAS,[114] the online application system used to apply for most permissions and approvals for research in health and social care in the UK. In May 2014, IRAS was further modified to interact with the newly established REC Central Booking System and, for the first time, to allow for electronic submission of applications. IRAS is seen as providing multiple benefits for researchers, not the least of which is streamlining the research application process by enabling researchers to enter information about their project once instead of duplicating information in separate application forms. Other benefits include using filters to ensure that the data collected and collated are appropriate to the type of project, and consequently the permissions and approvals required; and helping researchers meet regulatory and governance requirements. IRAS allows researchers to use a 'Project Filter' to select the type of research and enable other sections and forms relevant to their project (e.g. ionizing radiation, new/existing tissue samples, adults unable to consent) to appear. The IRAS NHS REC application form, and especially the questions it poses to researchers, has become central to the work of RECs, as will be seen later in this book.

3.2   Ongoing Criticisms and the 2011 Academy of Medical Sciences Report

At this point in the historical tracing, it would be beneficial to step back and situate the criticisms of and reforms to RECs in a broader context. If many in society support the concept of prospective ethics review of a research project by a committee of qualified people, many others have not supported the past practices of RECs. For as long as they have existed, RECs have been the source of opprobrium by the research community and other commentators, mainly because they are seen as under-, over- or simply mis-regulated bureaucratic bulwarks against otherwise ethical, minimally risky, or non-risky research. Empirical

---

[114]   IRAS <www.myresearchproject.org.uk/>.

research has indicated a high level of variation of decision-making processes in RECs[115] and dissatisfaction from various stakeholders.[116]

Many of the problems encountered in RECs have been due paradoxically to accusations of both weak regulation and decentralization (leading to duplicative review, procedural inconsistency, and substantive inconsistency of decision-making), and also over-regulation and centralization (leading to cumbersome rules and complex thickets of disproportionate regulation for minimal risk research). Yet, unlike other jurisdictions, RECs in the UK remain governed relatively lightly through statutory regulation. RECs hold a long tradition of independence from central or institutional control. Indeed, that NHS RECs are not formally associated with any specific research institution is what distinguishes them most from US IRBs and Canadian REBs that also evaluate research involving patients in hospitals and healthy volunteers. Though RECs in the NHS system have existed sporadically and informally since the late 1960s, as discussed, they had no formal standing until guidance was put forth by the Department of Health in 1991, and it must be emphasized that this was merely guidance, backed with no legal enforceability. Effectively, these guidelines were the standards governing their practice, though RECs had the discretion to exercise their judgement as to what their primary function should be—and indeed some did not abide by or accept the guidelines.[117] As a consequence, RECs were permitted to thrive and self-regulate independently. Across the UK, local RECs created separate fiefdoms of customs, standards, and rules that caused, it is said, administrative nightmares for researchers embarking on multi-site and even single-site studies.

The response by the UK government in the last decade to the criticism against RECs and health research regulation more broadly has been to streamline the regulation of health research, and to make the regulation

---

[115] See e.g. Bernard Barber and others, *Research on Human Subjects: Problems of Social Control in Medical Experimentation* (Russell Sage Foundation 1973); Mary Dixon-Woods and others, 'Written Work: The Social Functions of Research Ethics Committee Letters' (2007) 65 Social Science & Medicine 792.

[116] See e.g. Paul Benson, 'The Social Control of Human Biomedical Research: An Overview and Review of the Literature' (1989) 29 Social Science & Medicine 1; Konrad Jamrozik, 'The Case for a New System for Oversight of Research on Human Subjects' (2000) 26 Journal of Medical Ethics 334; Charles Warlow, 'Clinical Research Under the Cosh Again' (2004) 329 BMJ 241.

[117] Neuberger (n 49).

more proportionate so as to facilitate (ideally) more research and greater economic prosperity.[118]

The persistent criticism levelled against the clogged regulatory space of 'human subjects research' was evidently (and some would add, eventually) heard by the UK government. In March 2010, the then-ruling Labour government (through the Minister of Health Andy Burnham) asked the AMS, an independent body in the UK founded in 1998 that represents medical science, to undertake a 'rapid independent review' of health research amid concern that strict regulation was driving research abroad.[119] The Academy convened a work group of senior doctors and scientists; only 3 of the 19 members were drawn from outside the NHS or the biomedical research sector. Its now well-cited report, *A New Pathway for the Regulation and Governance of Health Research*,[120] published only several months later in January 2011, found much to criticize and sounded alarm bells: 'UK health research activities are being seriously undermined by an overly complex regulatory and govern- ance environment',[121] it intoned, and there was no evidence of improved participant or patient safety attributable to the regulatory framework.

The AMS report recommended that the UK's regulation and govern- ance framework around health research be underpinned by four prin- ciples, the first two of which were 'to safeguard the well-being of research participants', and 'to facilitate high-quality health research to the public benefit'.[122] Crucially, similar to the RCP Guidelines but dissimilar to the GAfREC and first edition of the RGF, when it came to discussing recommendations for RECs, the report pinned them with two equal responsibilities: 'Research proposals are reviewed [by RECs] to consider whether they provide sufficient protection for the interests and safety of research participants and to enable ethical research that is of benefit to society.'[123]

---

[118]   Jean McHale, 'Reforming the Regulation of Health Research in England and Wales: New Challenges: New Pitfalls' (2013) 1 Journal of Medical Law and Ethics 23.

[119]   Donald Asprey, 'UK Government Asks Academy to Review Regulation of Research' (2010) 340 BMJ c1770.

[120]   Academy of Medical Sciences, *A New Pathway for the Regulation and Governance of Health Research* (Academy of Medical Sciences 2011).

[121]   ibid 5.

[122]   ibid 6. The other two principles were: '3. To be proportionate, efficient and coordinated. 4. To maintain and build confidence in the conduct and value of health research through independence, transparency, accountability and consist- ency' (ibid).

[123]   ibid 73.

Though RECs came away relatively unscathed in the AMS report, the health research regulatory and governance environment as a whole was seen by the AMS in need of substantial pruning, including the need for 'a proportionate approach to ethics review' in line with US and Canadian approaches.[124] With respect to ethics review, the AMS report found that:

> High ethical standards in research can only be partially achieved through regulation and governance and researchers need support to identify and address the ethical issues arising in their research, outside of applying for an ethics opinion. In addition to the need to embed a proportionate approach within the ethics system, including implementation of 'proportionate review' following the NRES pilot, we recommend that [...] NRES should lead on improving support and advice for researchers by providing centralised, coordinated guidance and training on ethical issues for health researchers. Institutions engaged in health research should also improve the local availability of ethics advice and the training of local support staff.[125]

Significantly, the AMS report recommended the establishment of an independent, central 'Health Research Agency' 'to rationalise the regulation and governance of all health research'.[126] It also recommended the establishment of a National Research Governance Service within the proposed HRA to perform all project-wide NHS governance (i.e. R&D) checks and recommend research projects as suitable for undertaking within the NHS. In the AMS's view, the HRA would be capable of providing 'the necessary oversight and impetus' to oversee the regulation and governance of health research, as well as 'removing complexity and streamlining the pathway as a whole'.[127] It would also provide a 'home for some aspects of regulation and governance that urgently require better coordination and clearer governance'.[128] Other recommendations included providing greater access to patient data for research while protecting individuals' interests and embedding a culture that would value research within the NHS.

---

[124]   ibid 76.

[125]   ibid 79.

[126]   ibid 7. The AMS report acknowledged that the proposal for a 'Health Research Agency' was a development of the Department of Health's recommendation in its July 2010 report to create a single regulator of health research. See Department of Health, *Liberating the NHS: Report of the Arm's-Length Bodies Review* (Department of Health 2010).

[127]   AMS (n 120) 100.

[128]   ibid.

3.3   Government Response: 2011 – Present

The coalition Conservative-Liberal Democrat government quickly took up the AMS report's recommendation as announced that same year in its March 2011 budget statement,[129] agreeing with the report's findings and emphasizing the economic gains to be reaped through streamlining of regulation: 'The complexity of health research regulation and governance has increased over the last twenty years through successive legislative changes. National complexity was then compounded by diverse local approval systems, inconsistent, sometimes risk-averse, local interpretations, and confusion about the standards for compliance that apply to different types of research.'[130] The government announced that it would:

> set up a new health research regulatory agency to streamline regulation and improve the cost-effectiveness of clinical trials. [...] At national level, the Government will create a health research regulatory agency to combine and streamline the approvals for health research which are at present scattered across many organisations. This will reduce the regulatory burden on firms, improve the timeliness of decisions about clinical trials and hence the cost-effectiveness of their delivery in the UK, and has clear support from the Academy of Medical Sciences Review of health research regulation and governance. As a first step, the Government will establish this year a Special Health Authority with the National Research Ethics Service as its core. The new agency will work closely with the Medicines and Healthcare products Regulatory Agency to create a unified approval process and promote proportionate standards for compliance and inspection within a consistent national system of research governance.[131]

Thus, the HRA was established by the UK government as a central health research regulator for the UK and a one-stop-shop for approvals and accompanying guidance.[132] As recommended by the AMS, and which was presumably already in line with the government's wishes, the HRA was created rapidly—on 1 December that same year—as an interim

---

[129]   HM Treasury, Department for Business Innovation & Skills, *Plan for Growth* (HM Treasury 2011) 91.

[130]   ibid.

[131]   ibid 92.

[132]   The UK government created the HRA in part, though, because the National Patient Safety Agency had recently been abolished. See HL Deb 15 November 2011, vol 732, col GC219. This said, the HRA was expected to act more boldly than NRES and the NPSA.

Special Health Authority.[133] The creating order made clear the HRA's role in promoting research:

Functions of the Authority

3.—(1) The Authority is to exercise—

(a) such functions in connection with—

(i) the facilitation and promotion of research;

(ii) the establishment of Research Ethics Committees, and the appointment and indemnification of members of Research Ethics Committees; and

(b) such other functions;

as the Secretary of State may direct.[134]

In May that year, the GAfREC was revised. Taking up the AMS report's call for a more proportionate ethics review, the revised second edition of the GAfREC introduced several streamlining moves, including the removal of required REC review for certain types of research (e.g. research involving NHS staff recruited by virtue of their professional role; research limited to use of or access to a care organization's premises or facilities). At the same time, however, it retained the language about primary and secondary responsibilities of RECs. (A new edition of the GAfREC was issued in 2018 but it is primarily a technical update to take account of legal, policy, and operational developments since the previous version was issued.)

Since its formation in December 2011, the HRA's mission has been to promote and protect the interests of patients, streamline regulation, and

---

[133] The Health Research Authority (Establishment and Constitution) Order 2011, 2011 No 2323. See also the Health Research Authority Regulations 2011, 2011 No 2341. The HRA was abolished as a 'Special Health Authority' in the Care Act 2014, s 109(3), when it became a statutory body corporate (i.e. Non-Departmental Public Body) as of 1 January 2015. See the Care Act 2014 (Health Education England and the Health Research Authority) (Consequential Amendments and Revocations) Order 2015, SI 2015/137 and see also SI 2014/3090. It is important to note that the Health Research Authority (Establishment and Constitution) Order 2011 applied in relation to England only. The HRA's legal remit covers England only; however, it works closely with the devolved administrations in Scotland, Wales, and Northern Ireland to support UK-wide compatibility.

[134] The Health Research Authority (Establishment and Constitution) Order 2011, s 3(1).

promote transparency in health and social care research.[135] Proportionate regulation and streamlined research processes are a driving aim of the HRA. Emphasis on research promotion was reflected explicitly in statutory regulation for the first time in the Health and Social Care Act 2012, which imposed new duties on the Secretary of State for Health and Clinical Commissioning Groups to promote research relevant to the NHS and to use the evidence obtained from such research.[136] Emphasis on research promotion is further reflected most pronouncedly in the most recent change in the regulatory apparatus of RECs (at least in England)— the Care Act 2014, which is a watershed piece of statutory regulation of health research.[137] It established the HRA as a Non-Departmental Public Body to foster the HRA's UK-wide responsibility for health and social care research governance.[138] The main objective of the HRA in exercising its functions is stated in the Care Act 2014 as twofold:

(a) to protect participants and potential participants in health or social care research and the general public by encouraging research that is safe and ethical, and

(b) to promote the interests of those participants and potential participants and the general public by facilitating the conduct of research that is safe and ethical (including by promoting transparency in research).[139]

In exercising its functions, the HRA—under the law—'must promote the co-ordination and standardisation of practice in the United Kingdom relating to the regulation of health and social care research; and it must, in doing so, seek to ensure that such regulation is proportionate'.[140] The Care Act 2014 requires the HRA and eight key regulators and government bodies involved in health research to 'co-operate with each other in the exercise of their respective functions relating to health or social care research, with a view to co-ordinating and standardising practice relating

---

[135]   Health Research Authority, 'About Us' <www.hra.nhs.uk/about-us/what-we-do/> accessed 17 October 2019 and Health Research Authority, 'Our Vision & Purpose' <www.hra.nhs.uk/about-us/what-we-do/our-vision-purpose/> accessed 17 October 2019.

[136]   NHS Act 2006, ss 1E, 14Y.

[137]   Most of the provisions in the Care Act 2014 extend only to England, save where specified otherwise. But see Care Act 2014, Explanatory Notes, Territorial Extent and Application (paras 34–54).

[138]   Care Act 2014, s 109. The HRA became a statutory body corporate on 1 January 2015.

[139]   ibid s 110(2).

[140]   ibid s 111(3).

to the regulation of such research'.[141] Similarly, the Act states that the 'HRA and each devolved authority must co-operate with each other in the exercise of their respective functions relating to the regulation of assessments of the ethics of health and social care research, with a view to co-ordinating and standardising practice in the United Kingdom relating to such regulation'.[142]

The Act also speaks directly to RECs in sections 112–15. The HRA is authorized by the Act to recognize, establish, and abolish RECs in England[143] and 'must ensure' that these RECs 'provide an efficient and effective means of assessing the ethics of health and social care research'.[144] In other words, the HRA now has statutory power to directly manage RECs, including, for example, the power 'to require RECs to impose conditions on approvals for clinical trials'.[145] The HRA must publish a 'REC policy document' (currently the GAfREC) that 'specifies the requirements which it expects research ethics committees it recognises or establishes [...] to comply with' and 'must monitor their compliance with those requirements'.[146] The HRA is also empowered to 'do such other things in relation to research ethics committees it recognises or establishes [...] as it considers appropriate'.[147] Explicitly mentioned examples include: 'co-ordinate their work; allocate work to them; develop and maintain training programmes designed to ensure that their members and staff can carry out their work effectively;' and 'provide them with advice and help (including help in the form of financial assistance)'.[148]

In sum, the Care Act 2014 has explicitly imported the rhetoric of participant protection and research promotion—language that has evolved from RCP Guidelines, literature from the research and academic community, commissioned reports, and governmental policy—to statutory regulation governing a central regulatory body that has direct managerial oversight of RECs. It is clear that the Care Act 2014 seeks to promote the collective value of health research through streamlining regulation.

---

[141] Care Act 2014, s 111(1).
[142] ibid s 111(4).
[143] ibid s 115.
[144] ibid s 112(1). See also s 110(1)(b) ('The main functions of the HRA are – [...] functions relating to research ethics committees').
[145] *R (on the application of Richmond Pharmacology Ltd) v The Health Research Authority* [2015] EWHC 2238 (Admin), para 4.
[146] Care Act 2014, s 112(3).
[147] ibid s 112(4).
[148] ibid.

Certainly, this reflects a broader push by the UK government, which through its statutory and thus binding Regulators' Code, requires regulators to 'avoid imposing unnecessary regulatory burdens through their regulatory activities', to 'choose proportionate approaches to those they regulate', and to consider, among other things, 'how they might support or enable economic growth for compliant businesses and other regulated entities'.[149]

What remains unclear, however, is how the HRA intends to 'streamline' regulation and deliver 'proportionate' regulation through the practical work of those regulators it governs, namely RECs. The AMS's report from 2011 recommended that the HRA 'should lead on the development of proportionate approaches to regulation and governance that take into account the benefits and risks of a research study, rather than applying a "one-size-fits-all" model. This should be embedded through a new edition of the Research Governance Framework.'[150] As the RGFs from each of the four nations have now been transformed into a harmonized UK Policy Framework for Health and Social Care Research, through what regulatory approach(es) will the HRA manage RECs? In turn, will RECs heed the HRA's steering (i.e. catalysing) or rowing (i.e. controlling) role—and what will be the response for RECs and other regulatory actors outside of England?

Based on white papers and policy papers from the Scottish and English governments over the past few years, there seems to be a strong degree of consistent approach. The Department of Health and Social Care has published several policy papers advocating further system efficiencies, such as a governmental commitment 'to simplify how research is regulated as part of our plans to increase innovation in medical science';[151] and bestowing upon 'the NHS a duty to encourage medical research, so more patients have the chance to take part in clinical studies'.[152] The most recent NHS Constitution for England now reflects this, stating: 'The NHS aspires to the highest standards of excellence and professionalism [...] through its commitment to innovation and to the promotion, conduct and use of research to improve the current and future

---

149   Department for Business, Innovation and Skills, *Regulators' Code* (UK Government 2014). The Regulators' Code came into statutory effect on 6 April 2014 under the Legislative and Regulatory Reform Act 2006.

150   Academy of Medical Sciences (n 120) 89.

151   Department of Health, *Policy Paper: 2010 to 2015 Government Policy: NHS Efficiency* (UK Government 2010).

152   ibid.

health and care of the population', and that the NHS 'pledges [...] to inform you of research studies in which you may be eligible to participate'.[153]

Likewise, but even more resoundingly, the Scottish Government released a report in 2015 stating while it was pleased with its nation's ethics review system, further efficiencies could be gained: 'it is imperative that Scotland continues to lead the agenda on streamlining the approvals process and reducing bureaucracy; and there is scope for further improvement'.[154] To that end, the Scottish Government announced that the CSO would seek to combine the Scottish RES and NHS Research Scotland (NRS) R&D Offices into a 'single integrated service for researchers while retaining the independence of the REC decision making function'; that the CSO would arrange for 'shared access to study data for ethics and R&D staff through the HRA's HARP database, streamlining access to electronic documents for R&D staff throughout Scotland'; that the CSO would 'work with the HRA to revise the Research Governance Framework and implement an efficient ethics and R&D permission system across the UK that both builds on the efficiencies already delivered through [NRS] and operates seamlessly for sponsors and researchers across the UK'; and that the CSO would 'refocus the early contact of ethics and NHS R&D staff with researchers on facilitating study approvals, with named R&D contacts being given to support the researcher in obtaining those approvals'.[155] As of the time of writing, this merger of the Scottish RES and NRS R&D Offices has not occurred.

As Hedgecoe writes, even as the REC SOPs have allowed for some regulatory control over REC processes by the state, 'the content of REC decisions remains largely outside Department of Health control'.[156] The HRA and CSO do not have the legitimacy or statutory authority to directly amend statutory regulation, and the independence of NHS RECs is a highly cherished value, as reflected in the Scottish white paper mentioned above. What the HRA and CSO can do, though, is transform the health research process by amending regulatory instruments affecting RECs, and acting itself, or helping RECs and the actors therein act, as a

---

[153]   Department of Health, *The NHS Constitution for England* (UK Government 2015).

[154]   Scottish Government, *Delivering Innovation Through Research: Scottish Government Health and Social Care Research Strategy* (Scottish Government 2015) 11.

[155]   ibid 16–17.

[156]   Hedgecoe, 'A Deviation from Standard Design?' (n 45) 74.

steward for researchers to guide them through the process (i.e. the multiple stages) of embarking upon a health research project.

The HRA is working closely with its equivalent regulatory bodies in the devolved nations to foster education and training for REC members, staff, and the research community.[157] It is also working to foster harmonization of ethics review processes through its publishing of multiple policies and guidance documents, and through HRA Approval, which is largely an instantiation of the recommendation in the 2011 AMS report to create a National Research Governance Service within the HRA.[158] Indeed, greater harmonization and simplification of forms is most recently manifest in the HRA's announcement in 2017 that a combined IRAS form that merges the REC and R&D forms, previously only in place for projects where the lead NHS R&D office is based in England, would be available for use across the UK, saving time and effort for applicants and sponsors and helping to build UK-wide consistency.[159] Almost certainly these arrangements will further assuage many of the concerns levelled against RECs over the years. Indeed, as this Chapter 3 has emphasized, fewer criticisms are levelled against ethics review and RECs today.

Consequently, many of the long-standing criticisms of RECs have been quelled, first through influential reports authored by the research community itself in the past decade that were directly taken up by the government, and more recently, through the alignment of the research community, industry (particularly as sponsors or funders of research), and government in designing a regulatory regime that optimizes competition (through efficiency and accelerated review pathways) and economic gain. This does cause one to wonder, though: how, if at all, does this next-generation regulatory reform impact the independence and primary function of RECs, which must, under the stewardship of the HRA and its mandate to streamline regulation, work to 'provide an efficient and effective means of assessing the ethics of health and social care research'?[160] As Kerrison and Pollock remarked a decade ago following the passage of the Clinical Trials Regulations 2004 and the creation of the UKECA, 'by taking control of the ethics review, a

---

[157] See e.g. Health Research Authority, 'Learning' <www.hra.nhs.uk/planning-and-improving-research/learning/> accessed 17 October 2019.

[158] Academy of Medical Sciences (n 120) 83.

[159] Health Research Authority, 'Four Nations NHS/HSC Compatibility Programme' <www.hra.nhs.uk/about-us/partnerships/four-nations-compatibility-programme/> accessed 17 October 2019.

[160] Care Act 2014, s 112(1).

government intent on seeing biomedical research as an economic driver will be in a good position to ensure that [ethics] committees do not raise difficult ethical barriers to such research'.[161] Increased regulatory speed, coded as 'efficiency' and embedded in the regulatory documents governing RECs and in the practices of RECs, certainly begs questions about the role of industry promoting competitive edges and in the wider implications of such a regulatory feature in health research.

IV. CONCLUSION

In this chapter, I have argued that while the value and REC role (or responsibility) of research promotion has emerged as a recent statutory phenomenon in health research regulation, perhaps as a kind of beacon to encourage a more proportionate or streamlined approach to regulating health research, it has nevertheless existed throughout the history of RECs, appearing in various disguises alongside the role of participant protection. I have also argued that, having become entrenched in the regulation of health research for more than half a century, and through 'steady, incremental institutional change',[162] RECs are now governed by the government and by central regulatory agencies, administrative staff and offices, standardized forms and communications, lengthy governance arrangements,[163] and SOPs—the latest version of which stands at a daunting 302 pages.[164]

As advisory but fundamentally research gatekeeping bodies, RECs are a key node situated in the health research regulatory space. The criticisms levied against them have been intense, historically marked by concerns of both under-regulation of RECs and over-regulation by RECs of research projects. As one REC member observed after 20 years of service:

In the 1980s the research ethics world seemed much simpler. The Declaration of Helsinki informed our discussions and decisions, and we supplemented this when the need arose from those few guidelines that existed. We weren't hamstrung by 'Europe,' acts of parliament, regulations, and a clock obsessed set of standard operating procedures; nor were we working in a climate of constant criticism. I feel increasingly caught between a rock and a hard place

---

[161] Kerrison and Pollock (n 84) 488.
[162] Hedgecoe, 'Scandals' (n 52) 590.
[163] See GAfREC (n 2).
[164] See Health Research Authority, *Standard Operating Procedures for Research Ethics Committees* (Version 7.4, Health Research Authority 2019). By comparison, version 1.0, released in March 2004, was 182 pages.

as we try to protect patients from silly research and researchers from silly regulations.[165]

What we have seen in the UK is a march, aided by health research interest groups such as the AMS, towards significant regulatory reform underpinned by a neoliberal discourse stressing market rationality and economic optimization. Hedgecoe suggests that ethics review is a form of 'professional self-regulation without a profession', where 'the overall aim of such review centers on the needs of researchers and research funders, as opposed to the idea that ethics review is driven by the need to increase protection for research subjects'.[166] Later chapters will test that claim. Undoubtedly, the march towards reform has culminated recently in a turn towards the law for a facilitative remedy—as indeed law is often seen as the ultimate guide for bringing order to rough regulatory terrain. Law, seen in the Care Act 2014, is viewed as a beacon of clarity and power, providing the HRA a firm legal footing and a legal mandate, albeit set within a flexible framework, for streamlining health research regulation and facilitating research.

But law alone cannot provide a complete remedy for the concerns expressed by so many for so many years. Ethical judgements and the workings of these committees of diverse individuals must operate in the regulatory gap that exists between documented law and everyday practice, and in the space between protection and promotion. The Care Act 2014, GAfREC, SOPs, and the UK Policy Framework alone cannot dictate the behaviour and everyday practices of RECs. As we will see, ethical behaviour and regulatory stewardship practised by regulatory actors must be co-produced with regulation, as indeed health research regulation and ethical judgement are co-dependent.

The critical questions that arise from the historically grounded argument laid out in this Chapter 3 are as follows:

(1)   What is the nature of the regulation that now governs RECs?
(2)   In turn, what is the nature of RECs' approach towards reviewing research projects, and what do these practices and ethical judgements look like against the backdrop of recent regulatory reform at the national and international level that seeks to promote a more proportionate and streamlined regulatory approach?

---

[165]   George Masterton, 'Two Decades on an Ethics Committee' (2006) 332 BMJ 615.
[166]   Hedgecoe, 'Scandals' (n 52) 591–2.

(3) More broadly, what ought a regulatory framework for realizing the objective—or reconciliation—of participant protection and research promotion look like?

In the next chapter, I explain how these questions were addressed in my empirical research, guided by qualitative research methods and a methodology informed by regulatory theory and anthropology—what I term an anthropology of regulation.

4.   Anthropology of regulation

I. INTRODUCTION

Chapters 2 and 3 provided a conceptual framework and historical regulatory tracing of RECs, arguing that the roles and practices of RECs may be shifting in response to next-generation health research regulation. I showed how the previous generation of regulatory design, which was notably marked by self-regulation of health research involving participants—that is, ad hoc ethics peer review largely conducted by fellow scientists based on local customs and guidance from the medical profession (and the RCP especially)—gradually gave way to stricter, stronger, more centralized forms of regulation, particularly through statutes and policies set by the government. This was done to provide better coordination and coherence for researchers, research sponsors, and publics, in large part as a response to years of criticism that generated a crisis of reputational risk to RECs, threatening their legitimacy. This was also done by necessity in response to developments in EU law, such as the Clinical Trials Directive 2001.

This chapter situates the conceptual framework and the historical tracing in the present context by sketching the possible regulatory techniques and behaviours employed by RECs and their managing regulators. Subsequent chapters will consider the empirical question of whether, and, if so, how these regulatory techniques and behaviours appear in practice. Here, I explain the research approach, theoretical underpinnings, and analytical concepts that drive my empirical research.

To make sense of my empirical data, I employ the method of thematic analysis (explained below), which is informed by 'sensitizing concepts'[1] drawn from regulatory theory and anthropology. Specifically, I explore regulatory theory, design, and strategy, focusing on the concepts of 'regulatory space', 'proportionate regulation', and 'risk-based regulatory approach'. These sensitizing concepts add further analytic weight to the

---

[1]   A sensitizing concept is an interpretive device for a qualitative study that informs the overall research problem. See Glenn Bowen, 'Grounded Theory and Sensitizing Concepts' (2006) 5 International Journal of Qualitative Methods 1.

historical tracing undertaken in Chapter 3. They also allow us to better understand the precise regulatory form and functions of RECs, as well as the regulatory strategies employed by RECs and other regulators of health research, which will be discussed in subsequent chapters.

The central question that will emerge from the theoretical discussion in this chapter is: what do the empirical research findings tell us about the nature of the interaction between central regulators (foremost the HRA) and RECs, and the functional operations and deliberative processes of RECs in an era of twinned regulatory objectives of participant protection and research promotion? Another central question that will emerge is: do the empirical research findings reflect and validate the suggestions supplied in Chapters 2 and 3 that RECs engage in risk-based regulation, and that health research regulation is increasingly streamlined and proportionate? In other words, are RECs *really* risk-based, proportionality-attuned regulators, or is something else going on, and if so, what? What might proportionate and 'streamlined' regulation mean?

I will argue in this chapter that the main approaches to investigating law empirically (e.g. legal anthropology, socio-legal studies) should be supplemented to adequately answer my research questions as these approaches are commonly designed to understand law and legal practice rather than regulation and regulatory practice—fields that I have endeavoured to show are ontologically distinct. I explain the justification for going beyond them and harnessing a novel methodological approach that I call an 'anthropology of regulation', which structures my overall empirical enquiry. I claim that this is a methodological supplement to existing anthropological and socio-legal research approaches. As anthropology of regulation draws explicit attention to processes, passages, and change, I further draw on the anthropological concept of liminality. Liminality thus also serves as a sensitizing concept, in addition to those concepts provided by regulatory theory. Together with regulatory theory, liminality helps us to better understand the nature of transformations of actors within the regulatory space, the form of regulation in this space, as well as the behaviours and experiences of actors as they go through processes of change. In short, anthropology of regulation as an approach and field of enquiry adds explanatory power to my empirical data and to the kinds of contributions that socio-legal work might also make.

Thus, the key aim of this chapter is to explain and justify my research approach. I do this in several steps. First, I show how regulatory theory provides a solid but ultimately insufficient foundation on its own for the empirical investigation. Second, I explain that there is a need for an empirically grounded discussion of regulatory practice, but that extant socio-legal and legal anthropology approaches need to be supplemented to address fully the research questions. Therefore, I propose an anthropology of regulation that blends the theoretical with the empirical, and which affords a methodological contribution to the fields of socio-legal studies and legal anthropology, in part by drawing attention to (regulatory) processes and change, which was illustrated in the conceptual framework and historical tracing in the previous chapters. I argue that this approach, underpinned by regulatory theory and liminality, serves as a robust platform for making sense of the empirical data, as well as setting those data in a more meaningful context relative to the historical account. It offers a richer account of the steady, incremental transitions in health research regulatory practice across time. It also offers new ways of imagining the regulatory framework for ethics review of health research, namely through regulatory stewardship, and of understanding how liminality provides a powerful, unique, and useful heuristic for making sense of how RECs navigate participant protection and research promotion in an era of next-generation health research regulation.

II. REGULATORY THEORY

Regulatory theory is defined as 'a set of propositions or hypotheses about *why* regulation emerges, *which actors* contribute to that emergence and typical *patterns of interaction* between regulatory actors'.[2] Regulatory theory serves as an important underpinning because it helps provide an explanation for what is going on.

RECs are regulators of health research in that they quite clearly serve as social controls of science. They are 'independent' bodies charged with assessing the ethical acceptability of health research proposals, and thereby determine whether the project *should* be undertaken. Since their establishment, RECs have been delegated authority from the government and regulatory agencies to determine, often through norms of practice set by the medical and science professions, the ethical acceptability of a research project. On a case-by-case basis, RECs set the conditions around how a given project should be conducted. Always, their independence from both managing regulatory authorities and other organizations (be it NHS Trusts or Health Boards, or otherwise) is emphasized.

While RECs regulate the activities of researchers, above them sits a RES (not always named such) in each of the four nations that regulate the RECs' activities. Each RES is itself situated within a regulatory authority

---

2   Bronwen Morgan and Karen Yeung, *An Introduction to Law and Regulation: Text and Materials* (CUP 2007) 16.

(e.g. CSO in Scotland, HRA in England) that issues sets of commands to be applied by the RES, and through them, RECs, within their respective but coordinated jurisdictions. The HRA is the primary authority for RECs in England but cooperates with equivalent authorities in the three other nations in the exercise of their respective functions relating to the regulation of assessments of the ethics of health and social care research, with a view to coordinating and standardizing practice in the UK relating to such regulation.[3] Thus, in many ways, the HRA is the UK's primary health research authority with regulatory command of RECs (*primes inter pares*) as seen through its control of regulatory instruments such as the REC SOPs, GAfREC, and the UK Policy Framework.

The ethnographic work of Neil Stephens and colleagues at the UK Stem Cell Bank[4] suggests, however, that even if a (meta- or managing) regulator has ultimate legal authority, it may not necessarily have day-to-day authority. Stephens and colleagues found that despite what formal regulations mandate regarding the quality and origins of the stem cell lines received from depositors, scientists engage in a kind of interpretive flexibility when it comes to interpreting and operationalizing the regulations. Scientists at the UK Stem Cell Bank engage in 'bridging strategies' to reconcile the written demands of regulators and the social demands of scientific practice. Efforts to resolve tensions in the practical implementation of regulatory guidance are done through 'instantiated regulation', which describes the processes of translating written regulatory guidance into practical action ('making the documented doable'), and which serves as 'a response to the interpretative flexibility of regulatory texts'.[5] For Stephens and colleagues, regulatory instantiation demonstrates the inherent interpretive and procedural flexibility of regulatory scripts and demonstrates that regulation is always distributed and locally managed by the actors on the ground. In the case of the UK Stem Cell Bank, regulatory instantiation was demonstrated in the (1) iterative modification of the Cell Line Information Form by the UK Stem Cell Bank working together with laboratories; (2) visits to the laboratories by the UK Stem Cell Bank, which built trust through networks; and (3) the shaping of both laboratory and UK Stem Cell Bank practices as a result of these interactions.

---

[3] Care Act 2014, s 111(4).

[4] Neil Stephens and others, 'Documenting the Doable and Doing the Documented: Bridging Strategies at the UK Stem Cell Bank' (2011) 41 Social Studies of Science 791.

[5] ibid 794.

The insight from Stephens and colleagues ties in with the discussion of the interstitial nature of many regulatory spaces within a formal regulated space. Their insight suggests that as both regulators and regulatees, RECs, too, must navigate situationally specific ways to implement regulations (from the SOPs, GAfREC, and so on) that govern their practice in determining the ethical acceptability of research proposals. It also further suggests that RECs may have more regulatory flexibility than we may think and that part of this flexibility is based on 'interpersonal trust in instantiating and maintaining system trust'.[6] In the following chapters, insights from Stephens and colleagues will be invoked in discussions surrounding the key theme of 'regulatory stewardship' and its connection with liminality.

Describing the nested regulatory structure of RECs and opportunities for instantiated regulation is distinct from exploring *why* ethics review regulation emerged in the first place, *which actors* contributed to that emergence, and the *patterns of interaction* between RECs, the RES, and other regulatory actors, to say nothing of what the day-to-day regulatory practice of RECs looks like. What constitutes ethics review in the practices of RECs, particularly as they become more institutionalized and this 'next-generation' regulation is brought to bear on them?

Regulatory theory helps frame these questions. As the historian Laura Stark has documented, ethics committees first emerged because of historical contingency and political manoeuvring by lawyers, policymakers, and legislators in Washington, DC in the mid-1960s. Out of concern for ongoing research scandals, potential legal liability, and governmental regulation, National Institutes of Health (NIH) policymakers enacted a delegated 'satellite regulator' model as an adaptation of the 'group consideration' structure from the NIH Clinical Center's Clinical Research Committee.[7] In this model, committees of self-regulating medico-scientific peers at local institutions would review protocols submitted by fellow physician-researchers at their institutions and give 'due consideration' to 'pertinent ethical issues'.[8]

In the UK, we saw a follow-on effect from this American creation, with hospitals establishing RECs beginning in the late 1960s as a

---

6   ibid 808.

7   Laura Stark, *Behind Closed Doors: IRBs and the Making of Ethical Research* (University of Chicago Press 2012).

8   US Public Health Service, 'Revised Procedure on Clinical Research and Investigation Involving Human Subjects', 1 July 1966 (Department of Health, Education and Welfare 1966).

pragmatic response from the US Surgeon General's policy.[9] But growth and development of RECs were incremental and patchy; they were distinctly not in response to research scandals.[10] Contrary to the US, it was not until the new millennium that statutory regulation was enacted that set legally binding requirements on RECs' form and function—and technically, this was only for CTIMPs. Thus, for much of their history, RECs were unique products of actively designed decentred regulation,[11] whereby the government shifted authority to and trust in the medical and scientific professions as well as independent regulatory authorities to set the principles and standards for REC operation. However, as we will see, RECs exhibit a unique kind of regulatory design as compared to common understandings of decentred regulation in that the locus of the activity of regulating RECs has been gradually shifting *towards* the state.

Surveying the history, three rationales appear to have been at play in the aim of creating health research ethics regulation beginning in the 1960s, both voluntarily from within the profession and top-down from state actors. These were: (1) to protect research participants from potential harm by minimizing the risks exposed to them by the proposed research; (2) to address information asymmetries between researchers and participants by requiring researchers to explain clearly (e.g. through information sheets) what would be involved in the project, including the potential risks and benefits, to allow (healthy) volunteers and patients to make an informed decision about whether to participate in the project; and (3) to broker a compromise between public welfare-attuned politicians and regulators concerned with safety and public trust (not to mention being perceived to act in the public interest), and professional physician-researchers who were concerned with maintaining freedom of science and minimizing the impact of external regulation that might hinder their research (the argument for 'clinical autonomy'). In the early

---

[9] US Public Health Service, 'Memo to the Heads of Institutions Conducting Research with Public Health Service Grants from the Surgeon General', 8 February 1966 (Department of Health, Education and Welfare 1966).

[10] Adam Hedgecoe, 'Scandals, Ethics, and Regulatory Change in Biomedical Research' (2017) 42 Science, Technology, & Human Values 577.

[11] Decentred regulation can be defined as 'a shift (and recognition of such a shift) in the locus of the activity of "regulating" from the state to other, multiple, locations, and the adoption on the part of the state of particular strategies of regulation'. See Julia Black, 'Decentring Regulation: Understanding the Role of Regulation and Self-Regulation in a "Post-Regulatory" World' (2001) 54 Current Legal Problems 103, 112.

age of RECs' creation, a mixture of public and private interests drove regulation in this nascent regulatory space.

However, the historical tracing in Chapter 3 also suggests that regulatory developments in this area have never purely been a matter of 'public' *or* 'private' interests (or some hybrid mix thereof), though certainly both exist, and the recent legal instantiation of research promotion may signal a surge of private interests, particularly from the research community (including industry). More is occurring in health research regulation than a prolonged war between public welfare and research autonomy, interspersed with battles or scandals. Instead, even from the nascent stage of the REC system's creation and the emergence of regulatory controls on science, there has been an emphasis on social processes and how they shape health research ethics regulation. The historical tracing in Chapter 3 demonstrates that the progression of regulatory controls, both *on* RECs and *of* research involving participants, is symptomatic of incremental *process* rather than action:reaction punctuated by nodal points in regulatory history. Through an anthropology of regulation, one is able to bridge the historical tracing with present understanding and with future outlook; we cannot understand where we are and where we are going with health research regulation unless we understand where we have been. The past, present, and future are inextricably linked in time and place and bonded by processes of gradual change reflected in the actions of various actors.

2.1 Regulatory Space

The analytic concept and metaphor of 'regulatory space', first described by legal scholar Leigh Hancher and political scientist Michael Moran,[12] and already referred to above, provides useful spatial-temporal framing of the processes here. Regulatory space proponents argue that local context and historical configuration (i.e. time and space), as well as institutional dynamics, affect the relevant regulation and influence the practices that happen within the space.[13] As to the metaphor itself, regulatory space focuses on *networks* of regulation and mixing of regulators and strategies:

---

[12] Leigh Hancher and Michael Moran, 'Organizing Regulatory Space' in Leigh Hancher and Michael Moran (eds), *Capitalism, Culture and Economic Regulation* (OUP 1989).

[13] See e.g. Colin Scott, 'Analysing Regulatory Space: Fragmented Resources and Institutional Design' [2001] Public Law 329.

The 'space' here is conceived of as a cluster of regulatory issues, decisions, or policies (a 'regulatory arena') that involves the interplay and competition between various interests. Regulatory authority is widely shared between private and public actors (therefore making the distinction largely meaningless), and regulatory approaches are shaped by location, timing, and history. [...] In the world of regulatory space, as in the world of regulatory networks, the idea of 'capture' makes only limited sense; regulatory authority is inherently shared, and private interests are driven to, or accept, playing legitimate roles in the regulation of themselves, of industry sectors (through associations), and of wider society.[14]

The legal scholar Colin Scott argues that regulatory space speaks to the 'resources relevant to holding of regulatory power and exercising of capacities [that] are dispersed or fragmented'; the resources 'are not restricted to formal, state authority derived from legislation or contracts, but also include information, wealth and organisational capacities'.[15] Moreover, 'the possession of these resources is fragmented among state bodies, and between state and non-state bodies'.[16] Scott elaborates:

Put another way, capacities derived from possession of key resources are not necessarily exercised hierarchically within the regulatory space, regulator over regulatee. We recognise the presence within the space not just of regulators and regulatees, but of other interested organizations, state and non-state, possessing resources to a variable degree. Relations can be characterised as complex, dynamic and horizontal, involving negotiated interdependence. This re-conceptualisation of regulatory processes is important in understanding the limits of law within regulation. The dispersed nature of resources between organisations in the same regulatory space means regulators lack a monopoly both over formal and informal authority. This observation draws our attention to the need to conceive of strategies of regulation as consisting of a wide range of negotiated processes, of which rule formation and enforcement are but two.[17]

Further elucidation of the regulatory space is provided by the legal and regulatory studies scholar Julia Black, who suggests that three principal regulatory functions can be mapped across a range of actual or potential regulators—standard setting, monitoring, and enforcement—and a wide variety of institutional actors can be 'enrolled' to carry out, alone

---

14 Hancher and Moran (n 12) 64–5.
15 Scott (n 13) 330.
16 ibid.
17 ibid.

or in collaboration, one or more of these regulatory functions.[18] Legal scholar Scott Burris and colleagues extend this concept with discussion of polycentric, or 'nodal' character of, contemporary governance, which 'is an elaboration of contemporary network theory that explains how a variety of actors operating within social systems interact along networks to govern the systems they inhabit'.[19] They posit that institutions (which I would broaden to 'actors') are substantially comprised in *nodes*, having a set of technologies, mentalities, and resources that mobilize the knowledge and capacity of members to manage the course of events: 'Networks are a prime means through which nodes exert influence.'[20] Burris finds that there are a number of nodes that do or could help regulators (including ethics committees) regulate how researchers treat research participants. This can range from medical journals to professional organizations to courts to ethicists, all of whom can act as 'norm entrepreneurs' in formulating and disseminating new standards.[21]

The concept of regulatory space, along with insights from polycentric contemporary governance, helps us understand why the current regulation of health research involving human participants is less a matter of public authorities versus private interests. Indeed, the underlying institutionalist framework of research ethics review by dispersed expert ethics committees and pluralist organizational involvement was established already by the 1970s, and this was in large part due to a conscious effort by the state to delegate much of the decision-making authority to private interests in the form of the RCP and other non-state actors.

Interestingly, then, what appears to exist in the UK, at least in the particular space of health research ethics as it pertains to RECs, is a shifting of the locus of regulating *towards* the state, with more 'centred' or truly polycentric regulation. State actors such as the NHS (via Trusts, Foundation Trusts, and Health Boards and the R&D offices within them), the Department of Health and Social Care (and their equivalents in the devolved administrations), and the HRA assert much firmer control with

---

18   Julia Black, 'Enrolling Actors in Regulatory Systems: Examples from UK Financial Services' [2003] Public Law 63. As I argue below, however, the enforcement function has limited application to RECs.

19   Scott Burris and others, 'Nodal Governance' (2005) 30 Australian Journal of Legal Philosophy 30, 33.

20   ibid.

21   Scott Burris, 'Regulatory Innovation in the Governance of Human Subjects Research: A Cautionary Tale and Some Modest Proposals' (2008) 2 Regulation & Governance 65, 71.

rules- and principles-driven regulation (e.g. the Clinical Trials Regulations 2004, Care Act 2014, UK Policy Framework, GAfREC, REC
SOPs) that both seek to streamline ethics review processes and also
remove a degree of autonomy (but not 'independence', they stress) from
RECs.

But the state is not the sole controlling entity, of course. It is situated
next to the long-standing and previously dominant presence of non-state
regulatory actors and sources of authority such as researchers and
physicians, industry (e.g. pharmaceutical companies), organizations
within the medical and scientific profession (e.g. RCP), and new(er)
organizations explicitly promoting a pro-research agenda (e.g. AMS).
Unlike standard accounts of decentred regulation, then, here we see that
the state has only recently asserted itself into the mix of regulatory
actors. Not unusually, each of these actors can exert cross-competing
demands and the polycentric nature of the space exhibits potentially
cacophonous forms of standard setting, monitoring, and enforcement. Put
another way, while the state has recently asserted itself and the HRA has
emerged as a central regulatory actor, one can today delineate multiple
actors (or 'nodes') that populate the health research regulatory space in
the area of research ethics, including:

- RECs;
- research sponsors and institutions;
- NHS (e.g. Health Boards, Trusts, Foundation Trusts);
- Department of Health and Social Care/devolved administration
  equivalents;
- HRA/devolved administration equivalents (including the RES);
- UKECA;
- MHRA;
- regulatory licensing authorities (e.g. HFEA, HTA);
- regulatory advisory committees (Confidentiality Advisory Group,
  Public Benefit and Privacy Panel for Health and Social Care;
  Administration of Radioactive Substances Advisory Committee);
- industry;
- Data Monitoring Committees;
- funders (e.g. Wellcome Trust; MRC);
- courts of law (through litigation and court decisions);
- professional organizations (e.g. RCP, British Medical Association,
  World Medical Association);
- interest groups (e.g. AMS);
- research colleagues;
- professional ethicists;

- academic journals;
- news media and journalists;
- research participants; and
- the broader public/civil society.

Clearly, many actors (or 'nodes') populate this regulatory space, which, it must be stressed, merely covers one discrete area: regulation of the ethics of health research involving human participants. Indeed, some argue that in health research the regulatory space is not unitary but in fact comprised of 'a multiplicity of spaces ostensibly engaged in the same endeavour but with little means to learn lessons between them'.[22] How, then, can we put these nodes under the analytic microscope and make sense of this space or these spaces?

Law is important to consider here, and it is worth highlighting that in the institutionalist and polycentric theory of regulation, law is facilitative rather than prohibitive, 'emphasising non-legal organisational and systemic dynamics as crucial to regulatory objectives', and helping 'to structure the interactions between regulatory participants rather than directly to shape the substance of the regulatory issue'.[23] Yet law can also police the boundaries of the regulatory space where actors interact, and may be limited in what it can achieve, or holds itself out to achieve. As Colin Scott observes:

> [L]aw is more marginal to actions within the regulatory space than lawyers might assume. That political systems seek to use law instrumentally for regulatory purposes does not give law the pre-eminence in ordering society which some argue it had when adjudication was a central form of governance in an earlier period. Indeed, the argument that law is increasingly used to co-ordinate 'pre-existing relationships of power' is at odds with the dominant, but symbolic conception of law as being exercised hierarchically.[24]

So, even if we find, for example, that the Care Act 2014 has bestowed formal legal authority on the HRA to regulate RECs (directly in England and indirectly in the three other nations) and that the HRA has a duty to promote the coordination and standardization of practice in the UK relating to the regulation of health and social care research, as well as a duty to cooperate with each devolved authority in the exercise of their

---

[22] Graeme Laurie, 'Liminality and the Limits of Law in Health Research Regulation: What Are We Missing in the Spaces In-Between?' (2017) 25 Medical Law Review 47, 50.

[23] Morgan and Yeung (n 2) 76.

[24] Scott (n 13) 334.

respective functions relating to the regulation of assessments of the ethics of health and social care research, this does not mean that the HRA necessarily possesses *actual* (read: in practice) regulatory authority over health research. What it means is that the HRA has ultimate (legal) authority, but this is not equivalent to saying that it can or does dictate what happens on the ground or within the regulatory space(s). Things might 'work well', but not in ways that the HRA foresees or would necessarily sanction. The insight from Scott about the limits of law tells us that 'authority' can take many forms, legal and extra-legal, depending on how it is defined, who wields it, when, and in what ways, and who in return is impacted by it. Scott's insight draws attention to the problems inherent in a law-centric research approach. We must be open to the possibility that authority may be wielded in myriad ways and at different times by RECs and other regulatory actors, such as R&D offices, researchers, and sponsors, who possess key resources of information and organization even if they are not sanctioned with these resources by law.

Thus, we see that the value of regulatory space as an analytic concept is its usefulness in demarking the range of actors and processes in health research, and for 'drawing in perspectives which question the capacities of instrumental law and regulation, and envisage greater reflexivity or responsiveness in systems characterised variously as post-bureaucratic or post-interventionist'.[25] As Scott writes, '[b]efore we conclude that all key resources are possessed by a single regulatory agency, we ask first whether those resources are in fact dispersed through a more fragmented pattern'.[26] Lastly, an openness to surprise is warranted when applying a nodal analysis of the regulatory space in this context. For Burris:

> The positive potential of a nodal [analytic] view is clear: when the available regulators are identified and their capacities assessed, 'unregulated' activities can be revealed as highly regulated, or potentially so. In the case of human subjects regulation, a diversity of regulators may be creating problems of over-regulation, over-punishment, and over-deterrence.[27]

Ongoing or further recourse to the law as a means of achieving a robust health research regime may, upon analysis, not be appropriate.

It bears noting that some commentators consider a drawback to the regulatory space metaphor to be its difficulties in 'accounting for the

---

25   ibid 352.
26   ibid.
27   Burris (n 21) 71.

boundaries of regulatory spaces and in explaining the different dimensions that characterize the "topology" of the space—notably: the relative power of the different actors; the distribution of resource dependence relevant to the space; and the nature of the communication flows between actors'.[28] As will be argued, this, in fact, is where liminality adds key support to the sensitizing concept of regulatory space, especially in better understanding the spaces in-between boundaries. Additionally, an anthropology of regulation rounds out the call for richer characterization of the 'topology' of the space by paying close empirical attention to the dynamics of interaction between actors and how resources are distributed. It complements socio-legal research approaches by investigating the extra-legal elements of social practices from the inside out and paying attention to the processual nature of regulation. Engaging in anthropological investigation of regulation accounts for a deeply contextual understanding of the behaviours and experiences of actors who intentionally intervene in the activities of a target population (i.e. regulators), as well as those actors whose activities have been regulated (i.e. regulatees).

2.2 Regulatory Approaches: Risk-Based and Proportionate Regulation

If regulatory space serves as a useful frame to make sense of the range of nodes that share regulatory authority of a given activity, what can be said of the structures, techniques, and strategies deployed by regulatory actors to accomplish their tasks? Risk assessment and management are classic *modi operandi* of regulators. Baldwin and colleagues observe that 'regulation can be seen as being inherently about the control of risks'.[29] Recent changes in health research regulation described in earlier chapters suggest a pronounced move towards this risk-focused approach, which also accords with the UK's Hampton Review in 2005 that recommended all UK regulators operate a risk-based system,[30] and the statutory Regulators' Code, which requires UK regulators to 'base their regulatory activities on risk' and 'choose proportionate approaches to those they regulate'.[31]

---

[28] Robert Baldwin and others, *Understanding Regulation: Theory, Strategy, and Practice* (2nd edn, OUP 2012) 65.

[29] ibid 83.

[30] Philip Hampton, *Reducing Administrative Burdens: Effective Inspection and Enforcement* (HM Treasury 2005).

[31] Department for Business, Innovation and Skills, *Regulators' Code* (UK Government 2014).

Risk, a pervasive theme in contemporary societies,[32] can be defined simply as an 'adverse event that may occur in the future'.[33] The CIOMS Guidelines define risk more specifically to the human research context as 'an estimate of two factors: first, how likely it is that a participant will experience a physical, psychological, social or other harm; and second, the magnitude or significance of the harm'.[34]

Risk-based regulation is defined as 'the prioritizing of regulatory actions in accordance with an assessment of the risks that parties will present to the regulatory body's achieving its objectives'.[35] Surveying the literature, one finds that it generally contains the following key elements (Box 4.1).[36]

Throughout their history, RECs have been charged with assessing, or weighing a favourable 'balancing' of, the harms (i.e. the adverse events) and benefits of a given research project, or phrased another way, risks against the probability of benefit. As the GAfREC state: 'The committee has to be assured that any anticipated risks, burdens or intrusions will be minimised for the people taking part in the research and are justified by the expected benefits for the participants or for science and society.'[37] Elsewhere, it states that 'RECs must be assured about the planned ethical conduct and anticipated risks and benefits of any proposed research'.[38] At least on paper, there would appear to be two general levels of risk in the assessments undertaken by RECs: minimal risk and greater than minimal risk.[39] For their part, researchers are expected to prepare descriptions of risks and intended benefits for REC members as part of their application,

---

[32] Iain Wilkinson, *Risk, Vulnerability and Everyday Life* (Routledge 2010).

[33] Robert Baldwin and Julia Black, 'Driving Priorities in Risk-Based Regulation: What's the Problem?' (2016) 43 Journal of Law and Society 565, 566.

[34] Council for International Organizations of Medical Sciences, *International Ethical Guidelines for Health-Related Research Involving Humans* (Council for International Organizations of Medical Sciences 2016), Guideline 4, Commentary.

[35] Baldwin and others (n 28) 281.

[36] Adapted from Baldwin and others (n 28) 281–90 and Gregory Bounds, 'Challenges to Designing Regulatory Policy Frameworks to Manage Risks' in OECD (ed), *Risk and Regulatory Policy: Improving the Governance of Risk* (OECD 2010).

[37] GAfREC para 1.2.2.

[38] ibid para 3.2.15.

[39] See Annette Rid, 'Rethinking Risk–Benefit Evaluations in Biomedical Research' in Daniel Strech and Marcel Mertz (eds), *Ethics and Governance of Biomedical Research* (Springer 2016) 153.

BOX 4.1.   ELEMENTS OF RISK-BASED REGULATION

1. There are three sequential phases in the regulatory approach: (1) assessment (framing and forecasting the probability/possibility and consequences of identified hazards); (2) management (designing and implementing actions and remedies to address risks through a consideration of potential risk treatments and selection of the most appropriate); and (3) review (decision-making processes are transparent and open to revision in light of new information);
2. The regulator's aim is to control relevant risks rather (or more) than achieving compliance with sets of rules;
3. Once assessed, a range of responses can be applied to manage the risks, such as risk avoidance, risk reduction, risk retention, and risk transfer;
4. There is clear identification of risks that the regulated organizations (i.e. researchers and their projects) may present to the achieving of the regulator's objectives;
5. There is a comprehensive system for assessing such risks and scoring these in either a quantitative or qualitative manner, underpinned by scientific evidence and a robust decision methodology;
6. There is a linkage of risk scoring mechanism/risk evaluation with resource allocation (e.g. more resources to regulate the higher risk organization or activity);
7. There is recognition that risk tolerance and use of a risk-based framework is more political art than pure technical application; and
8. The risks that the regulator is concerned with may not align with the risks on which regulatees (i.e. researchers) are focused.

---

and they are expected to discuss them with research participants as part of the consent process as well. Together, the risk-benefit calculus is said to operationalize all three of the 'classic' research ethics principles of beneficence, respect for persons, and justice.[40]

Assessing the elements outlined in Box 4.1 and turning our attention to the context of ethics review, we can speculate that RECs most often engage in risk management techniques of risk reduction (e.g. setting conditions on the research project for it to be ethically acceptable) and risk avoidance (e.g. prohibiting certain research projects or activities within them by not granting a favourable opinion).

Further and relatedly, we can surmise that risk-based regulation is linked with notions of 'proportionate' regulation. In law and regulation, proportionality connects 'the exercise of legal power with doctrines and

---

[40]   Robert Levine, *Ethics and Regulation of Clinical Research* (2nd edn, Yale University Press 1988) 38.

ideas of reason, fairness, fittingness, and order circulating within broader political and indeed cultural discourse'.[41] As the legal scholar and bioethicist Michelle Meyer notes, there has been 'a global trend toward "risk-proportionate" regulation of [human subjects research]' [...] It aims for two politically unassailable goals—the safety and welfare of research participants and the efficient use of scarce resources—and wraps these goals in the seemingly unobjectionable language of "proportionality"'.[42] An OECD report from 2010 observes that '[a] risk-based approach to regulation explicitly acknowledges that the government cannot regulate all risks and that regulatory action, when taken, should be proportionate, targeted and based on an assessment of the nature and magnitude of the risks and of the likelihood that regulation will be successful in achieving its aims'.[43] It finds that for central regulators (in this case, the HRA for example): 'A significant objective of incorporating a better treatment of risk in regulatory management is to improve regulatory design and administration, to reduce the fiscal costs of administering regulation and minimise the burden that regulation imposes on business and the community.'[44] This language accords with the UK's Regulators' Code, which states that: 'Regulators should carry out their activities in a way that supports those they regulate to comply and grow', which means that, among other things, they 'should avoid imposing unnecessary regulatory burdens through their regulatory activities' and 'should consider how they might support or enable economic growth for compliant businesses and other regulated entities [...]'.[45]

For RECs specifically, an early shift towards risk-proportionate regulation can be traced to the Lord Warner Report from 2005 (discussed in Chapter 3), which recommended proportionate ethics review such that '[t]he remit of NHS RECs should not include surveys or other non-research activity if they present no material ethical issues for human participants'.[46] COREC's response publication in 2006, *Building on*

---

[41] Nicola Lacey, 'The Metaphor of Proportionality' (2016) 43 Journal of Law and Society 27, 35.

[42] Michelle Meyer, 'Regulating the Production of Knowledge: Research Risk-Benefit Analysis and the Heterogeneity Problem' (2013) 65 Administrative Law Review 237, 294–5.

[43] Bounds (n 36) 16.

[44] ibid 26.

[45] Department for Business, Innovation and Skills, *Regulators' Code* (UK Government 2014) paras 1–1.2.

[46] Lord Warner Report 15.

Improvement, acknowledged that the Lord Warner Report sought 'proportionality of review' as a means to streamline the extant regulation, and in
response, COREC recommended introducing 'a research ethics service
incorporating RECs working in structured networks, where decisions are
made as a result of review proportionate to the level of risk provided by the
study'.[47] As noted in Chapter 3, in 2010, following the earlier pilot study
from 2009 based on the recommendation from the Lord Warner Report,
the PRS was introduced across the UK to operationalize a proportionate
regulatory approach based on the level of risk a study proposed.

Similarly, the AMS emphasized the need for proportionate regulation
in its report from 2011, recommending it as a key principle underpinning
health research regulation (indeed, it was one of the four principles they
advocated): 'the application of regulation should be both proportionate
and symmetrical. A "one-size-fits-all" approach to regulation damages us
all. Instead, regulation of health research should be proportionate to the
risks and benefits to individuals and society.'[48] Throughout its report, the
AMS recommended that an 'ideal' health research regulatory system
would, among other things, apply regulatory requirements in a way that
is proportionate to the potential benefits and harms of the research.
Within ethics review, the AMS encouraged NRES (as it then was) to roll
out Proportionate Review to all RECs, opining that:

> It is particularly important to adopt a proportionate approach to ethics review
> because of the diversity of research that undergoes this assessment, which
> includes: questionnaires for staff and patients, minimally interventional stud-
> ies and clinical trials of new drugs. The benefits of a proportionate approach
> are recognised in both the US and Canadian ethics review systems ...[49]

Even after the HRA's creation, the research community has continued to
advocate for a turn towards streamlined and proportionate regulation in
the hopes of 'increasing value and reducing waste in biomedical research
regulation and management'.[50] In an influential article published in *The
Lancet* in 2014, clinical neurologist Rustam Al-Shahi Salman and colleagues (including Janet Wisely, then Chief Executive of the HRA) wrote

---

[47]   COREC Report 9.
[48]   AMS, *A New Pathway for the Regulation and Governance of Health
Research* (Academy of Medical Sciences 2011) 5. Principle 3 from the report is:
'Be proportionate, efficient and coordinated.'
[49]   ibid 76.
[50]   Rustam Al-Shahi Salman and others, 'Increasing Value and Reducing
Waste in Biomedical Research Regulation and Management' (2014) 383 Lancet
176.

alarmingly of 'the increasing burden, inconsistency, and complexity of regulation in the past two decades, sometimes out of proportion to the risk of the research'[51] that ultimately had led to a 'threat to public health'.[52] Chief among their concerns was that: 'Although the conceivable risks of research vary, regulatory requirements do not seem to have been designed to be proportionate to the extent to which safety of patients is likely to be jeopardised.'[53] In this context, they cited the example of requiring consent for 'low-risk' epidemiological research and biobanking and the application of the EU Clinical Trials Directive to non-commercial trials assessing licensed treatments that have already been adopted in practice. Though they noted examples from the UK of solutions to some sources of waste and inefficiency in regulation of clinical research (e.g. the development of COREC to NRES to the HRA and the latter's strategic plan from 2013), they also noted much more could be done to reduce 'wasteful regulation and management of research'.[54] As they wrote: 'The main solution to disproportionality is to limit regulation to whatever is essential, both to protect the autonomy and wellbeing of research participants and to be proportionate to the plausible risks posed to them.'[55] The authors did not explain what might comprise 'essential' regulation.

A final example of proportionate regulation is seen in the Care Act 2014, which mandates the HRA to 'promote the co-ordination and standardisation of practice in the United Kingdom relating to the regulation of health and social care research; and it must, in doing so, seek to ensure that such regulation is proportionate'.[56] Operationalizing this legal mandate in practice, the UK Policy Framework for Health and Social Care Research 'recognise[s] the value of [...] proportionate application [of recognized ethical standards and models of good practice] to different types of research'[57] and, throughout, emphasizes a proportionate approach, including as a principle for regulators: 'The HRA has a specific role to ensure the following. [...] a. The regulation of health and

---

51 ibid 177.
52 ibid 183.
53 ibid 178–9.
54 ibid 183.
55 ibid 181.
56 Care Act 2014, s 111(3) (emphasis added).
57 Health Research Authority, 'UK Policy Framework for Health and Social Care Research' (2017) <www.hra.nhs.uk/planning-and-improving-research/policies-standards-legislation/uk-policy-framework-health-social-care-research/> accessed 17 October 2019, para 5.1.

social care research is proportionate, so that research that is clearly lower-risk gets processed accordingly.'[58]

Based on the foregoing discussion, a question arises as to whether this next-generation health research regulation implements a risk-based and proportionate approach for RECs that fulfils the elements described in Box 4.1. Are RECs' deliberative processes 'informed by an assessment of the probability of harm expected to arise' from a given research project, or if the probability of harm cannot be calculated, do RECs demonstrate 'a rational and transparent consideration of other relevant factors that for want of evidence remain uncertain'?[59] This is a critical and empirical question that will be explored in the following chapters. At this stage, it may be beneficial to look at what the UK regulations state.

In short, what the regulations state about risk assessment by RECs is minimal. The REC SOPs provide no detailed guidance on how risk is to be assessed. Somewhat clearer guidance is provided by international regulatory instruments such as the CIOMS Guidelines,[60] but as the bioethicist Annette Rid points out, 'there is no explicit upper risk limit when informed consent is obtained, provided the net risks to participants are reasonable in relation to the scientific or social value of the research'.[61]

Risk-proportionate assessment also lacks clarity. The REC SOPs state that: 'The Proportionate Review Service (PRS) provides for proportionate review of research studies raising no material ethical issues, including projects involving straightforward issues which can be identified and managed routinely in accordance with standard research practice and existing guidelines.'[62] It then proceeds to discuss procedural guidance on how the PRS is to operate. The GAfREC specify that 'REC review is proportionate to the scale and complexity of the research proposed',[63] neither of which are attributes that necessarily equate to risk, but nevertheless are seen as linked. A Proportionate Review guidance document published by the HRA lists seven categories (i.e. types of research) considered to present no material ethical issues (e.g. research using prospectively collected data or tissue that is anonymous to the

---

[58]   ibid para 9.19.

[59]   Bounds (n 36) 16–17.

[60]   See e.g. Council for International Organizations of Medical Sciences, *International Ethical Guidelines for Health-Related Research Involving Humans* (Council for International Organizations of Medical Sciences 2016) Guideline 4.

[61]   Rid, 'Rethinking Risk–Benefit Evaluations' (n 39) 156.

[62]   REC SOPS para 4.1.

[63]   GAfREC para 3.2.4.

researcher), followed by an eighth category, which is described as 'Studies which do not fit categories 1–7 but do not have any "Material Ethical Issues"'. According to the HRA, these categories prima facie raise no material ethical issues because they 'have minimal risk, burden or intrusion for research participants'.[64]

Such is how the ethics review system is currently designed for the purposes of assessing risk. Detailed regulatory guidance is lacking, which can raise conceptual and practical challenges. Rid argues that 'frameworks for risk-benefit evaluations of biomedical research remain surprisingly vague',[65] that they 'arguably place too much emphasis on informed consent as a condition of acceptable net risk to participants',[66] and that the 'documented variation and inconsistency of risk judgments between RECs'[67] raises concerns about both over- and under-protection of participants from risks, not to mention possible stifling of 'valuable research for overall marginal gains in subject protection'.[68] In the following chapters, we will consider the extent to which RECs engage in risk-based regulation in practice, and examine how RECs (and the HRA) address the conceptual and practical challenges raised by the lack of clarity surrounding risk assessment.

So far in this chapter, I have argued that sensitizing concepts from regulatory theory, namely regulatory space and risk-based regulation, along with its related concept of proportionality, help us understand why regulation emerged in this space and the different array of actors who partake in regulating health research. However, regulatory theory has its limitations. On its own, it cannot validate whether models (or propositions) hold up in reality; regulatory theory can be highly abstracted and pay too little attention to the 'human' roles in regulatory practice.

We have learned from an ethnographic study of the UK Stem Cell Bank[69] that instantiated regulation brings nuanced insight into how

---

[64] Health Research Authority, 'Proportionate Review: Information and Guidance for Applicants' <www.hra.nhs.uk/documents/1022/proportionate-review-information-guidance-document.pdf > accessed 17 October 2019.

[65] Rid, 'Rethinking Risk–Benefit Evaluations' (n 39). See also Annette Rid and David Wendler, 'Risk–Benefit Assessment in Medical Research: Critical Review and Open Questions' (2010) 9 Law, Probability & Risk 151; Annette Rid, 'How Should We Regulate Risk in Biomedical Research? An Ethical Analysis of Recent Policy Proposals and Initiatives' (2014) 117 Health Policy 409.

[66] Rid, 'Rethinking Risk–Benefit Evaluations' (n 39) 160.

[67] ibid 156.

[68] ibid.

[69] Stephens and others (n 4).

regulation is actually done on the ground, and what it means to be a regulatee who—it turns out—has more of a regulatory role than theory or law might suggest. Other behaviours and experiences of actors may be missing from law and theory that require a fresh perspective and a new lens. In the following sections, first, I unpack the methodological contribution of anthropology of regulation; then, I argue that liminality is a critical component to anthropology of regulation and a strong response to the need to fill in the knowledge gaps of process and transformation in regulation.

III. ANTHROPOLOGY OF REGULATION

This book presents an empirical study of the form and function of regulation, and of the behaviours and experiences of those that impact and are impacted by it. Here, I want to make the claim that a novel methodology is required to drive this study forward in a comprehensive way. The rationale behind anthropology of regulation can be summed up by paraphrasing a well-known quote from the socio-legal scholar Lawrence Friedman:[70] regulation is a massive vital presence in the world; it is too important to be left to regulators alone—or even to the realm of pure thought. Anthropology of regulation is a methodology grounded in interdisciplinary dialogue and mixed research methods. It sits neither fully within anthropology nor within law or regulatory studies; it is a mode of enquiry in its own right within the broader social science tradition. It is a study of the nature of regulation and of the behaviours and experiences of actors within a given regulatory space (or spaces), and explores ways in which these actors are affected by regulation and in turn how these actors affect regulation.

Anthropology of regulation contributes to the fields of legal anthropology (also known as anthropology of law) and socio-legal studies. Legal anthropology is a similar field, of course, as it aims to understand the nature of law and how it is integral to culture, and likewise how culture is integral to law; in other words, it explores how law is a window into the nature of culture itself. Socio-legal studies (and its disciplinary cousin, legal sociology) employ 'various empirical methods to study

---

[70]   Lawrence Friedman, 'The Law and Society Movement' (1986) 38 Stanford Law Review 763, 780.

what is *legal* about legal processes, legal institutions and legal behaviour'.[71] It draws attention to the interfacing social context within which law exists, and concerns itself with the empirical study of law as a set of social practices or as an aspect of a field of social experience.[72]

The limitation of legal anthropology and socio-legal studies is that they tend to take law and legalities as the primary foci of investigation. As the above discussion of regulatory space elucidates, in making sense of the form and function of regulation, law fundamentally provides boundaries around space(s). Or, as the legal scholar and political scientist Austin Sarat and colleagues put it: 'In its basic operation, law attempts to create, police, and occasionally transgress social, spatial and temporal boundaries. [...] Within law's spatio-temporal grid, complex classifications are established, creating boundaries that define individuals, communities, acts and norms ...'.[73] I have argued earlier in this chapter that law's role within the regulatory space is limited; fundamentally, a focus on law alone would inadequately answer research questions that examine not the logic of boundaries, but rather the logic (or illogic) of processes and regulatory spaces. Moreover, the regulatory spaces with which I am concerned—being those occupied by RECs that are explicitly focused on ethics and *not* law—require an approach to their study that does not presume law is the central object of attention. This said, anthropology of regulation does not appear out of thin air; in at least three ways, it builds on and complements the work of different strands of methodology from legal anthropology and socio-legal studies.

First, scholars have undertaken ground-breaking observational studies of human behaviour in the context of regulatory compliance or regulatory enforcement by a public agency or official.[74] To some extent, anthropology of regulation owes its allegiance to these pioneering observational

---

[71] Reza Banakar and Max Travers, *Theory and Method in Socio-Legal Research* (Hart Publishing 2005) Introduction.

[72] Roger Cotterrell, 'Sociology of Law' in David Clark (ed), *Encyclopedia of Law and Society: American and Global Perspectives* (SAGE 2007).

[73] Austin Sarat and others, 'The Concept of Boundaries in the Practices and Products of Sociolegal Scholarship: An Introduction' in Austin Sarat and others (eds), *Crossing Boundaries: Traditions and Transformations in Law and Society Research* (Northwestern University Press 1998) 3–4.

[74] See e.g. Keith Hawkins, *Environment and Enforcement: Regulation and the Social Definition of Pollution* (OUP 1984); Bridget Hutter, *Compliance: Regulation and Environment* (OUP 1997); Clare Hall and others, *Telecommunications Regulation: Culture, Chaos and Interdependence Inside the Regulatory Process* (Routledge 1999); Garry Gray, 'The Regulation of Corporate Violations:

(and typically ethnographic) studies. However, to my knowledge, none of these studies have investigated non- or semi-public regulatory bodies such as RECs. Nor have these studies attempted to branch out from compliance and enforcement reflected in command-and-control regulation so as to analyse both the form and function of non-rules-based regulation and its impact on regulators and regulatees. This book explores risk-based approaches and ethical reflection and governance rather than rules-based compliance or enforcement. In the world of RECs, there is limited 'stick-beating'; at worst, a research project is not approved by the REC and thus cannot commence, or the REC revokes its ethics approval following a material ethical breach. The focus of anthropology of regulation, and specifically my research, is different. As I discuss further below, anthropology of regulation builds on these empirical regulatory studies through its theoretical underpinning of liminality, which draws attention to the processual nature of regulation and the importance of human experience during periods of uncertainty and transition. Anthropology of regulation also extends this work as it does not seek merely to identify, document, and understand observed regulatory practices. Through its multi-method approach, it also seeks to provide larger theoretical and normative insight into regulatory processes within a given space and within a given society. That is, it aims to prescribe and evaluate the desirability of different regulatory strategies and styles.

Second, Sally Falk Moore's ground-breaking 'sociological study of reglementation', which she defines as 'the study of the way partial orders and partial controls operate in social contexts',[75] provides foundational support to anthropology of regulation. As a legal anthropologist, Moore, too, desires a qualitative exploration of social processes and order that occur beyond state-based law, considering 'reglementation' as covering both 'government law and non-governmental sites of rule-making and/or rule-enforcing'.[76] Moore recognizes that 'reglementary control can be only temporary, incomplete, and its consequences not fully predictable'.[77] Nevertheless, Moore quite clearly bases her approach on rules, coded as elements of order and control, which consequently envelops regulation within a relatively narrow paradigm. I have made clear that my empirical study concerns itself with regulation, which is much broader than law,

Punishment, Compliance, and the Blurring of Responsibility' (2006) 46 British Journal of Criminology 875.

[75]   Sally Falk Moore, *Law as Process: An Anthropological Approach* (Routledge & Kegan Paul 1978) 30.

[76]   ibid 18.

[77]   ibid 30.

even if law is defined as including non-state forms of normative ordering. And, to reiterate, unlike Moore, I believe regulation must include not only rules, but also principles, mechanisms, strategies, or activities promulgated by state or non-state actors that either affect behaviour as an incidental effect or are designed to steer behaviour in a socially, politically, and/or economically desirable way. This notion of regulation privileges neither the state nor rules. It does, however, accept and incorporate Moore's message that a researcher should take 'into account that there is a constant struggle between deliberate rule-making and planning, and other more untameable activities and processes at work in the social aggregate, [which] should be inspected together'.[78]

Third, institutionalism (e.g. sociological institutionalism, historical institutionalism, political institutionalism) is an approach that examines, often through empirical methods, how actions and decisions by individual actors may be influenced (or structurally determined) by higher-level institutional factors and contexts.[79] While anthropology of regulation certainly acknowledges that social processes shape regulation (and indeed it is influenced by the institutionalist approach of regulatory space), it does not presume that institutions and institutional frameworks influence or constrain decision-making. More importantly, it does not focus its analysis on the structural level of institutions (e.g. laws, the HRA, RECs) to explain processes and outcomes at a lower level (e.g. decision-making by a REC or individual REC members). It does not ask how institutions affect the behaviour of individuals, nor how individual behaviour affects the evolution of institutions. Rather, anthropology of regulation engages in investigation of regulation itself as both an ontological and functional concern. It examines the ways in which regulatory actors affect and are affected by processes of regulation, which in turn sheds light on regulation as a social form. The unique contribution of anthropology of regulation is that it focuses on the behaviours and experiences of regulatory actors within a space (or spaces) and the ways in which they themselves are affected by regulation, but it does so by scaling up of the units of analysis, from the individual level to the social level and drawing insights from empirical research to accomplish what the regulatory space metaphor seeks to do: examine 'how the actions and intentions of regulatory actors are embedded in larger systems and

---

[78]   ibid 29.

[79]   Edwin Amenta and Kelly Ramsey, 'Institutional Theory' in Kevin Leicht and J Craig Jenkins (eds), *The Handbook of Politics: State and Civil Society in Global Perspective* (Springer 2010) 15.

institutional dynamics'.[80] And indeed, the research questions in this study explore and explain—through documentary research comprised of historical tracing and present-day regulatory analysis that explicates the internal constitution of regulation, as well as through observation and interviews—the experiences and behaviours of specific individual actors (i.e. units or nodes) in the health research regulatory space governing the ethics of health research involving participants, namely RECs and their managing regulators.

In sum, there are limits to law-based or even rules-based methodological approaches. Anthropology of regulation allows me to investigate both the nature of regulation as a social form (an ontological concern) and what regulation does to actors and what actors do to regulation (a functional and experiential concern). In so doing, it permits recognition of the limits of regulation, taking up Moore's apt message (at least through the prism of rules) that we should be cognizant of 'social processes which operate outside the rules, or which cause people to use rules, or abandon them, bend them, reinterpret them, side-step them, or replace them'.[81] Regulatory theory is necessary to help provide potential explanatory background; empirical research is equally necessary to help provide understanding of everyday practice. In essence, anthropology of regulation allows us to bring theory and practice meaningfully together.

Anthropology of regulation consists of theoretical underpinnings drawn from regulatory and anthropological theory and is grounded in a trinity of empirical research methods to provide 'a confluence of evidence that breeds credibility'.[82] The approach is interpretivist rather than positivist: it considers people as products of their environment and as those who construct the environment through their understandings of it. The focus is on subjective understandings: the 'inner worlds' of people and their understanding of the world.[83] It does not seek to produce 'objective' findings about human activities (of which regulation is part) precisely because it rejects that such a position is possible. Documentary research uses interpretive methods to examine sources of regulation to

---

[80]   Morgan and Yeung (n 2) 59.

[81]   Moore (n 75) 4.

[82]   Elliot Eisner, *The Enlightened Eye: Qualitative Inquiry and the Enhancement of Educational Practice* (Collier Macmillan Canada 1991) 110, quoted in Glenn Bowen, 'Document Analysis as a Qualitative Research Method' (2009) 9 Qualitative Research Journal 27.

[83]   Lisa Webley, 'Qualitative Approaches to Empirical Legal Research' in Peter Cane and Herbert Kritzer (eds), *The Oxford Handbook of Empirical Legal Research* (OUP 2010).

determine how regulation has developed and been applied over time. It asks both what the law is on a particular issue and how an activity is regulated and how that regulation has developed over time. It is, in other words, research into regulation, regulatory concepts, regulatory practices, and the symbioses between them. The result of such interpretation is both descriptive analysis (explaining how a segment of regulation fits within the larger regulatory space) and normative evaluation of the processes of regulating an activity. The empirical evidence gathered through observation and interviews adds to our understanding of human behaviours and experiences, and also is analysed qualitatively. While the specifics of the epistemological and ontological positions, as well as the detailed steps in the empirical research, are described in Appendix 1, the claim I wish to make here is that anthropology of regulation's detailed attention to regulatory sources and human behaviours and experiences allows us to take special notice of context—historical, political, legal, economic, social, cultural, organizational—to explain and understand the nature of regulation as well as the experiences of regulatory actors who both regulate and are regulated. While this might, tangentially, touch on understandings of law, legal concepts, and even legal consciousness of actors,[84] this approach extends socio-legal studies and legal anthropology by fundamentally focusing on that which is regulatory. Box 4.2 summarizes the key elements of anthropology of regulation.

I have mentioned that anthropology of regulation focuses on the processual and is underpinned in part by theory drawn from anthropology. I have not yet discussed the intricacies of anthropological theory and why it serves as a crucial component of the anthropology of regulation. In the following section, I expand on liminality as a key anthropological concept (and as another 'sensitizing concept') that underpins this methodology and is a crucial component of my investigation of RECs and next-generation health research regulation. As I will argue, liminality helps us to understand the processual dimensions of regulation—the passages of actors from one stage to another, to document and understand experiential dynamics in regulatory spaces, and to reconceptualize the nature of health research regulation.

---

[84] For discussion of legal consciousness and the fluidity of legalities as experienced in everyday life, see generally Susan Silbey, 'After Legal Consciousness' (2005) 1 Annual Review of Law and Social Science 323.

BOX 4.2.   KEY ELEMENTS OF ANTHROPOLOGY OF
            REGULATION

1. **Definition**: the study of the nature of regulation and of the behaviours and experiences of actors within a regulatory space (or spaces), and the ways in which they themselves affect and are affected by processes of regulation.
2. **Theoretical underpinnings**: informed by theoretical underpinnings from regulatory theory (i.e. regulatory space) and anthropology (i.e. liminality) that together draw attention to the human factors that determine the nature of regulation and how regulators actually work, as well as the connections between regulated objects and the subjects (e.g. humans) connected to them.
3. **Methodological approach**: empirical research set within an interpretivist tradition that is constructed around a multi-method approach[85] ('research trinity') of document analysis, interviews, and observations to make sense of the form and function of regulation (i.e. what it is and how it is expressed) and its impact on regulators and regulatees (i.e. how it is experienced).
    o   Document analysis: qualitative analysis (e.g. content analysis and thematic analysis) of regulatory sources (e.g. texts) covering a particular area that provides context and historical tracing of how regulations developed and have been applied over time. This includes analyses of the relationship between regulations and regulatory actors. The research is a two-part process that first involves locating regulatory sources (historical and current), and then involves interpreting and analysing the sources to make sense of processual developments. The outcome of the analysis can be both descriptive and normative.
    o   Observations and interviews: evidence of the behaviours and experiences of regulatory actors who both regulate and are regulated gathered through direct observation. The gathered evidence is typically analysed qualitatively (i.e. thematic analysis), which, as with document analysis, can be both descriptive and normative. The observation may be naturalistic or participant-based; the interviews may be unstructured or semi-structured.
4. **Goals**: (1) to explain and understand the processual nature of regulation *and* the behaviours and experiences of regulatory actors who both regulate and are regulated (i.e. how they understand their own actions); and (2) to provide larger theoretical and normative insight into regulatory processes within a given space and within a given society.

---

[85] I avoid the term 'ethnographic approach' as ethnography implies a particular set of features, whereas anthropology of regulation's features are broader and may be non-ethnographic, e.g. naturalistic observation for a short period of time.

IV. LIMINALITY

4.1 The Value of Liminality to Anthropology of Regulation

As defined by Bjørn Thomassen, liminality is an anthropological concept that 'refers to moments or periods of transition during which the normal limits to thought, self-understanding and behaviour are relaxed, opening the way to novelty and imagination, construction and destruction'.[86] Thomassen argues that liminality is a universal concept because 'cultures and human lives cannot exist without moments of transition, and those brief and important spaces where we live through the in-between'.[87] Given its universality, Thomassen argues liminality should be posited as a central concept in the social sciences, akin to 'structure' and 'practice', for it gives meaning and understanding to how humans experience and react to change—and indeed, liminality is foremost based on experience, because to experience something means, etymologically, to go *through* something. Liminality is thus not so much an explanatory concept as it is a state of affairs: it exists, it happens, and humans 'react to liminal experiences in different ways'.[88] It constantly 'emerges in the in-between of a *passage*'[89] and through its constant appearance, it helps us understand transition periods and social processes of change. Liminality can apply to individuals, groups, and even societies, and may occur in a single moment, over a period, or across an epoch. Similarly, liminality has a spatial dimension that can relate to specific places or thresholds (e.g. a doorway in a house), areas (e.g. airports, border areas between countries), and countries or larger regions (e.g. ancient Palestine).[90] Examples of liminal experiences include marriage, baptism, puberty, graduation ceremonies, New Year, natural disasters, and revolutions.

Liminality serves as an integral component of anthropology of regulation and, as further advantage, accords well with regulatory theory. Both regulatory space and liminality affix themselves to the temporal and spatial dynamics of various actors. However, whereas regulatory space affords a metaphysical mapping of the actors involved in the space (or spaces), liminality affords a processual and experiential understanding of those actors and the ways in which they are affected by regulation,

---

[86] Bjørn Thomassen, *Liminality and the Modern: Living Through the In-Between* (Ashgate 2014) 1.
[87] ibid 4.
[88] ibid 7.
[89] ibid 2.
[90] ibid 90–91.

particularly at moments or periods of transition where uncertainty is paramount. The value of liminality is that it serves as a lens to make sense of the processual nature of health research regulation and RECs (and individuals therein) as key nodes in the health research regulatory space. It shines analytical light on the kinds of potentially transformative activities RECs both perform and experience. It offers perspective on what it means to be a regulator of health research, and also indirectly through my empirical investigation, draws attention to the experiences of researchers and research participants who, individually and collectively, undergo the transformative experience of becoming these embodied actors.

Liminality also supplements the concept of risk-based regulation. Risk-based regulation is about dealing with uncertain futures through the prism of risk identification and management. Liminality often—indeed, usually—occurs when there are moments of change and uncertainty. A lens of liminality therefore helps us both to recognize uncertainties, embrace them to a certain extent, potentially even exploit them, and pay attention to what is required to work through them. Liminality thus has the potential to yield novel insights into the nature of health research and its regulation—and the limits thereof, namely by helping us to uncover alternative paths to governing the behaviour of various actors and enforcing norms across sites of authority in research ethics oversight. It further helps us consider the importance of transition and transformation among critical components of health research.

In what follows, I trace liminality's conceptual evolution.

4.2   The Conceptual Evolution of Liminality

Liminality as a concept emerged at the beginning of the 20th century. In 1909—a period marked by progressivism and trust in scientific methods—the anthropologist Arnold van Gennep wrote that upon analysis of 'detailed descriptions and monographs concerning magico-religious acts' throughout the world, he could 'attempt a classification of these acts, or rites, that would be consistent with the progress of science'.[91] Van Gennep found that all cultures exhibit ritual behaviour (i.e. ceremonies or rites) to mark the passage of an individual or social group from one status to another. However, van Gennep singled out 'rites

---

[91]   Arnold van Gennep, *The Rites of Passage* (University of Chicago Press 1960 [1909]) Introduction.

of passage' in his study as he found them to serve as a critical component of the reproduction of social order:

> The life of an individual in any society is a series of passages from one age to another and from one occupation to another. [...] The underlying arrangement is always the same. Beneath a multiplicity of forms, either consciously expressed or merely implied, a typical pattern always recurs: *the pattern of the rites of passage.*[92]

In each of these series of passages, ceremonies are invoked by the society in which individuals are situated to enable them 'to pass from one defined position to another which is equally well defined',[93] and consequently, these ceremonies share a wide degree of similarity (seen, for instance, in birth, childhood, marriage, and funerals).

Though he did not invoke the noun 'liminality' as such, nor ever define it, van Gennep posited a tripartite conceptual schema of these ceremonial patterns that 'accompany a passage from one situation to another or from one cosmic or social world to another',[94] and selected rites of passage as a special category of transition, which he then subdivided into: (1) the symbolic separation of individuals (or a group) from their existing social position (rites of separation); (2) the transformation of their social status as they pass through an adjacent space (liminal or transition rites); and (3) their spatial and symbolic reincorporation into society (rites of incorporation). Van Gennep clarified that 'although a complete scheme of rites of passage theoretically includes preliminal rites (rites of separation), liminal rites (rites of transition), and postliminal rites (rites of incorporation), in specific instances these types are not always equally important or equally elaborated'.[95] Indeed, van Gennep reiterated several times in his seminal work that the 'liminal' stage often takes on an autonomy of its own.

Often during the transition (liminal) periods in the rites of passage, van Gennep observed that:

> a special language is employed which in some cases includes an entire vocabulary unknown or unusual in the society as a whole [...]. This phenomenon should be considered of the same order as the change of dress,

---

[92] ibid 2–3, 191.
[93] ibid 3.
[94] ibid 10.
[95] ibid 11.

mutilations, and special foods (dietary taboos), i.e. as a perfectly normal differentiating procedure.[96]

Van Gennep further found that the passage from one social position to another is associated with a territorial passage, seen for example in the crossing of streets or entrance into a house or moving from one room to another. 'This identification explains why the passage from one group to another is so often ritually expressed by passage under a portal, or by an "opening of the door".'[97] This focus on territorial passage draws attention to the passages that research protocols go through as they wend their way through the stages of the research lifecycle, an observation that I will return to in the following chapters.

Liminality has been further developed in recent decades by scholars who apply the concept from various disciplinary perspectives to modern social settings and social theorizing of modernity, be it political revolutions, earthquakes, gambling, or bungee jumping.[98] Thomassen argues that liminality is omnipresent in modernity, thus completing a circle from what might otherwise seem like a marginal and antiquated anthropological account of status passages in exotic lands to a central conceptual device that helps to capture key features of many moments of modern life.[99] Scholars increasingly have plumbed the analytic depths of liminality as well. Árpád Szakolczai contends that any rite of passage 'must follow a strictly prescribed sequence, where everybody knows what to do and how' and that 'everything is done under the authority of a master of ceremonies, the practical equivalency of an absolute ruler [...] whose word is Law – though only during a rite, when there is no law'.[100] Other scholars, however, qualify Szakolczai's observation by suggesting liminal experiences need not always be demarcated with an institutionalized transition 'rite' and with identifiable masters of ceremony,[101] such as in moments of 'spontaneous liminality' which is unforeseen and resulting from crisis.[102] Yet Szakolczai's contention that there is often an independent actor serving as a master of ceremonies to guide people through

---

[96]   ibid 169.

[97]   ibid 192.

[98]   Thomassen, *Liminality and the Modern* (n 86); Agnes Horvath and others (eds), *Breaking Boundaries: Varieties of Liminality* (Berghahn 2015).

[99]   Thomassen, *Liminality and the Modern* (n 86).

[100]   Árpád Szakolczai, 'Liminality and Experience: Structuring Transitory Situations and Transformative Events' in Horvath and others (n 98) 18.

[101]   Bjørn Thomassen, 'Thinking with Liminality: To the Boundaries of an Anthropological Concept' in Horvath and others (n 98) 39.

[102]   Laurie (n 22).

rituals, moments, or periods of transition may have some powerful resonance in health research regulatory encounters; it is one I will return to in the following chapters.

For this empirical study, the key relevant and important features of liminality are its focus on processual change and transformation, and the numerous actors that experience uncertainty and transformations as a result of health research and regulation, both of which in turn cause reflection on how regulatory apparatuses structure process and transformation. Liminality also draws attention to authority figures that may guide actors through status passages. The regulatory theory literature notes that significant coordination challenges can arise in getting actors within a regulatory space to operate effectively. Various modes can be devised in response. One such mode is hierarchy, where, often through a legal framework, a top-down arrangement is instituted such that a central control body lays down rules that direct lower-rung institutions within the network. Through the lens of liminality, this is something to consider as existing between the HRA and RECs. For example, the HRA Approval process could be seen as a liminal period in itself. This new procedure was launched in 2016 for researchers and RECs in England, with direct impact on how they do their work (researchers in putting together the application; REC members in changing which aspects they should be reviewing). The HRA instituted HRA Approval with the express purpose of smoothing the regulatory approvals process for researchers. Yet the roll-out was somewhat controversial for REC members, a fair number of whom were, at least in my discussions with them, unfamiliar with the regulatory changes and felt left in the dark from the HRA about how these changes bore upon them. Not uncommonly, REC members expressed concern to me that the HRA had imposed something top-down on them, perhaps for a good reason, but in a way that also created uncertainty and frustration. A second example of a liminal period includes the HRA's gradual move to a paperless system via the HARP—a significant change when one considers the amount of paper that dominates REC operations—which also has caused some controversy among REC members as a fair number consider paper-based documentation crucial to their undertaking of a thorough ethics review.

Another key feature of liminality is the attention drawn to rituals, which reflect the fundamental values of a group of actors. Additionally, a regulatory network coordination mode itself can be based on rituals. Rituals can function as 'structured processes that serve to organize not only the actions taken by network members but the meanings that participant individuals or organizations give to events or decisions'.[103] They may be imposed or voluntarily adopted by the network, 'but the essence of ritualistic network coordination is that embedded processes drive forward the collaborations that are found within the network'.[104] For many regulators, the central motivation is to employ ritualistic processes 'in a manner that serves their own organizational interests. Their broad attitude will be that interactions with other agencies can best be seen in terms of their impact on achieving success in rituals. Claims and responses will be processed through embedded procedures and will be structured accordingly.'[105] From within the literature on regulatory theory, Baldwin and colleagues explain:

> In *ritualistic cohabitations*, processes can be used to allocate institutional roles and to encourage the development of common aims and approaches by ordering experiences, creating shared meanings, building feelings of community, and encouraging trust. They may be used to facilitate the development of discourses that generate bodies of common knowledge, generalized ways of seeing challenges and problems, and authoritative versions of situations and values. The difficulty, however, is that, in the absence of authority, rituals may not suffice to reconcile all interests and perceptions and this may impede the establishing of objectives and an organized regime for delivering on these. Rituals, moreover, can lead to stultification if they are following unthinkingly.[106]

Yet, despite recognition of rituals in regulatory theory, the notion is underexplored both theoretically and empirically. Nora Machado and Tom Burns, two of the few scholars to explore rituals in regulation, explain that 'complex social organizations' (e.g. a state, university, corporation, nuclear system, regulatory agency, large-scale medical system) contain heterogeneous modes of organizing, with each mode containing its own principle, constitutive rules, norms, identity, and so on.[107] These heterogeneous modes can generate benefits, such as creativity, reflectivity, and innovation, but they also can sometimes contribute to incongruences, tension, and conflict. To mitigate these problems, organizational spacing, mediators, discourses, and rituals can play a key role. Rituals for Machado and Burns are defined as 'a type of patterned or

---

[103]   Baldwin and others (n 28) 161.
[104]   ibid.
[105]   ibid 162.
[106]   ibid 163.
[107]   Nora Machado and Tom Burns, 'Complex Social Organization: Multiple Organizing Modes, Structural Incongruence, and Mechanisms of Integration' (1998) 76 Public Administration 355.

institutionalized symbolic action, collectively defined and constituted within a group or organization. It consists of words, gestures, and actions and use of objects and artefacts to express a conception, symbolic meaning, feeling or sentiment within a group or collectivity.'[108] They are 'one of the most important devices to define and "re-structure" the experience of situations and events'.[109] Machado and Burns explain that rituals minimize incongruence and tension in non-discursive and non-rationalized ways; this is seen, for example, in hospital rituals that range from rituals of caring (e.g. fixing pillows, touching the patient, taking temperature, writing down information) to rituals of authority and deference such as medical rounds, consultation, case conferences, and mortality and morbidity conferences. These rituals are embedded to a significant degree in the schedules, procedures, and practices of a hospital: 'Through institutionalized rituals within hospitals, professionals structure their own experiences and the experiences of their clients and avoid or negate considerably incongruent or disequilibrating information and experience.'[110] As they further elaborate:

> Ritual helps to: (a) order the experience in critical situations by creating and re-creating a sense of order in a chaos of experiences, and gives a sense of security through a pattern of predictability (where for example an individual knows what is, has and will be done in such situations); (b) enforce a given meaning in an unclear situation; and (c) strengthen the sense of community that shares knowledge about what is to be done in ambiguous and critical situations. *An important characteristic of ritual (and ritualized behaviour) – that to a large extent accounts for its effectivity and cultural persistence – is that it enables actors to collectively handle ambiguous and incongruent situations in a non-discursive (i.e. non-verbalizable) way.*[111]

We can draw a parallel here to the HRA and the RECs they manage, and in turn, to the interface between RECs and researchers. There are rich linkages between rituals, regulation, and liminality, especially the notions of transition from one stage or threshold to another. Liminality is particularly helpful in adding value to the analytical framing. It demonstrates how rituals and processual developments across time and space in fact play a crucial role in regulatory coordination when we consider the ways in which an activity (e.g. research) may be regulated by a network of regulators (e.g. RECs, MHRA, HRA) through a variety of rituals

[108] ibid 372.
[109] ibid 373.
[110] ibid.
[111] ibid 373–4 (emphasis in original).

(e.g. the informed consent process, the drafting of a research protocol and ethics review application, the rituals performed by REC members at meetings) that work across numerous thresholds, and which in turn can have a tangible impact on the regulatory actors' behaviour—particularly when those rituals are disrupted by regulatory change. Liminality thus supplements regulatory theory by encouraging us to identify and pay attention to symbolically and practically significant stages or thresholds. And, given the processual nature of regulation and the regulatory spaces that exist within health research, liminality also buttresses anthropology of regulation by providing a lens for understanding human experiences within health research and the roles of regulation within these spaces.

V. CONCLUSION

In this chapter, I described the research approach, theoretical under-pinnings, and analytical concepts that drive this empirical investigation of RECs and health research regulation. Particular attention was drawn to ideas from regulatory theory and anthropology, namely the metaphor of the regulatory space, risk-based and proportionate regulation, and limin-ality. I argued that there are limits to what regulatory theory can tell us about 'what is going on', how and why anthropology of regulation complements common socio-legal research approaches, and how it naturally aligns with liminality. Anthropology of regulation draws atten-tion to experience, time, and space(s) that are otherwise often overlooked in analyses (too narrowly) fixated on law as the object of investigation or (too broadly) fixated on social patterns of interaction. I closed this chapter with discussion of the evolution of liminality and its contribution as a sensitizing concept to anthropology of regulation.

Having described the methodological approach, I now turn to present what the empirical research findings tell us about the nature of the interaction between central regulators and RECs in the health research regulatory space, and the functional operations and deliberative processes of RECs in an era of twinned regulatory objectives of participant protection and research promotion. We will see whether the empirical research findings reflect and validate the suggestions supplied in earlier chapters—that RECs engage in risk-based regulation, that health research regulation is increasingly grounded in a principle of proportionality, and that health research regulation is increasingly 'centred' such that the state, especially through the HRA, is exercising growing influence and control.

5. Operationalizing 'next-generation' health research regulation—what is happening in practice?

I. INTRODUCTION

The principal aim of this and the following chapter is to engage with the empirical data collected from the interviews and observations and, coupled with the findings from the document analysis, make sense of them through an anthropology of regulation approach, as outlined in Chapter 4. In this chapter, I explore what happens in REC meetings, consider the operationalization of 'next-generation' health research regulation (particularly in light of the twin aims of protection and promotion), and investigate the procedures and substance behind risk-based regulation. I do this by querying whether risk-based regulation is actually being practised by RECs and the HRA, and more fundamentally, by querying the nature and function of the interactions among RECs, researchers, and the HRA. Throughout, I draw on the implications of space and time in the process of research ethics review, signifying the contribution of liminality to the normative discussion that follows in Chapter 6.

In what follows, I present three themes (subdivided into categories) that emerged from the data. These findings consist of evaluative statements based on an overall assessment of the raw data informed by an anthropology of regulation. I rely on direct quotes or extracts of fieldnotes where they specifically enrich the analysis. Given the wealth of data in my notes, however, I cannot do this everywhere. A significant category within the third theme—regulatory stewardship and its connection with liminality—will serve as a bridge to Chapter 6, which, taking up the normative dimension of anthropology of regulation, provides recommendations for refining the health research regulatory framework.

II. THEMES

Each of the three themes focuses on different aspects of regulation and transition. Combined, they paint a picture of a health research regulatory system that both REC members and regulators support, but do not always praise. For REC members and regulators, the current system demonstrates vast improvement in the last decade. To this end, most members were supportive of the HRA's efforts to further centralize research ethics and create common standards to improve quality and consistency, as well as efficiency. At the same time, however, many REC members were also critical of certain aspects within the system, including the at times fraught relationship between the HRA and its equivalent bodies in the devolved administrations, and—perhaps surprisingly—between the HRA and RECs themselves.

My findings suggest that research promotion is *not* a 'new' twinned role for RECs—some additional primary responsibility only recently foisted upon members—but, the findings reveal that the practices of REC members vary greatly in how this role is both conceptualized and instantiated. In enacting their regulatory roles, whether for risk/burden-benefit analysis, assessment of the consent process, or legal and scientific checks (itself a questionable role), REC members and regulators demonstrate the value of stewardship—most notably expressed through the work of REC Managers, REC Chairs, and Scientific Officers—to set an example for others to follow, and guide REC members and researchers alike across the stages of the research application process. Within this latter observation, we uncover key insights into the liminal spaces RECs occupy and the potential role they may play across various thresholds of the research lifecycle, including those beyond the current *ex ante*-dominant positioning of ethics review.

The following subsections investigate three themes, namely: (1) the 'black boxes' of ethics review; (2) regulatory connectivity; and (3) regulators as stewards. In light of the methodology described in Chapter 4, we will find that elements of anthropology of regulation appear in each of the three themes identified.

1.   Regarding the first theme of 'black boxes' of ethics review, anthropology of regulation helps frame the regulatory behaviour of RECs as an instance of internal flexibility, where individual and group behaviour impacts and indeed helps shape a regulatory space wherein RECs and researchers alike explore and deliberate the 'ethics' of a research project. Liminality, in turn, draws our attention

to rituals and how they play a crucial role in regulatory coordination. The rituals in ethics review serve to organize the REC's actions and reinforce its authority, but they also drive collaboration and coordination with other actors, particularly researchers.

2. Regarding the theme of regulatory connectivity, anthropology of regulation invites us to consider the influence of law, science, and ethics in REC work. Rather than viewing each of these as disciplinary and regulatory 'boundaries', we are better placed to view them as connected regulatory spaces that call for guidance to work through and across each of them. Law, science, and ethics are all wrapped up together in the making of an ethics opinion.

3. Finally, regarding the theme of regulators as stewards, anthropology of regulation suggests that particular actors can serve as 'masters of ceremony' in guiding other actors (most often researchers and sponsors) through stages and thresholds of regulatory processes, where uncertainty often is paramount. This last theme therefore teases out the crucial finding that actors within and connected to RECs serve as 'regulatory stewards' who help guide researchers, and their applications, across stages of the research lifecycle, and that the HRA as a managing regulatory authority can take a leading role here.

I now proceed to explore each of the three themes, commencing with the 'black boxes' of ethics review.

2.1   The 'Black Boxes' of Ethics Review

2.1.1   Learning by observation

As earlier chapters have underscored, much is unknown about how REC members learn to 'do' ethics reviews and what actually happens in the course of their work before, during, and after a committee meeting. As anthropology of regulation aims to investigate the nature of regulation and the behaviours and experiences of actors within a regulatory space (or spaces), and the ways in which they are affected by, and in turn affect, regulation, I was interested in understanding how people learn to become REC members and perform the regulatory task of assessing the ethics of research. I was interested in knowing whether REC members felt their knowledge—or indeed expertise—was formed primarily by formal training sessions and regulatory documents, or by the experience itself—learning by doing, in other words.

By and large, REC members felt that they learned how to 'do' ethics reviews by observing other REC members in action. They watch, listen, and learn, but what REC members pick up is not necessarily carbon-copied into their own particular ways of doing committee work. Their observations are individually interpreted and subsequently manifest themselves in unique ways based on their own values, experiences, and expertise. Training, such as the mandatory induction for new members, provides a cursory overview of research ethics and points them in the right direction for additional resources if they are uncertain about specific areas, but the actual practice of ethics review—the process of working through applications; adopting the rituals, mannerisms, and jargon during meetings; evaluating forms; questionning researchers face-to-face; and writing up reports—is learned by observing other members who have obtained this experience. It is through this that members come to contribute 'effectively' and produce a culture of ethics review. As one REC member explained:

> I wasn't expected to contribute for the first few meetings—so if I wanted to I could have done—but it was mostly, 'You're here to learn about how things operate and what sorts of things we're going to be discussing', and then just picking it up from those meetings. [...] The best way to learn is by listening to what the other members come up with. (P6)

If REC members learn by observing other members and also individually interpret applications based on their own values and experiences, what might the process of an ethics review look like? How might one describe it? An HRA regulator described ethics review as a 'black box' where the process of review itself constitutes the outcome:

> To some extent you just have to sometimes, I think, look at the RECs as a black box and you just say, 'Well, that's how we have decided in this country and across the world to deal with that ethical decision making.' That's it, that's the black box—it's up to 18 people around a table discussing it and out pops the opinion. And it's a bit of a difficult one to get into that black box and mess around with it. It's almost that the process is the ethical decision. We've just decided that's the process and what pops out and we'll live with it. You know, you can train the people who are inside the black box and do everything you can, but I think to some extent this is probably as good as it gets when you get [86] committees with up to 18 people sitting around a table making ethical decisions. (P1)

It was the reference to RECs as a black box and the *process* of deliberation as constituting the ethics opinion in this first interview that propelled me to look more closely inside RECs. Does the practice of ethics review align with what the regulations would suggest happens, or should happen? Do REC members have any sense of what other RECs do, any curiosity about it, or any desire to know if they are being 'consistent'? As opposed to a singular black box, could there be a multiplicity of unconnected black *boxes* operating in fairly splendid isolation—and yet with still a fair degree of homogeneity in culture? How exactly does the process of ethics review itself constitute an opinion—not input and then output, but input *as* output, and arguably process as product?

2.1.2   Ethics review—peering inside the black boxes

The HRA's guidance document, 'Information for Potential Research Ethics Service Committee Members', outlines a process of ethics review in RECs that focuses on the utilitarian calculus of risk-benefit, a robust consent process, and adherence to the REC SOPs and relevant guidance and legislation.[1] The evidence from my research suggests that RECs follow this guidance. A great deal of effort and time at meetings is dedicated to three areas: (1) ensuring that the consent process is robust, such that participants are fully informed of all material issues in a Participant Information Sheet (PIS) and are able to make a voluntary decision to participate in a project; (2) ensuring that the burdens and risks to participants are minimized as far as possible, and risks to the researchers are minimized; and (3) ensuring that there is methodological robustness to the project, that is, that 'the science is right' (this focus on scientific quality is discussed further below).

Within these three areas of focus, all five RECs I observed approached research projects liberally. As one REC Chair explained: 'I think sometimes we have to remind ourselves that if the risks to the participants are minimized as far as possible then that research should probably be allowed to happen' (P3). The prevalent view that I observed is that provided risks are outweighed by potential benefits (or there is a 'fair balance' between risk or burden and potential benefits), and participants are provided with all material information during the consent process, then the choice to participate should be theirs to make, not the REC's. A member elucidated this liberal approach as follows:

> sometimes you have to be careful not to be paternalistic in that actually … well, so long as people have a choice, they don't have to do the study, and if they don't like the fact that they're not going to get paid or they're not going to get travel expenses, we might suggest, 'Well, it would be nice if you could

¹   Health Research Authority, 'Information for Potential Research Ethics Service Committee Members' <www.hra.nhs.uk/documents/1025/standard-application-pack-rec-members.pdf> accessed 22 October 2019.

pay them, but if you're not going to pay them then the person won't do the study.' There's a fine balance between thinking a participant hasn't got the brains to work things out for themselves and they have to be mollycoddled every step of the way. It's really hard to think of things that you just want to go: 'No, you can't do that.' (P8)

In REC meetings, ethical issues within the three areas mentioned above are transformed into questions of refinement, or what might be called technical questions (e.g. inconsistencies between the research protocol, PIS, or IRAS form; missing information in the PIS; clarification of the participant recruitment process; whether there will be continuation of the study drug after the clinical trial ends). Fundamental questions demanding meta-ethical reflection (e.g. the ethics of gene therapy; the ethics of 'me-too' drug applications) rarely manifested themselves in REC meetings. Instead, there was a cumulative gathering of information: members tended to reinforce other members' comments through adding their own, often in complementary ways. This may be a pragmatic matter driven by time and resource constraints. Or, this may be a matter of REC members thinking it inappropriate, or thinking themselves incapable, of engaging in deep ethical reflection or debate. After all, RECs do not function as a bioethics council (such as the Nuffield Council on Bioethics) where there are resources and an explicit mandate to deep dive into matters of ethical concern. Rather, RECs function more as regulatory event licensing bodies that individually evaluate and collectively deliberate on submitted documents and render a decision underpinned by standards, principles, and intuition. This reinforces legal scholar Carl Schneider's claim that the REC system 'is not an engine for abstract ethical thought. It is an agency *regulating* research',[2] and legal scholar Jonathan Montgomery's claim that a REC 'rarely engages directly in ethical reflection, but is concerned with ensuring compliance with established standards'.[3]

As such, to the extent that there is an underlying ethos guiding these RECs, it appears most strongly as liberalism and pragmatism. Each member is tasked with interpreting and applying ethical standards and principles (and to some degree, laws and regulations) to specific research projects. How these standards and principles are instantiated vary among individual members and, to some extent, among RECs. But, while the individual interpretations can vary, they are not limitless.

---

[2] Carl Schneider, *The Censor's Hand: The Misregulation of Human-Subject Research* (MIT Press 2015) 107 (emphasis added).

[3] Jonathan Montgomery, 'Bioethics as a Governance Practice' (2016) 24 Health Care Analysis 3, 11.

In her ground-breaking empirical work on IRBs in the US, the historian Laura Stark invokes an 'ethics of place'[4] to denote the peer review model of IRBs—*institutional* review boards—that attaches ethics to a specific physical place—a particular building—rather than a classic code of ethics that attaches to an individual physician or researcher. Peering further into the 'black box' of ethics review in the UK, several key findings emerge that suggest NHS RECs, unlike their institutional counterparts in the US, symbolize an *ethics of space*. Ethics is attached to the REC within their meeting space at an NHS Trust hospital, Health Board, or hotel conference room, yet as a node within networks (RES, NHS, and others), theirs is also an ethics informed by a larger regulatory framework such that moral authority for a decision rests not just in the REC itself, but also in the institutional apparatus of the RES(s). As bodies that have become increasingly centralized, their independent 'room to roam' is still wide, but it is not infinite. Ethically appropriate research must fit within the personal sensibilities of REC members, as well as institutional sensibilities set by the HRA and equivalent bodies that prescribe boundaries of ethical (and legal) acceptability. Invoking an anthropologically informed view of regulatory practice by RECs, we find that the 'ethics' within research *ethics* committees is a proving ground of debate, deliberation, and negotiation, and a regulatory space that accommodates diversity, disagreement, and dissent across applications and across time.

Within this ethics of space, a common behaviour exists across RECs. Intriguingly, relative to each other, RECs are black boxes, existing in multiple spaces. Several REC members I spoke with perceived a top-down command from the HRA, while HRA regulators told me they perceived a collaborative ethics co-produced with RECs. Several REC members also perceived that they had little interaction with other RECs. Beyond the regional REC Chair meetings held twice a year (across regions in England), 'ordinary' REC members do not have common opportunities to engage with other RECs, and they do not seem to have much desire to do so. Yet, despite these black boxes existing between black boxes, there exists a surprising degree of group homogeneity in terms of approach and rituals. What drives this homogenous REC group culture across the different black boxes may be in part HRA standards driving consistency, but this can only be a partial explanation. Many of the rituals and routine performed by REC members are not simple

---

4 Laura Stark, *Behind Closed Doors: IRBs and the Making of Ethical Research* (University of Chicago Press 2012) 83.

instantiations of HRA standards. Even if RECs maintain a relatively wide latitude in which to roam, they appear to roam in similar ways and in similar spaces. Even more intriguingly, elements of REC culture—interpretive flexibility, self-policing behaviour, sensitivities with regard to relationships with researchers—would ordinarily suggest heterogeneity, not homogeneity. What might explain this?

The ethics of space illustrates the symbolic importance of inviting various actors, such as researchers, into the black box of ethics review, and it illustrates how the physical dimensions of space impact on the processes of review. The space that is created is on the REC's terms, even if it may be part of the physical space of the NHS or another's community. For instance, a clinical researcher may be on her 'home turf', residing in the same NHS Trust hospital as where the REC meets monthly, but she must still face the black box by entering the conference room, presenting her research project before the members, and submitting to their judgement as the REC casts its opinion on whether her application is ethically acceptable. One might think that this is a recipe for adversarial conflict, driven by a desire for research promotion versus a desire for participant protection. Quite on the contrary, researchers invariably seem to submit to the REC and work together alongside them in moving the research application along towards ethical acceptance. Indeed, only once did I observe an overtly hostile situation where a researcher was unwilling to participate in the REC's ethics of space and overtly demonstrated an unreceptive attitude. The REC Manager later told me that this researcher had been to the REC several times before and had a bit of a 'reputation'. Even so, this hostile situation and ostensibly unfriendly relationship did not seem to have any bearing on the REC's view towards the research application. The outcome recommended by the Lead Reviewer and subsequently agreed by the REC as a whole was 'favourable with conditions'.

In sum, an ethics of space constitutes a connected network of RECs across the UK where cultural homogeneity is paramount. A researcher can submit an application in Southampton in the south of England or Aberdeen in the north of Scotland and is likely to experience a very similar ethics review (and a REC whose members are rather similar in demographic composition), even if the ultimate outcome may differ (e.g. favourable opinion versus provisional opinion requiring further information). RECs themselves may not be aware of how similar they are culturally. More than once REC members asked me how their REC 'compared' to the others I was observing, and whether I found any differences. As I responded to them, the differences are few and far between. Despite, or perhaps because of this homogeneity, there is a strong desire by RECs, including REC Managers, to preserve the sanctity of *their* black box and ethics of space. As will soon be shown, initiatives by the HRA that try to improve the regulatory pathways for researchers can backfire if there is improper consultation with RECs. Specifically, the 'Ethics Officer' pilot, discussed later in this chapter, can be interpreted as an invasion of this ethics of space. Researchers who enter this space do not create tension, yet other regulators who enter into it can. The irony, then, is that in the present context, regulatory tension or failures exist between regulators, not between regulators and regulatees.

2.1.2.1   A liberal approach to risk and expected benefit

2.1.2.1   A liberal approach to risk and expected benefit   The GAfREC state: 'The [REC] has to be assured that any anticipated risks, burdens or intrusions will be minimised for the people taking part in the research and are justified by the expected benefits for the participants or for science and society.'[5] Elsewhere, the GAfREC state that 'research can sometimes involve an element of risk, because research can involve trying something new. It is important that any risks are minimised and do not compromise the dignity, rights, safety and well-being of the people who take part.'[6] Specific guidance is not provided as to how this evaluation of anticipated risks and benefits is to be conducted, or how risk minimization may be done. As we saw in Chapter 4, this concerns scholars such as Annette Rid, who argues that 'frameworks for risk–benefit evaluations of biomedical research remain surprisingly vague'.[7]

Compared to Jan Federici Jaeger's ethnographic study of IRBs in the US, which found that '[m]ost of the time that an IRB spends on a proposal review is focused on identifying and deliberating about risk',[8] my findings suggest that RECs spend *some* time per application discussing risk, but it does not comprise a majority of the REC's meeting time. Moreover, to the extent that the risk-benefit or burden-benefit calculus is invoked in decision-making, a number of REC members tended to focus their discussion more on the prospective evaluation of burdens to participants (usually framed as 'mere inconveniences', typically of a temporal or financial variety) than risks of a physical, psychological, or

---

5   GAfREC para 1.2.2.
6   ibid para 2.2.1.
7   See Annette Rid, 'Rethinking Risk–Benefit Evaluations in Biomedical Research' in Daniel Strech and Marcel Mertz (eds), *Ethics and Governance of Biomedical Research* (Springer 2016) 153.
8   Jan Federici Jaeger, 'An Ethnographic Analysis of Institutional Review Board Decision-Making' (PhD thesis, University of Pennsylvania 2006) 94.

social variety. Only on occasion were expected benefits of the research project discussed.

One Scotland A REC member agreed that, at least as far as her REC was concerned, the members look at 'the burden probably more than the risk actually. We do occasionally get quite risky looking things, but they're usually in people who are really not well, I mean, really end of life' (P12). This may be because many REC members feel that risks in most projects are in fact relatively minimal (even though they are not non-material as compared to Proportionate Review applications); that there is a high level of unambiguity and certainty in the risks present in most research projects (and thus they do not need to be assessed in any systematic way); or that the scientific aspect of risk assessment is beyond their scope (unlike, say, the MHRA).

Discussions of risk in REC meetings were often limited to their identification, that is, a listing of what they were as identified by both the researcher in the application materials and the REC members in their review of the materials. The majority of the time, this was done by the Lead Reviewer. Explicit risks, burdens, and benefits may be gathered from the IRAS form: question A22 of the form asks the Chief Investigator (researcher) to list 'potential risks and burdens' for research participants and explain how they will be minimized; question A24 asks about the potential for benefit to research participants; and question A26 asks about potential risks for researchers themselves. Non-explicit forms of risk, burden, and benefit may be drawn out in the HRA Ethical Review Form's question 3, which asks REC members to consider whether the risks to the research participant are proportionate to the benefits to the research participant and society. Thus, some risks and burdens are explicitly identified already by the researchers; others may be implied (i.e. drawn out by REC members in their review and discussion); and still others theoretical (i.e. remote) or unknown (i.e. risks or burdens that the REC cannot identify due to missing or inaccurate information).

Chapter 4 explored risk-based regulation, which can be defined as 'the prioritizing of regulatory actions in accordance with an assessment of the risks that parties will present to the regulatory body's achieving its objectives'.[9] Looking back at the elements listed in Box 4.1 in Chapter 4, risk-based regulation tends to encompass a broad sweep of risk assessment (or appraisal), risk management, and review, including scoping the various dimensions of a risk, considerations of framing (i.e. how different

---

[9]   Robert Baldwin and others, *Understanding Regulation: Theory, Strategy, and Practice* (2nd edn, OUP 2012) 281.

stakeholders may have conflicting views concerning a risk), scientific risk assessment, and the broader social, institutional, political, and economic contexts that must be taken into account in risk-related decision-making.[10] RECs do provide written opinions and allow for appeals and at times engage in analogical reasoning, but they do not seem to follow specific rules governing particular aspects of the risk assessment process. As the legal scholar Lars Noah argues, risk assess-ment is a separate endeavour than burden or risk-benefit assessment;[11] the latter may not necessitate 'objective', scientific measurement so much as an intuitive balancing and effort to minimize (i.e. manage) risks that may manifest.

And indeed, in the full committee meetings I observed, RECs, and in particular REC Chairs, strived to enact a liberal approach in ethics review while avoiding a paternalistic stance towards risk. No member seemed wantonly unconcerned about risk; none would allow unfettered risks to be placed on participants. At the same time, though, the REC meeting discussions did not give me the impression that risk assessment and management were often the central focus. Members did not frame their approach to ethics review as a calculus such that their level of scrutiny of a research project was definitively determined by the level of risk it posed to participants. Rather, risk was discussed as part of a much larger whole of ethics evaluation. Commonly, risk was a matter to be made clear and explicit in a PIS, and for a potential participant to weigh. As a Scottish REC member explained: 'Nobody wants to stop research being done; we just want it to be done so the person being studied is fully aware of everything that's going to happen to them and to make an informed choice about whether they want to participate or not' (P18).

An example of this liberal approach can be drawn from my fieldnotes. As I was leaving at the end of one REC meeting, I stopped to chat with the REC Chair. I explained that I was interested in how issues such as risk are conceptualized and assessed by RECs. The Chair thought for a moment and said, 'I don't think this is really a philosophical issue; it's a practical issue. Most research is not at all risky. Where's the evidence that research is risky, beyond a Phase 1?' he asked. He then continued: 'Who's died from research? Some people have, but more people have died from unresearched care. Actually, if you look at the meta-analyses, taking part in Phase 3, Phase 4 research is neither good for you nor bad

---

[10]   International Risk Governance Council, *An Introduction to the IRGC Risk Governance Framework* (IRGC 2012) 8–10.
[11]   Lars Noah, 'Deputizing Institutional Review Boards to Police (Audit?) Biomedical Research' (2004) 25 Journal of Legal Medicine 267.

for you.' Pausing a moment for further reflection, he then added, 'I wonder what health research regulation would look like if we considered research to be good for you.'

This liberal approach towards risk may work at some level to address the 'heterogeneity problem' raised by the legal scholar and bioethicist Michelle Meyer.[12] While RECs as a group appear to exhibit homogenous cultural and regulatory behaviour, scholars such as Meyer argue that individual research participants are heterogeneous in their preferences and other circumstances; thus the same research protocol will offer a different risk-benefit profile for different participants. Likewise, individual members of ethics committees assess risks and benefits based on their individual interpretation of their regulatory mandate to do so. Thus, REC members can engage in interpretive flexibility[13] when it comes to interpreting and operationalizing the regulations regarding risk-benefit assessment. As Stephens and colleagues demonstrate, interpretive flexibility can be a positive outcome in regulation. To overcome this heterogeneity problem, Meyer advocates greater private ordering whereby individual prospective research participants, rather than the ethics committee, decide whether it is reasonable for them to accept the risks of participating in a particular research project. In the REC meetings I observed, the liberal approach enacted a form of private ordering. RECs fulfilled their regulatory mandate to assess burdens, risks, and potential benefits, yet the most common occurrence for the REC was to insist on clear provision of risks (and honest portrayal of expected benefit) in a PIS. It was then for individual prospective participants (or their proxies) to decide whether it was reasonable for them to accept the risks of taking part in a given research project.

In my view, then, it cannot be said that RECs operate solely as risk-based regulators. Were they acting as such, we would expect to see, among other things, more objective forms of risk assessment (e.g. a system for assessing risks and scoring them, beyond Proportionate

---

12   Michelle Meyer, 'Regulating the Production of Knowledge: Research Risk-Benefit Analysis and the Heterogeneity Problem' (2013) 65 Administrative Law Review 237; see also Michelle Meyer, 'Three Challenges for Risk-Based (Research) Regulation: Heterogeneity Among Regulated Activities, Regulator Bias, and Stakeholder Heterogeneity' in I. Glenn Cohen and Holly Fernandez Lynch (eds), *Human Subjects Research Regulation: Perspectives on the Future* (MIT Press 2014).

13   Neil Stephens and others, 'Documenting the Doable and Doing the Documented: Bridging Strategies at the UK Stem Cell Bank' (2011) 41 Social Studies of Science 791.

Review applications), management, and review; systematic improvement of decision-making processes based on new evidence and insights into potential risk; and allocation of resources where risk is greatest (e.g. more time and effort spent on gene therapy and Phase 1 clinical trials).[14] Instead, RECs' regulatory positioning towards research applications encompasses elements of risk assessment and risk management (such as communicating risks to participants), although the regulatory positioning extends beyond this. RECs regulate not on the basis of risk alone. The social and scientific value of a research project and its likely risks, burdens, and benefits are weighed by RECs; RECs decide whether burdens and risks to participants are ethically justified in light of, and reasonable in relation to, the potential benefits and scientific and social value of a project.[15] Thus, just as critical to RECs' operative deliberation is the *facilitation* of a context in which a fair choice is offered to participants whereby they can decide whether to participate in a project that presents ethically acceptable risks and burdens (as determined by the REC) and is likely to answer, or at least contribute to, the research question it purports to address. Moreover, the facilitation is directed not just to research participants, but also to researchers themselves, as I discuss further below.

This focus on facilitating participant choice aligns with the 2015 Nuffield Council on Bioethics' report on children and clinical research, which suggests that:

> the fundamental role of ethical review is to ensure that an invitation to participate in research would constitute a *'fair offer'* to children, young people and their parents, where the value of the research and its likely risks, burdens and benefits have been carefully weighed up.

> In focusing on the role of the REC in ensuring that research involving children constitutes a fair offer to children and parents, it is also important to recognise *the REC's second and equally important function: its facilitative role*, which arises in recognition of the essential social good of well-designed and well-conducted research. It is not an ethically neutral act to say 'no' to a research proposal that might potentially lead to better outcomes for children's and young people's healthcare.[16]

---

[14] See e.g. OECD (ed), *Risk and Regulatory Policy: Improving the Governance of Risk* (OECD 2010).

[15] See also Jeffrey Cooper and Lindsay McNair, 'Assessing Research Benefits: Practical Ethicist' (2017) 12 Journal of Empirical Research on Human Research Ethics 191.

[16] Nuffield Council on Bioethics, *Children and Clinical Research: Ethical Issues* (Nuffield Council on Bioethics 2015) xxvii (emphasis added).

To preview the discussion to follow, here we begin to see one element of (ethical) research promotion. To the extent risk is assessed, managed, and communicated, RECs concern themselves with risk vis-à-vis its identification and mitigation (as set forth in the HRA Ethical Review Form) in a personalized (read: subjective) and socialized way (i.e. in the course of REC deliberation), but the scope of risk assessment and management is mitigated by a liberal, facilitative approach.

A final key finding within this theme is that different moral considerations apply to different types of research projects, in a twist to the risk-proportionate approach advocated by the HRA, which focuses on reducing the regulatory burden for research that presents 'no material ethical issues' for human participants. RECs approve research projects involving high-risk treatments for late-stage cancer patients (e.g. Phase 2 and 3 clinical trials), even though this means there might be known (quantifiable) risks associated with the treatment, or even unknown risks. They approve such projects on the basis that participants could accept the treatment with the full knowledge of the risks, and that *without* taking the treatment, they could well die rapidly. One reason for this is that, unlike a Phase I (first-in-human) healthy volunteer study, at least some of the risk-bearers may well also stand to benefit from the risks taken. As the ethicists Allison Ross and Nafsika Athanassoulis argue, 'while we normally tend to think of risks as something we want to avoid, research risks can be very attractive, especially for those whose last hopes for a treatment lie with the potential research benefits'.[17] In these situations, RECs do make ethical decisions knowing that there are associated high(er) risks. For them, the emphasis is placed on making that knowledge explicit and clear to the participants. The REC cannot speak on behalf of potential participants, but it can ensure that potential participants have accurate, up-to-date, and understandable information. From there, liberal autonomy seems to dictate: the choice is theirs to make.

This was evident in a REC review of a gene therapy trial that I observed. Here, unsurprisingly, risk discussions predominated. The REC's main concern was the balancing of safety and efficacy of the therapy. Following the initial discussion, three representatives from the research project were invited into the committee room, where the REC Chair began by asking them to describe their project. In a calm, cool, and well-spoken manner, the Chief Investigator described the proposed project. When the REC Chair then asked him about weighing safety and

---

[17]   Allison Ross and Nafsika Athanassoulis, 'The Role of Research Ethics Committees in Making Decisions About Risk' (2014) 26 HEC Forum 203, 205.

efficacy, the Chief Investigator, with powerful rhetorical flourish, narrated a story about how participants understand risk better than we think. A potential participant once asked the Chief Investigator to sign his will before participating in a clinical trial, in case death occurred. The Chief Investigator, slowing his cadence at this point, said to the REC: 'And I didn't sign that will. And you know, I was glad not to because the man had planned to give everything to his girlfriend, and they then broke up six months later!' This drew laughter from the REC. 'He knew he was putting his life on the line,' the Chief Investigator continued. His point, of course, is that RECs should not assume participants cannot understand risks in research, much less substitute their judgement for a competent adult participant. If the information provided to them is honest and complete, the research should proceed. Following the face-to-face discussion, when the researchers got up to leave, the REC Chair beamed and said to the Chief Investigator, 'Thank you very much, that was fascinating!' After they left, the REC Chair looked around the table at his fellow committee members and said: 'What do you want me to do, team? He's quite persuasive, isn't he?' All agreed, and the outcome of this application was a 'happy provisional' opinion.

2.1.2.2 Pragmatic ethics The HRA disseminates ethics review guidance and policies driven by procedures; they do not offer guidance on how to conduct an ethics review by reference to substantive ethics. It is, as I discovered, up to REC members and key 'stewards' such as REC Chairs and Scientific Officers (as I further discuss below) to help guide the REC members towards an ethically informed decision. REC members were hard-pressed to pinpoint the ethical deliberative content in a committee decision. When asked to explain the process, they provided a procedural description that focused on the steps involved in working through the contents of the application form and attendant documents. Members reach an ethically informed decision of some type, but the decision-making process appears to be performed intuitively or pragmatically. Just as researchers rarely frame ethical scenarios in the moral philosophical language of deontology, consequentialism, and virtue ethics,[18] rarely was an ethical principle relied upon to justify a stance on an issue within an application. Members might have taken utilitarian perspectives or objective dignitarian perspectives when considering risk-benefit analysis (i.e. weighing risks against benefits, as the regulation

---

[18] David Johnson and Elaine Howard Ecklund, 'Ethical Ambiguity in Science' (2016) 22 Science and Engineering Ethics 989.

largely dictates, or suggesting a particular risk of harm could never be justified, regardless of any consideration of benefits), but none articulated them as such. Foremost, educated (and experiential) gut reactions and feelings drive ethical decision-making processes to render an opinion that seems suitable to and workable in the context at hand.

This finding accords with philosopher Mary Warnock's argument that 'morality cannot be divorced from sentiment'[19] and '[e]thical decisions cannot be taken without the examination of ethical feelings'.[20] Each REC member brings their own culture of moral reasoning to bear on applications, which is then negotiated contextually and situationally in the circumstances that arise for a given application before the committee. This moral intuition, built up from a lifetime of cultural experience, manifests in an ethics assessment undergirded as much by reason as it is by feeling, as one member explained:

> I think in ethics committees, as in life, we make very quick decisions, 'Oh, that's right', or 'That's wrong', and most of the time we're okay. And if there's very little contention, if there are no particular problems, it's a very efficient way to make decisions. (P10)

This is not to say RECs and individual members were incapable of justifying their reasoning; rather, it is that the moral reasoning could manifest *ex post* rather than a priori, or as one REC Chair put it: 'The actual ethical review process is almost tick-box' (P3).

Part of this can be explained both by the growth in volume of procedural forms provided by the HRA to REC members, and by the lack many REC members have in formal ethics education and training. REC members receive basic induction in research ethics issues and are encouraged to engage in self-directed learning,[21] but no member I spoke with thought such training would transform them into ethicists. Indeed, few members were interested in academic ethics articles or abstract ethical debates. In this sense, pragmatism drives the decision-making process: members apply rules, standards, and principles in ways that are practically useful for rendering a decision and that work best for the situation at hand. As one HRA regulator told me, 'there's a disconnect

---

[19] Mary Warnock, 'Moral Thinking and Government Policy: The Warnock Committee on Human Embryology' (1985) 63 The Milbank Memorial Fund Quarterly: Health and Society 504, 518.

[20] ibid 520.

[21] Health Research Authority, 'REC Member Learning Resources' <www.hra.nhs.uk/planning-and-improving-research/learning/rec-member-learning-resources/> accessed 22 October 2019.

between where ethics is going as an academic discipline and where it talks about research ethics, and the knowledge of RECs about that and that sort of coming together to discuss, so that one informs the other' (P1). This seems to bother neither the HRA nor RECs—nor, from what I saw in my observations, researchers and sponsors. The important point that regulators and REC members equally stressed is that a REC must be able to justify an outcome that is reasonable: provided so, it will be seen as valid, legitimate, and ethical. As a REC Chair elaborated:

> I can't tell you how [as a REC member] to think, and that actually what I want to try and do is to get people to think: 'How am I deciding? What are the reasons for my decision? How am I reflecting on this? Where can I turn? What questions should I ask myself?' I think if one can provide that sort of framework, then it has to be down to the individual to look back to see, 'What are my own values?' When you come to an ethics committee, when you come to induction training at say whatever age you are, 30, 40, 50, 60, there's so much in your life that you bring to that, that this meeting for one day is going to barely touch. So I try to help people and say: 'Look, if you're going to make decisions, just work out what your reasons are because those are the crucial ... Why have you made that decision?' By and large, if people think about reasons and think through their reasons, I think they usually come to the right decision. (P10)

As I continued to peer into these black boxes, I also discovered that in bringing their life experiences to bear in the ethics review process, REC members engaged in rituals that helped coordinate relationships, overcome potential disagreement, and achieve a consensus opinion.

2.1.2.3 Rituals in ethics review   Ritual patterns are often present in highly 'rationalized' settings such as hospitals, and are embedded to a significant degree in the schedules, procedures, and practices of the setting.[22] RECs and the spaces in which they meet and constitute form a highly rationalized setting. In creating and reinforcing their ethics of space, REC members adopt rituals—that is, a type of patterned or institutionalized symbolic action[23]—that manifest throughout the process of ethics review. These include:

---

[22]   Nora Machado and Tom Burns, 'Complex Social Organization: Multiple Organizing Modes, Structural Incongruence, and Mechanisms of Integration' (1998) 76 Public Administration 355, 372.

[23]   ibid.

- the refrain of phrases expressed by a REC Chair to the REC and attending researchers to induce comradery (a REC Chair might say to the attending researcher: 'Thanks very much for attending today. We've had a *really* good discussion of your application, and as you might expect, have a few questions for you'; following a face-to-face meeting with a researcher, a REC Chair might jokingly say to the researcher, 'Right, now run for the hills!'; or always begin the group deliberation following the face-to-face researcher meeting with, 'What do we think, team?');
- the ordering of questions gathered by the REC Chair (i.e. distilling the REC's discussion of an application into three or four key questions for the attending researchers so as to keep the meeting on time and also not overwhelm researchers);
- rituals of placement, such as the seating arrangement of REC members, researchers, and staff (e.g. the Chair and Manager always sitting side by side, researchers sitting at a right angle to the REC Chair and Manager, as opposed to directly across from them, which minimizes a sense of confrontation and encourages a more research 'promotionist' approach);
- the shuffling of the bundles of papers as RECs move through the applications, which perpetually swathe the conference tables during meetings;
- the presentation by the Lead and Second Reviewers to the REC by reading from their filled-in HRA Ethical Review Form;
- the meeting structure (e.g. on-time starts and a strong collective desire to stick to the allotted times for the agenda items); and
- the formalized structure of working through an application (i.e. the structure of Lead and Second Reviewer presentations followed by structured discussion by other REC members).

Rituals play a crucial role in structuring how members formulate comments on an application and approach their ethical decision-making. Similar group rituals were present across all five RECs, and within each, members had individual rituals vis-à-vis their review process. Thus, how rituals of ethics review played out varied across members. REC members bring their own idiosyncrasies and predilections to their reviews; they have 'certain bugbears' that can make them sound like 'a bit of a broken record' (P12), but this, members explained, helps ensure a well-rounded and consistent review. As a Scientific Officer told me: 'You also have to find your own way [as a REC member], because if everybody reviews an application the same way, you're going to miss something' (P23). Indeed, subjectivity and idiosyncrasy of individual members is a natural outcome of most independent committee structures. The committee structure allows for a more thorough review than if only one reviewer is to pore over an application. Yet, it was rarely the case that subjectivity among individual members led to diametrically opposing viewpoints on the ethical acceptability of an application. Consensus forms the backbone of ethical deliberation, which is reached in large part through rituals:

> if there wasn't at least an element of opinion and subjectivity in the review process you wouldn't need committees. You could do the entire review with checkboxes on a computer. [...] But I also think it's true to say that if you canvassed the committee members about what the decision for this month's applications would be before the meeting started, there would be almost complete unanimity on every application. (P14)

Some members review applications from only a narrow perspective, such as through their niche area of expertise (e.g. statistics, pharmacology). Others, particularly lay members, invoke a process of relationality: they read applications from the perspective of a potential participant, reminding themselves to 'think like a patient' and raise issues that may concern even only a few patients. In 'thinking like a patient', the lens may not be ethical per se; instead, it may be grounded in relationality with participants, tied in with an ethic of care:

> I take a step to the side and I think from the patients' or the participants' perspective; not that I sit and think I'm here because I'm a professional with a background in certain things. I would definitely highlight if I thought that the scientific integrity of a protocol wasn't robust, but really because I'm there as not a specialist or not an expert person. I give my opinion from the more personable side, patients' side. (P22)

Some members think it inappropriate, however, to substitute their opinion on whether to participate in a given project with that of an adequately informed potential participant. For these members, relationality with participants is risky; avoidance of paternalism should predominate. An ethical research project for them is one that discloses all material information to participants:

> I remember commenting on a particularly onerous ... I think it was pancreatic cancer study. Even if I had the cancer and was as sick as I needed to be to enter the study, I personally would not be prepared to enrol in the study because of the demands it would place on me. It was too onerous. Having said that, was it ethical? Yes, absolutely, because you're telling the patients precisely what's going to be required of them. And whilst I wouldn't agree to it, that doesn't mean to say that other people can't. And that's actually

potentially a difficult distinction to make. [...] It was an interesting one for me because I wouldn't volunteer for the study, but I wouldn't say it's wrong for other people to do it. (P14)

As noted, one of the key rituals is the meeting and agenda structure for RECs. Established by the HRA in a template form, the meeting agenda was consistent across all five RECs I observed, namely in the order of:

1. Apologies for Absence;
2. Minutes of the Meeting Last Held;
3. Matters Arising;
4. Items for Information and Discussion;
5. REC Manager's Report;
6. Declarations of Interest;
7. New Applications for Ethical Review (led by the Lead Reviewer and then Second Reviewer);
8. Any Other Business; and
9. Date of Next Meeting.

Within this structure, the timing was constant, too. Items 1–6 rarely extended beyond five minutes discussion in total. The vast majority of each meeting was dedicated to Item 7: New Applications for Ethical Review. Following the presentation by the Lead Reviewer (which typically ranged from 7 to 15 minutes), the Second Reviewer added a few comments (typically ranging from 3 to 7 minutes) in a gap-filling manner, raising further queries to be posed to the researcher or areas of concern within an application. Then, the REC Chair would invite other REC members to comment on the application. Following this open discussion, the REC Chair would write down the 'main issues' to discuss with the researcher, assuming the researcher was attending in person. (REC Managers were always taking minutes of the meetings, portions of which would then be transformed into opinion letters sent to the researchers.) Once the list of questions was formulated to all members' satisfaction, the REC Chair or Manager would retrieve the researchers (along with, on occasion, a representative from the sponsor or a student's supervisor) waiting outside (assuming they were attending in person), invite them inside, and ask questions regarding the application. Following this back-and-forth dialogue, the researcher would leave, and the REC Chair would invite members to deliberate further on the application, culminating in a decision.

Rituals of expertise manifested themselves often in meetings. For REC members with a particular niche area of expertise, such as statistics, quite often the REC Chair would turn to a specific member and ask, 'Are the statistics okay?' The member would reply, and then the REC Chair would move on. The power of the member's expertise was such that other members did not feel able to adequately comment on the specific matter of concern, though often other REC members would ask general questions about a niche area to the expert member, such as a pharmacist, prefacing their question with self-effacing and self-professed ignorance of the area.

Routine in the ethics reviews undertaken by individual members and routine in the meetings themselves do not necessarily mean there is a predictable outcome in any given application, even though the vast majority of applications (71 per cent from the meetings I observed) are deemed 'provisional'.[24] Interestingly, a provisional opinion is a *forward-focused* step in ethics review. The application moves from the pre-review threshold at submission to the threshold of approval during the REC meeting. A provisional opinion rendered by a REC almost always leads to a favourable opinion once the researcher has addressed the REC's concerns, which are expressed in the opinion letter. Indeed, members in all five RECs I observed sometimes would use the phrase 'provisional favourable' in announcing their verdict on an application, which symbolically differs from the HRA's term of 'provisional opinion', which signals no pre-determined final outcome. Upon receiving a provisional opinion, a researcher likely will amend the relevant documentation, which is then reviewed by the REC Chair and sometimes one or two other members, and then this 'sub-committee' will render a final decision.

With an array of rituals, idiosyncrasies, and moral intuitions, even if ethics is 'situated'—constrained by the limits of the committee structure, the predominance of scientific experts, or the desire for consensus and efficiency—any given REC's output, as with the input, is uncertain. For example, certain cues in the course of ethics review (e.g. the type of research under review, a REC's trust in the researcher, the quality—such

---

[24] Out of the 24 REC meetings I attended, I observed deliberation of a total of 119 new applications for ethics review. Six were approved outright as favourable, 22 were granted favourable with conditions, 85 were deemed provisional, and 6 were rejected as unfavourable. This is on par with the HRA statistics for RECs in England, which indicate that, of applications reviewed at full committee meetings, on average over 70 per cent are deemed provisional. See Health Research Authority, 'Annual Report Summary for RECs in England April 2016 to March 2017' <www.hra.nhs.uk/documents/1515/Annual_Report_Summary_for_RECs_in_England_April_2016_-_March_2017.pdf> accessed 22 October 2019.

as lack of errors and comprehensiveness—of the IRAS form and attendant documents) can help make an outcome more predictable, but not
necessarily certain. There is always an element of uncertainty in the
outcome of an application after REC review. As well, intra-REC precedent (i.e. comparing current applications to past applications and
decisions) occasionally was invoked in deliberations to serve as a
reference and maintain consistency, but this was not done formally or
systematically. Instead, group experience, or a 'memory within the
group' (P19), predominated the aiding of a decision. As one REC Chair
phrased it, 'group moral maxims that we all generally share' (P10) helped
determine if the past opinions were relevant to the current application.
Collective memory and experience, along with these 'group moral
maxims', maintained order and propelled the REC towards a decision
that they believed would be consistent within their REC and, ideally,
across others.

Liminality draws our attention to rituals and how they play a crucial
role in regulatory coordination. The rituals in ethics review serve to
organize the REC's actions, reinforce their authority, but also drive
collaboration and coordination with other actors, particularly researchers.
Rituals constitute embedded processes of ethics review that work to
create shared meanings, establish order, build feelings of community, and
encourage trust in the process and outcome. At the same time, in
considering the ways in which research may be regulated by a network of
regulators (e.g. RECs, MHRA, HRA) through a variety of rituals (e.g.
rituals of consent, rituals of placement at meetings, rituals of words and
phrases), we see that rituals have a tangible impact on the regulatory
actors' behaviour, particularly when those rituals are disrupted by regulatory changes, or impositions 'from above', such as the HRA's ShED
exercise or push for Proportionate Review. Liminality invites us to
identify and pay attention to symbolically and practically significant
rituals and how they organize a REC's regulatory behaviour and structure
a REC's relations with other actors.

2.1.2.4 Ethics as an act of faith   As a final key finding discovered
when peering inside the 'black boxes' of RECs, ethics review can be an
act of faith shared between the REC and researchers. This finding aligns
with the sociologist Adam Hedgecoe's observation that RECs and
researchers can interact as 'work groups' and co-construct 'organizational
deviance' through 'cultures of production' that contain various features,
including trust that RECs place in research applicants' abilities and

openness.[25] REC members receive 'marvellous bits of paper' in research applications, some of which may be 'meaningless' (P12), and yet they must make a definitive judgement on what they see and hear. For applications from commercial sponsors especially, REC members feel they must act on faith to trust the researcher or research team to act ethically. For them, there is a risk—but an acceptable one—in approving an application based on their assessment of 'bits of paper' and perhaps a 15-minute discussion with the Chief Investigator or another member of the research team.

A vital component that makes this act of faith acceptable to the REC, researchers, the HRA, and others is the face-to-face meeting with the researcher. This meeting follows the presentation of the application by the Lead and Second Reviewers and the general discussions around the conference table. REC members place a tremendous degree of value on meeting the researcher (or research team) in person, and likewise, though I did not interview them, researchers seemed to value the face-to-face meetings as well.

There are two purposes behind asking a researcher to attend a REC meeting. The first is to discuss key issues in the application that may be resolved in the meeting, thus saving time and perhaps even turning an application from a provisional to a favourable opinion. Efficiency and research promotion drive this purpose. As one REC member told me, 'because we can ask them questions straightaway and sometimes they can give answers very quickly, it just resolves the problem in a way' (P20). The second purpose is to get a sense of whether researchers seem trustworthy—something that cannot be investigated nearly as thoroughly through a document review alone. RECs want to get a sense of the researcher's character and probity. A good presentation by a researcher is almost as valuable as a well-put-together application. If the REC is comfortable that a Chief Investigator has participants' welfare at heart—and some members believe this is 'easy to convey in an interpersonal interaction' (P14)—then it will go a long way towards delivering a favourable opinion. Given that a number of researchers choose to apply to the same REC, either because the REC is in their local area or because they think highly of the particular committee, the rapport and trust established between REC and researcher can lead to more efficient—but potentially also shortcutted—reviews:

---

[25]   Adam Hedgecoe, 'A Deviation from Standard Design? Clinical Trials, Research Ethics Committees, and the Regulatory Co-Construction of Organizational Deviance' (2014) 44 Social Studies of Science 59.

So [this researcher had] done all that she'd needed to do to use [the medical device]; she just hadn't explained it particularly well in the IRAS [form]. And she put us completely at ease [in the face-to-face meeting] that the safety wasn't going to be an issue. So along comes the second application [from the same researcher a couple months later]. It has essentially the same defect in terms of explaining the safety. But because we knew it was her, we knew it wasn't an issue and we didn't need to spend any time on it, because it was the same piece of kit. The same researcher, and she'd convinced us beforehand. So that was very helpful. (P14)

At the same time, the inability for the REC to observe the researcher in action, to monitor what is actually occurring, given its *ex ante* positioning in the research lifecycle, troubles some members. Even if they have a good 'feeling' based on the face-to-face meeting, how sure can they be that the researcher will conduct the project ethically? Again, faith must be placed in the researcher to act ethically: 'All we're approving is the paperwork in effect, and we have no control about what actually goes on' (P8). To sustain this faith, RECs must work together with other actors to share responsibilities, approve projects that are designed to be ethical throughout, and inculcate virtuous behaviour in researchers. And, in working with other actors, RECs must connect across regulatory spaces. I now unpack this as the second theme.

2.2   Regulatory Connectivity

Law and science occupy an uncertain relationship with the work that RECs do. The GAfREC indicate that RECs are not responsible for assessing the scientific quality and legality of a research project; after all, RECs are neither a scientific review nor legal advisory body. In regard to science, the GAfREC state that: 'A REC need not reconsider the quality of the science, as this is the responsibility of the sponsor and will have been subject to review by one or more experts in the field (known as "peer review").'[26] In regard to law, the GAfREC state: 'It is not the role of the REC to offer a legal opinion on research proposals, but it may advise the researcher, sponsor or host organisation whenever it considers that legal advice might be helpful to them.'[27] In regard to regulatory responsibilities (e.g. those undertaken by the MHRA or HTA), the GAfREC encourages RECs to defer to other bodies where responsibilities may overlap: 'Where others have a regulatory responsibility, a REC can expect to rely on them to fulfil it. If the law gives another body

---

[26]   GAfREC para 5.4.2(a).
[27]   ibid para 3.2.11.

duties that are normally responsibilities of a REC according to this document, RECs do not duplicate them.'[28]

Even if RECs 'need not reconsider' scientific quality, should not offer a 'legal opinion' on research proposals, and should not 'duplicate' other bodies that have regulatory responsibilities, it remains the case that often they perform all three roles.

2.2.1 Ethics and science

REC members find it a 'constant struggle to try and separate out the idea' that RECs already should be assured that the science is 'good' and that the application has had appropriate peer review (P1). As a body partially comprised of past or current researchers, it is a challenge for many to disentangle science and ethics, as even HRA regulators recognize:

> you have a certain number of experts 'round there who are all jobbing scientists and jobbing researchers, or much of them are, or at least acquainted with research at that level, you know, who can't help but pick over the carcass and the bones of the methodology … It's really difficult … where does ethics stop? Where do you stop thinking it's an ethics issue? But I think they do predominantly, a lot of committees do focus on the methodology, talk about the methodology. (P1)

Indeed, the HRA seems to implicitly acknowledge this potential for a connected ethics-science regulatory space in its push for committees to include a statistician among their membership. The GAfREC state that: 'The REC will be satisfied with credible assurances that the research has an identified sponsor and that it takes account of appropriate scientific peer review.'[29] But how does a REC satisfy itself with such credible assurances? A good deal of discretion is given to them. Not surprisingly, even REC members who are not 'jobbing scientists' also think it vital to ensure the science 'is right'. Three different members I interviewed repeated a well-worn line in research ethics: Bad Science is Bad Ethics. But they also acknowledged that RECs cannot simply mimic scientific review committees. In consequence, RECs engage in a secondary form of *self-policed* science review.

There were times that I observed RECs expressing uncertainty with the scope of their scientific review, particularly in their communications with researchers. For example, when a statistician expressed serious concern

---

[28]   ibid para 5.4.2(c).
[29]   ibid para 5.4.2(a).

about the stated scientific accuracy of a CTIMP application, the Vice Chair remarked, 'this is a MHRA issue, though'. The statistician countered that the MHRA advises on research design, but not accuracy. Self-policing itself, the REC as a whole discussed how best to express this to the applicants, deciding that they could *not* say in the opinion letter that they disagreed with the scientific design, but instead they would ask the researchers to more clearly explain their rationale for the project design, given 'concerns' the REC had. In other instances where I observed that RECs felt the science of a proposed research project was not up to par, they policed themselves in terms of not having it colour their overall assessment of the application; their concerns would be expressed in the opinion letter, but the opinion was to be based on a constricted view of the 'ethics'. There was an ongoing challenge, therefore, in teasing out the ethics from the science. Invariably, the resulting opinion was not a favourable one—not surprising in itself when only six applications were granted 'favourable' outright, which equates to 5 per cent of the total new applications I observed.[30] The evidence suggests that RECs constrain themselves within their own linguistic and operational paradigm or 'space', implicitly recognizing there is another regulatory space (i.e. science review) that they ought not to enter explicitly. Through these constraints or workarounds, RECs can satisfy themselves that the ethics of an application has been fully reviewed to their satisfaction, and in a way that does not penetrate too deeply or too explicitly the scientific space.

Is this an instance of 'double jeopardy'?[31] I do not believe so. The ethics-science divide is an artificial boundary incapable of being rationally adhered to in this process of review.[32] RECs do not seek to expand their jurisdictional control over science. If anything, REC members admitted hesitancy in assessing scientific quality, but the process of ethics

---

[30]   This practice endorses David Hunter's argument that bad science is poor ethics, but not necessarily bad ethics, and thus not grounds for rejection alone. See David Hunter, 'Bad Science Equals Poor not Necessarily Bad Ethics' in Jennifer Gunning and Søren Holm (eds), *Ethics, Law and Society: Volume III* (Ashgate Publishing 2007).

[31]   Stephen Humphreys and others, 'Science Review in Research Ethics Committees: Double Jeopardy?' (2015) 10 Research Ethics 227.

[32]   See also Angus Dawson and Steve Yentis, 'Contesting the Science/Ethics Distinction in the Review of Clinical Research' (2007) 33 Journal of Medical Ethics 165 (arguing that the science versus ethics distinction is incoherent and that RECs have an 'obligation' to consider a research project's science).

review necessarily entails a verification of the scientific quality.[33] The CIOMS Guidelines endorse this position in their latest version, which states: 'Although in some instances scientific review precedes ethical review, research ethics committees must always have the opportunity to combine scientific and ethical review in order to ensure the social value of the research.'[34] My empirical findings also accord with those of other researchers who found that scientific issues (e.g. sampling; choice of methods; the research question; the measuring instrument; analysis; bias; feasibility; equipoise) are frequently raised in opinion letters to researchers and are often considered a quality problem by RECs.[35] One REC Chair explained the connectivity thusly:

> [An application] might have the best question in the world, it might have the best hypothesis, but if the way the research is designed has not been able to answer that question, then there is a danger that time, effort, and money are all going to be wasted. Participants' time could be wasted and for me that is unethical and shouldn't be allowed to happen. (P3)

RECs want to be satisfied the science is sound, so unverified reliance on the scientific review alone will not suffice.[36] To the extent there is a 'problem' of regulatory overlap, it is not one of double jeopardy, but rather one of a science paradigm that is prevalent within RECs (unsurprising when we consider that so many members are current or former medics or scientists) and of a failure in regulatory frameworks to

---

[33] This runs against the logic circulating in the EU Clinical Trials Regulation No 536/2014, which separates ethics review from the review of the science. Controversially, the latter review explicitly includes assessment of the risk-benefit ratio. Unsurprisingly, the Regulation has been criticized for the effect it will have on REC operations and the adequate protection of research participants. See e.g. Eugenijus Gefenas and others, 'Application Challenges of the New EU Clinical Trials Regulation' (2017) 73 European Journal of Clinical Pharmacology 795; Carlo Petrini, 'What is the Role of Ethics Committees after Regulation (EU) 536/2014?' (2016) 42 Journal of Medical Ethics 186.

[34] Council for International Organizations of Medical Sciences, *International Ethical Guidelines for Health-Related Research Involving Humans* (Council for International Organizations of Medical Sciences 2016), Guideline 23, Commentary.

[35] Emma Angell and others, 'An Analysis of Decision Letters by Research Ethics Committees: The Ethics/Scientific Quality Boundary Examined' (2008) 17 BMJ Quality & Safety 131.

[36] See also Sarah Edwards, 'The Role, Remit and Function of the Research Ethics Committee—2. Science and Society: The Scope of Ethics Review' (2010) 6 Research Ethics Review 58.

acknowledge the *necessary* overlap in review as between ethics and science. If RECs are constituted to review, among other things, risk to participants, they necessarily must have due regard to the scientific design that generates such risk, and not merely regard to the value of the science alone.

Previewing discussion to come on regulatory stewardship, some REC members suggested that they could focus less on the science in their reviews if there were better support for a research design service at the nascent stage when researchers and sponsors are planning their projects. Stewards such as the four Scientific Officers in the Scottish RES, though highly qualified and experienced in both science and ethics reviews, cannot perform this role alone:

> It's great having Scientific Officers, but it's, like, how far can we go into the science of the application? And there isn't an obvious other person to send [researchers] to, you know, 'cause you're thinking, oh I should ... the science of this ... this hasn't been designed very well, this study. ... they're overlapping, aren't they, science and the ethics. But you, kind of, feel that you can only go so far down a certain line. So it is a great service up here, but, you know ... there's always something missing, isn't there. (P27)

2.2.2　Ethics and law

Similarly, many REC members thought it necessary to have due regard for relevant laws. An ethics opinion is not a legal opinion, but it is certainly informed by the law. Moreover, for some RECs, such as the Scotland A REC, they *must* have due regard for legislation in their functions.[37] Statutory regulations now ascribe specific functions to ethics committees (e.g. the Clinical Trials Regulations 2004, Mental Capacity Act 2005). REC members are aware of the importance of law in undertaking their reviews, as a REC Chair told me:

> When I joined my committee back in 2003 ... when I first applied, I was turned down, and the reason I was turned down was because one of the questions I was asked was whether the ethics committee should consider the law or not. And my response was, 'Yes, we should consider the law.' And that was the reason I was turned down. It was the wrong answer! At the time, the

---

[37] For the Scotland A REC, this includes the AWI Act and the Adults with Incapacity (Ethics Committee) (Scotland) Regulations 2002/190, as amended. Notably, again evidencing the regulatory connection between ethics and science, Regulation 6 of the Regulations makes clear that the Scotland A REC 'must take into account' in its review 'the objectives, design, methodology, statistical considerations and organisation of the research'.

view was ethics committees consider ethics and the law to lawyers. Nowadays, that would be the right answer. You cannot undertake an ethical review without considering the law, and very many bits of it. But whether we reference it an awful lot, I don't think we do. Other than the Data Protection Act … (P3)

Yet unlike scientific quality, which most REC members feel is important to consider and discuss regularly, as the REC Chair above indicated, rarely did I observe RECs explicitly considering the law when discussing an application at a meeting, and members did not suggest to me that they consulted the law when conducting an ethics review remotely prior to the meeting. Rather, I observed that RECs encouraged researchers to see it as their (and their sponsor's) responsibility to assure compliance with the law, both when designing their project and when conducting the research. REC members agreed that their opinion is not a 'legal opinion', but they strive to ensure their opinion is *intra vires*—that is, to provide an ethics opinion that sits within the bounds of legality. Most REC members interviewed did not feel a lawyer was needed on a committee. As a member of NREAP told me:

> the ethics committee is not making a legal judgement—what they're doing is providing advice that's consistent with the legal framework that they're having to operate within. That's how I see it. Now, is that operating according to a legal framework or not? I think it is. And it's daft to say the law doesn't have a grip on ethics committees. It does. But it's not on everything. Again, you might say, well practice is around consent, or data management, being engaged with the common law as well as statute. I don't think you can escape from it, but you don't have to be a lawyer to be on an ethics committee. (P4)

The HRA does provide training on relevant areas of the law, such as patient confidentiality; data protection; research involving children; the Mental Capacity Act 2005; and the Human Tissue Act 2004. For REC members, that was seen as sufficient. After all, they are charged with only having 'regard to statutory provisions for ethical review of particular types of research'.[38] Much of the assurances about legality provided previously from the R&D (i.e. research governance) directorate or R&D offices in England are now from the HRA Approval team, known as 'HRA Assessors', who conduct the review remotely. REC members do not want to render an opinion that is blatantly illegal, but they also do not want to carry the weight of expectations that their opinion is as much legal as it is ethical. As with science, the ethics opinion necessarily

---

[38]   GAfREC para 3.2.10.

incorporates consideration of the law. The regulatory spaces are connected, but not necessarily combined. As one member of the Scotland A
REC told me, again emphasizing the liberal approach:

> I think there is a bit of a tension between training people in, say, the Data
> Protection Act, that you are sort of handing them a mantle, in a sense, and
> empowering them to believe they understand the law and, therefore, are
> making legal decisions around data protection. I think that's a mistake. [...]
> [I]t ought to be around the sort of ethical issues involved in handling data and
> whether it's appropriate, and whether it's clear and open, and people
> understand what the deal is and it's a fair choice that's being offered. (P12)

This liberal approach manifests itself most clearly when RECs confront
grey areas of the law. RECs must make a good judgement that is
consistent with the law, even if they may be unsure of whether their
opinion is suitably legal. For example, when a REC reviews an application where adults with incapacity might be enrolled in a project, a
specific checklist is consulted so that members ensure that all relevant
elements of the Mental Capacity Act 2005 or Adults with Incapacity
(Scotland) Act 2000 (AWI Act) (whichever applies) are observed. The
HRA assures RECs the checklist is not meant to be seen as rigid; rather,
it serves as an aide-memoire, for the Lead Reviewer in particular, to
consider when reviewing an application.

Other times, RECs are genuinely uncertain of the legal effects of a
research project. One REC in England I observed, for instance, was
uncertain whether researchers looking to start a UK-wide research
database legally required a separate REC approval in Scotland. In another
REC meeting I observed, a REC member queried other members what
would happen if participants lost capacity during a Phase 1b CTIMP. The
REC Chair recalled that, under the Medicines for Human Use (Clinical
Trials) Regulations 2004, if a patient has capacity to consent at the
beginning of the trial, that consent continues through for the duration of
the trial, unlike for research projects subject to the Mental Capacity Act
2005. But he also expressed some doubt. He then looked at me and said,
'Edward?' I pointed to my 'Observer' name plate, reminded the REC of
my duty to not speak during the meeting, and everyone laughed. 'Oh,
twist his arm!' the Chair joked. 'Okay, I'll look this up and get back to
everyone on what the rules are,' he added.

Members of the Scotland A REC have particular expertise with the
AWI Act, and those who have served for a long time on the committee
are critical of the Act's provisions relating to research. Indeed, this
REC's special focus on the AWI Act seemingly enables them to be more
flexible in their interpretation of the law than other RECs I observed,

who are mindful in obeying and strictly interpreting the research-related provisions of legislation such as the Human Tissue Act 2004 (only one section of which applies in Scotland). The AWI Act's provisions state that research involving an incapacitated adult is forbidden unless: (1) research of a similar nature cannot be carried out on an adult who is capable in relation to such a decision; and (2) the purpose of the research is to obtain knowledge of the causes, diagnosis, treatment, or care of the adult's incapacity; or the effect of any treatment or care given during the adult's incapacity which relates to that incapacity. One of the conditions of such research is that consent *must* be obtained from any guardian or welfare attorney who has power to consent to the adult's participation in research or, where there is no such guardian or welfare attorney, from the adult's nearest relative.[39] What does this mean for research projects on emergency treatment? A strict interpretation would suggest that it can hardly ever be performed. However, Scotland A REC members found that both ethics and law have shades of grey in interpretation, and part of their role is to craft an ethics opinion that respects the spirit of the law without taking a necessarily conservative view:

> People often say, well, of course, ethics is very grey, but the law is very black and white. And you go, well, no, actually it really isn't. And I think there is … yeah, and I think that's the problem actually with the AWI thing and this absolute requirement for consent. It's never been tested in court, got no idea if there is actually an absolute requirement. No one has ever challenged it and said, well, hang on a minute, I wouldn't normally ask people [for consent] who are capable. There is no other way of doing it, this is a really important question, it's an emergency situation, for example. It's just a complete nonsense. I think you could well find that actually a judge might say, yeah, you're right, it's complete nonsense and start to refine it, but there's never been that. So there's this belief that it's against the law but actually as you know, laws don't really work like that. (P12)

In sum, the connections between ethics, law, and science cross-cut across regulatory spaces. RECs and other actors such as the HRA Assessors who assess governance and legal compliance as part of HRA Approval can receive the same pile (or digital file) of documentation but approach them with differing goals and perspectives. A REC strives to focus its assessment on ethical issues, but inevitably there is some duplication in the process, as RECs and other bodies move across fluid spaces of ethics, law, and science. The research application and its attendant documents

---

[39]   Adults with Incapacity (Scotland) Act 2000, s 51.

involve a network of regulatory actors and resources embedded in several interconnected and overlapping spaces. These documents form a dynamic nexus or focal point that circulates throughout the network. The HRA wants its guidance for REC members on relevant legislation (e.g. Mental Capacity Act 2005) to be reflected in the REC opinion letters, but this appears to be more for quality control check purposes. Adding reference to the law changes the force of an ethics opinion letter. As one REC Manager (P15) told me, 'they're not just ordinary letters that we do. I think of them as legal documents.' If a researcher appeals a REC decision, the HRA and another REC can always look at the initial REC and trace what has happened, including whether there was inappropriate information or opinion given about relevant legislation. In this sense, then, a REC must not only always be aware of the legal implications, but also strive to provide adequate assurance that a participant's legal rights are being protected and due process is followed.[40] This is a shared task; other actors involved in health research regulation also must play a part in reaching an outcome that is ethical, scientifically robust, and legal. Thus, despite what the GAfREC state, and despite what some critics label a fundamental problem, RECs do engage in scientific and, to a lesser degree, legal review. This is seen as a responsibility that may be shared with, but not delegated to, other bodies.

To conclude this theme, RECs are embedded in multiple overlapping, interconnecting regulatory spaces. The REC floats within and between these spaces. The evidence suggests that in regard to science and the law, the REC space is the connecting bridge between these other spaces. In this sense, the REC is truly liminal. Rather than viewing these over-lapping regulatory spaces as a problem, we would be better served to view them as evidence that regulators can act as stewards—that is, they can help researchers and others navigate the various spaces.

2.3   Relationships, Protection and Promotion, and Stewardship

A final theme to emerge from the empirical investigation concerns the nature of the interactions between RECs and the HRA, the variation in mechanisms to work through the ostensibly twin roles of participant protection and research promotion, and the value of regulatory steward-ship in guiding researchers across the stages of the research lifecycle. The research findings reinforce Árpád Szakolczai's contention that in

---

40   Christopher Roy-Toole, 'Research Ethics Committees and the Legality of the Protocol: A Rejoinder and a Challenge to the Department of Health' (2009) 5 Research Ethics Review 33.

liminal moments, there is often an independent actor serving as a 'master of ceremonies' to guide people (and things) through rituals, moments, or periods of transition.[41] It is here where I wish to bridge to Chapter 6 in drawing out implications for health research regulation as it concerns embedding 'processual regulation' and regulatory stewardship more visibly into regulatory frameworks.

2.3.1 Interests and responsibilities

REC members view themselves relationally, as key nodes in a network of regulatory spaces that, together with other actors, perform tasks that aim to mediate between science and society and between the spaces themselves. Vis-à-vis researchers, REC members found that only in rare instances would researchers fail to appreciate the value of an ethics review, dismissing it as a bureaucratic step that they should not have to face.[42] Quite often, REC members reported that researchers view RECs as a helpful body that can improve their research and ensure risks towards participants are minimized. In turn, REC members viewed their committees as stewards that can encourage researchers and support them in conducting robust and ethical research.

Members expressed that the interests of RECs, researchers, and the HRA are aligned, and the common bond is in facilitating meaningful research. We should recall that a good number of REC members are or have been researchers themselves; they do not sit in a silo, viewing research from only one side. As a REC Chair explained it, 'it's all tied up' (P3), and as another Chair added, REC members, researchers, and other stakeholders form a common community: 'I don't see it as two different communities. I see it as one community trying to learn together. We all have common aims—researchers, research ethics committees, the public—and that's relevant, meaningful, and valid research. And promoting that I think is a shared task' (P10). Linking this to the above discussion about scientific quality and the discussion to follow about research promotion, RECs are confident in suggesting changes to applications to support researchers, not just in terms of ethics, but also in

---

[41] Árpád Szakolczai, 'Liminality and Experience: Structuring Transitory Situations and Transformative Events' in Agnes Horvath and others (eds), *Breaking Boundaries: Varieties of Liminality* (Berghahn 2015).

[42] REC members tended to dismiss these researchers as 'older researchers who don't fill in our IRAS application forms, don't know how to, because they get their juniors to do it'. They were viewed as unchangeable; RECs simply must wait 'until they retire' (P23).

terms of scientific quality. This is something that the HRA recognizes and encourages:

> [REC members are] strongly encouraging in terms of what different parts of the application could be changed or how things could be done slightly better. They're just good at giving advice to researchers. Often, we receive feedback from the researchers saying it was really helpful to attend the meeting and encouraging. And one thing—we have used the satisfaction reports and we added a question to it to say, 'Do you think the REC review enhanced your study?' And we felt that that was quite a brave question for us to put on. We weren't sure what sort of feedback we'd get, but I think about 75 per cent are saying, yes, they do feel the REC review enhanced their study. So that's been really good to see as well. (P26)

While the relationship between RECs and researchers may be seen as healthily aligned, as already noted above, the relationship between RECs and the HRA is more complicated. As we saw from Chapter 3, for years, RECs, and especially LRECs, operated as local fiefdoms. The move towards centralization with COREC and NRES caused entrenched positions to be taken. One regulator told me that a running joke among RECs was that every time NRES put out guidance to RECs, it was dismissed as yet 'another missive from central bunker' (P1).

None of the members I interviewed took such a negative view of the HRA, but their assessments were certainly mixed. A REC Chair described the relationship today as 'collaborative' and 'a team effort' (P3) with regard to sharing aims. A few other REC members I spoke with were generally supportive of the HRA, finding there is a 'reasonably open channel' (P7) of communication with them. However, others I spoke with felt that they were 'completely unaware of what goes on at the HRA' and that constant regulatory changes served as a distraction. A REC member expressed her frustration to me as such: 'Who do they [the HRA] think they're collaborative with? To me, they send an email to the REC Managers and then the REC Managers forward that on. That's as collaborative as it gets.' She explained that she and other members adopt a cynical approach to dealing with the HRA:

> So, I think at the last meeting that you were at, somebody said, 'What's this for, what's HRA Approval mean?' [...] And honestly, as a REC member, we don't really get told anything in a way that is digestible, understandable. And, to be honest, it wouldn't actually change how we reviewed the documentation anyway. A study is a study regardless. With my researcher's hat on, my real-world job, we have to be very aware of what's going on, and, to be honest, it's not communicated brilliantly. Because all my colleagues, our mantra is don't bother to learn the system because the next time you come to

put in an application it will be completely different. So, let's go with the flow. If we do it wrong, they'll tell us. (P8)

Similarly, members offered mixed assessments about the ShED exercise and Proportionate Review. Focusing on the former, members felt that ShED provides the HRA with some idea of whether and where RECs are broadly consistent or inconsistent. One member described it as 'very helpful' for training purposes and improving 'everybody's education' in terms of what to 'look for' in an application (P7). Similarly, an HRA regulator explained that they find ShED adds a lot of value in highlighting where the differences are across RECs and how they can 'be addressed through further training' (P17). The same REC member who adopts a cynical approach to dealing with the HRA, however, described ShED as 'absolute dross':

> Oh God, when we used to get them at [XXX] we used to go, 'Oh, not another one, what is the point?' So we'd do it, and I will tell you this, I always realized that I was always leading on it, and then the REC Manager admitted to me, 'Oh yes, because I know it will get done properly [...], we need to make sure it's done properly so we look good.' Okay. Honestly, everybody's heart sank every time we got one. So you'd review it, and you would do it properly, and then several months later you'd get this consolidated report of, well, so many committees said this and so many committees said that. ... And the point of that is? So, what is the actual answer? [...] What is that actually teaching us? I've no idea. [...] ... utter nonsense. There must be a better way of doing it. I mean, it's to ensure consistency. [...] Maybe it's useful for them because they can tick a box. That's me being cynical again. But I can't say I've ever learned anything from doing it. (P8)

A Scientific Officer told me that the HRA acknowledged members are 'quite unenthusiastic about' the exercise (P26) and were working to improve the individual feedback to RECs. The HRA was of the view that individual feedback would provide RECs with an 'incentive to review [the ShED application] well and show how good they are, in a way' (P26). Yet even with these improvements, in discussions with members, scepticism seemed to predominate. Two members told me the last time their REC received a ShED application, they were assigned as Lead and Second Reviewers. Yet they were not told it was a ShED application, much to their frustration, and so they 'wasted three hours on it', complete with typed up notes. 'ShED is about the principles, not the practice. And they never told us! Needless to say, the HRA got some choice words from us,' one of the members told me. Laughingly, he then added that their REC had not received another ShED application since.

I also observed ongoing frustration with the HRA when a ShED application appeared before one of the RECs. The Lead Reviewer began her presentation by stating, 'I've put at the top of my paper, "Many queries".' The members laughed and nodded in agreement. The Lead Reviewer then added that she only realized *after the fact* that it was not a real application. Reading from her typed up HRA Ethical Review Form, which included sections highlighted in yellow that warranted particular discussion, she read out a litany of problems. 'Well done so far!' the REC Manager said as she was copying down each 'problem' noted by the Lead Reviewer. 'Are there any other ones?' she asked. 'As if that wasn't enough?' a member retorted. Nevertheless, other members then chipped in to add several more concerns. It became quickly evident to me that as part of this 'game', the more 'ethical problems' spotted by a REC, the more favourably the HRA would view them. A long-standing member, visibly frustrated, stated that previous ShED exercises had 'somewhat normal applications. But I gave up halfway through this one because I found it an insult, with a bunch of doctored information.' Other members verbally voiced their agreement. In response, the REC Manager explained the background to this particular ShED application. A private clinical trials unit sent this 'case' to the HRA's Director of Operations with a list of all the issues to spot. The REC Manager, sympathizing with the committee, added that she had already explained to the HRA her problems with this kind of 'spot the error' game, including how it is a poor use of the REC's meeting time. All REC members agreed with this assessment. The long-standing member added: 'I think the Shared thing is a good idea. But this ...', she trailed off, waving her hand over the application. The consensus from the members was that the application contained too many small issues and not enough 'meaty ethical issues'. A member opined that a lot of the issues in the ShED application had been seen in real applications, but they were points more for researchers to pick up and learn from than for REC members. The discussion closed with the REC Manager asking the REC if there were 'main ethical issues to flag'. The REC members listed what they considered to be the main issues, with the REC Manager taking careful notes.

For some, then, the HRA was seen as an active central regulator that served the interests of the research community, but not always those of the REC community. Some REC Chairs were unclear who to contact when they had broad ethical questions or concerns. REC Managers and Regional Managers were seen as 'so overworked and busy just managing the day job of running committees' that they lacked 'any kind of mental space' (P11) for addressing broader concerns or issues. Members indicated that they would appreciate more interaction with the HRA to understand the context of the next-generation regulations—but only to a certain degree. Just as they would appreciate more value for the work they do, members also wanted to retain their independence. A growth in procedural regulation and centralization caused some to worry that they were 'being told how to think' (P10); achieving a balance between quality ethics review (through consistency and standards set by managing regulators) and independent ethics review (freedom for an individual and a group to engage in ethics deliberation) was an ongoing struggle.

In sum, RECs viewed themselves as having aligned interests with other actors in regulatory spaces. Specifically, they perceived a close bond with researchers, sharing the same goal of facilitating meaningful and ethical research. RECs and the HRA also share this goal, but the relationship is more strained. The HRA was not always perceived as working collaboratively with RECs and at times was instead seen as interjecting itself into their ethics of space, causing tension and political controversy. What this suggests is that there is a plurality of regulatory spaces and a relationship between regulatory actors that constitutes a space at times filled with tension. But it also suggests that there are spaces between spaces. As we will see, there is a stewardship role *within* these spaces that appears to work well for Scotland and could work for other nations. If RECs perceive aligned interests, the question remains how they work to operationalize those interests. Specifically, how do they work through participant protection *and* research promotion?

2.3.2 Working through protection and promotion

I now return to one of the driving questions of this study—that of how RECs act among themselves and interact with other actors within the context of 'next-generation' regulation that aspires to both protect research participants from harm *and also* promote health research through streamlining perceived regulatory barriers. Going into the empirical research, I was expecting a number of REC members to express concern on two levels: first, that they had noticed a recent change in the regulatory architecture governing their practice as ethics reviewers; and second, that this change—an imposition of research promotion—was having detrimental effects on their ability to protect research participants.

As I discovered, REC members expressed a different viewpoint. For them, protection and promotion could be a challenge to work through (and at times was seen as being in 'tension'), but it was a twin role they recognized *and supported*. This twinned objective was therefore viewed not as a recent development or challenge in light of the Care Act 2014 or other statutory regulation, nor was it necessarily 'felt' by REC members. Rather, statutory regulation instantiating research promotion was seen as a form of next-generation regulation that embedded in law what had been occurring in practice for a number of years. That it was now embedded in law did not translate into a shift in the relationship between RECs and the HRA, nor with researchers themselves. No member I spoke with was aware of explicit instructions issued by the HRA or other managing regulators encouraging or mandating them to look towards facilitating research while protecting participants. There was no explicit change in approach, and none felt that protection had been or was being sacrificed on the altar of a research promotionist agenda. To the contrary, some even thought RECs had become *more* protectionist in certain areas, such as no longer permitting researchers to look through patient notes without consent.

Many viewed research promotion as an example of their REC's independence and a key role for them to play, particularly for research that was independent (i.e. not funded by pharmaceutical companies) or may otherwise have been neglected (e.g. rare disease research). And, the aligned interests between RECs and researchers was such that the latter came to appreciate the assistance RECs provide in tweaking their application, be it on research design or a more standard 'ethical' component such as the consent process. The RECs I observed and members I spoke with wanted researchers to come to them with enquiries; they saw part of their role as being educational for researchers. They wanted researchers to regard ethics review as a favourable experience where RECs offer guidance and suggestions to improve their research project, foremost ethically but also scientifically. In this way, if researchers were to apply to the same REC, the REC would hope researchers take on board the issues they raised with them in a previous 'round' so that there would be a general improvement of standards.

This said, some recognized that the twinned protection and promotion role has become more pronounced compared to the previous generation of the ethics review system before COREC and subsequent efforts to centralize and standardize the RESs in the UK. If participant protection was the 'be-all and end-all' of RECs in the prior generation, next-generation regulation encourages all to view research as a civic good that requires promotion; part of the HRA's role is to 'help facilitate the set-up' of research (P2) and provide confidence to the public that good research is being conducted. Research promotion is intertwined with a bioeconomic imaginary that sees the UK as a favourable jurisdiction in which to conduct research and bring economic benefit to the country.[43] As an HRA regulator explained:

> I think there's been a wholesale change if we just focus, say, on ethics committees, a change of emphasis ... Before when I joined 20 years ago, running ethics committees, it was all about protection of the individual participant and that was pretty much it. That was the be-all and end-all, that's what we were there to do, protecting the individual participant. [...] I think over time that's changed, that now we see research as a kind of civic good, something that people should have access to. You know, we need to break down barriers so that everyone can get access to research, so I think there's a shift between being protected from research and now being given access to it because it's a good thing. Also, our dual mission now is this sort of protection of the individual but facilitating ethical research and the whole making the UK a good place to do research, so that it comes in a UK PLC business kind of focus to what we're doing, that it's not about just protecting individuals, it's about making sure that the UK attracts research and money, and so that's the change, and people will have their views about that. I remain neutral on that. [...] I think I just observe that that's been that shift, that things have become, well, commoditized, I suppose, in a way that research is part of UK PLC, attracting research here, doing research, making research easier, less bureaucratic, everything else, is all good for the, as I say, UK PLC. So there's been a shift there, I think, for ethics committees. Now whether that has been reflected in the people who sit on ethics committees ... (P1)

RECs, however, were not consciously aware of any political pressure to realize this bioeconomic imaginary. They were cognizant of drivers that exert a strong influence on research promotion through streamlining initiatives, such as HRA Approval, the IRAS application, and changes in regulations that build the UK's research capacity and seek to harness patient records from the NHS. But they viewed their role, and the HRA's role in this drive, as but a 'small piece of a much larger jigsaw' (P5). Their independence is well preserved; they did not fear a present or future context in which they were pressured to 'skim' through application materials. 'I'll be honest with you,' a Scottish REC member confided in me, 'sometimes I think the UK wants to be seen as a biomedical hub and it is becoming a biomedical hub and it's good that it becomes [one], but it should never be at the expense of ethics and of protecting patients, never' (P20). This member was adamant that RECs would not allow this to happen.

---

[43]   Rustam Al-Shahi Salman and others, 'Increasing Value and Reducing Waste in Biomedical Research Regulation and Management' (2014) 383 Lancet 176.

If the HRA regulator I interviewed above was uncertain whether REC members embodied this dual mission of protection and promotion, accepting that it was indeed present in REC practice, there was also widespread variation regarding how this dual mission was to be worked through. As I came to discover, in the absence of specific guidance on how to work through protection and promotion, members approached this twin role through various heuristics. The HRA regulator speculated that protection and promotion is an *irreconcilable tension*, or as one REC member labelled it, 'an inherent contradiction' (P14), which simply must be acknowledged:

> I think we just acknowledge that tension [between protection and promotion]. Well, some people say there's no tension, other people say that's clearly a tension between those two things and you can't do both and there's a conflict of interest in doing both. I would love to tell you there was some practical way in which we sort of tell people how you balance that ... like this is how you balance these two competing ... but in practice, there is no guidance. We don't have a position on how you do that, we just hold these truths to be self-evident. You've got to protect but also you have to promote. (P1)

Yet later, when I pushed for clarification on how the HRA expects to foster an environment of protection and promotion if they do not offer practical guidance for RECs on how to work through this dual role, several interviewees came to view protection and promotion not as twin aims to be balanced, but rather, as aims to be treated *sequentially*, working from protection as a primary question that establishes a track record of trust, and only after to address a secondary question of research promotion:

> I suppose it's resolved by you treat[ing] them sequentially. The first one is you have to make sure that it's safe, risk-free and protected, and ethical, and if it is, well, you do everything you can to promote and facilitate that. So maybe it's resolved by that sort of sequential looking at it. You're not holding them at the same time, you're focusing first of all on the protection. Once you're assured of that protection, then we need to make sure that we don't then hang around on giving a decision for six months or something, that our processes are ... that we can give that full due consideration to the protection in the time that we need to do that, but also make sure we deliver those opinions sort of rapidly so that that facilitates the research and it can go ahead. (P1)

> the protection is almost you have to get in the right order. We can't promote until we have something to promote and in order to promote it we need to make sure that everything is safe, is protected, because otherwise there's no point promoting something that no one has any trust in. [...] In order to build

up trust you need a track record. You can't just say, trust us, we're the NHS. It doesn't work. People don't work like that. I would say track record is more important. (P2)

Some REC members reiterated to me that 'participant safety and the ethics are always going to come first', as one put it:

Standing back and looking in, definitely it's most important to promote research. Absolutely. But as a REC member, when that 12-inch thick pile of paperwork lands on my desk, my job is, as I see it, to read and evaluate those documents to make sure that those studies are scientifically sound or ethically sound and, on balance, no harm is being done to any participant. That's the bottom line. Whatever goes on from a management, HRA point of view, at that point I don't actually care. I care about that cancer patient or that healthy volunteer, that's what's important and that's what I'm assessing, as I see it, for me. (P8)

On the ground, facing research applications, other REC members saw protection and promotion *as working together*, as 'all tied up in one' (P3), with RECs and researchers both aiming for high-quality research. But how exactly do they work together? RECs will not often 'stop research from happening' (P3). The vast majority of research still goes ahead; indeed, the RECs I observed were extremely hesitant in rendering an unfavourable opinion and spent a significant amount of meeting time trying to work an application with a number of issues or concerns into a provisional opinion. When in the few instances I observed that a REC did render an unfavourable opinion, they aimed to phrase the opinion letter in a positive light, 'welcoming a resubmission' to the REC provided the researchers took their (suggested) points into account.

Some see the 'proportionate' approach taken by RECs to research applications as a mechanism to instantiate research promotion. By treating a 'simpler' project with a lighter touch than a more 'complex' or 'risky' project—typically seen as Phase 1 CTIMPs—RECs are contributing to the research enterprise. Others see protection as being '*balanced*' against promotion—or as one described it, as a 'halfway house' (P14)—with promotion as a value that can reign in a tendency to go overboard with protection:

The idea that RECs are there to support ethical research for the common good, I think, is an appealing principle. It's one that I certainly support. But it's also one in which you're trying to balance the interests of the vulnerabilities of participants, the resources in health care and those kinds of thing. RECs definitely do feel very much, and they ought to, as they're there to offer a layer of protection for participants. But they can overstep the mark on that

I think, and sometimes become too protectionist, or make some kind of claim about their own expertise, which oversteps what they can do. (P4)

Both a REC Chair in England and a Scientific Officer in Scotland opined that balance manifests in weighing the rights of the community against the rights of the individual, a balance that is difficult to achieve but fundamental to modern research. The primary interests will always be participants, but in contrast to the Declaration of Helsinki's Paragraph 8 precautionary intonation that medical research can *never* take precedence over the rights and interests of individual research participants, sometimes, the REC Chair told me, we must 'recognize that there's more than one person at this party and that we have to accommodate their interests' (P10); RECs must support research for the benefit of the community. Humorously, he added that RECs should promote research as a civic good to the community, to 'educate them and say, actually, research is a good thing for you. Research, like Guinness, is good for you' (P10).

Research that was poorly designed disappointed REC members, not so much because it was seen as a waste of their time, but because the underlying research question could be valuable and could 'save some lives'. A delayed research project was a delay to potentially innovative medical treatments and health care improvements. 'We want to find a way; we always want to find a way,' the Chair of one REC said as they were agonizing over the potentially too burdensome consent process for patients in an emergency setting. 'I love the idea of this proposal,' a Secondary Reviewer of a CTIMP said at one meeting, who went on to express concerns about how the researchers planned to execute it (specifically, the changing of dosages). 'It's such a shame,' he lamented. 'The study needs to be done, but perhaps in a different way.' Others agreed. 'I think it should be done, but they've got to get the application right.' In this instance, following a face-to-face interaction with the research team, the REC reached consensus on a provisional opinion, in which they would reiterate their concerns and hope to prod the research team to consequently redesign part of the CTIMP.

Whether through 'balance', 'ranking' or 'proportionality', RECs strive to work through protection and promotion, performing a twinned task that aligns their interests with that of their managing regulators, researchers, participants, and the public at large. The ways in which RECs help researchers navigate through thorny regulatory and ethically challenging areas can vary. In Chapter 6, I argue that this is in fact a *benefit* of next-generation regulation. Law, especially through the Care Act 2014, has provided sanctioned spaces in which RECs and other actors can engage in 'regulatory play', with more flexibility to work through challenges and interact with others. Before I turn to this argument, however, in the final part of this theme, I further suggest that actors within and connected to RECs serve as 'stewards' who help guide researchers (as well as sponsors), and their protocols, across stages of the research lifecycle.

2.3.3 Regulatory stewardship

Regulatory stewardship can be defined as the prudent guidance of one or more actors across regulatory thresholds—without which there is risk of failure, impairment, or harm—with a view to fulfilment of regulatory objectives and collective betterment.[44] In this book, I have already ascribed importance to specific actors within regulatory spaces, and specifically those actors connected with RECs. Regulatory stewardship draws attention to more than just the REC; it highlights the role actors within or connected to them play in helping researchers, sponsors, REC members themselves, and others navigate difficult regulatory spaces and improve the overall quality of the research enterprise. In addition to the HRA, certain REC actors, namely REC Chairs, REC Managers, and Scientific Officers (as well as the REC as a unitary actor), play a critical role in assisting researchers and sponsors navigate the demands of putting an application together and channelling it through the various thresholds in the research lifecycle. These actors can serve as regulatory stewards that help researchers cross thresholds, serving as 'ethical research promoters'.

How does regulatory stewardship manifest in the operations of regulatory actors? An HRA regulator provided me with early insight in describing that Authority's vision for improving regulatory pathways, in part by providing support and working in partnership with other actors:

> ethics committees 90-something per cent of the time say yes to research, so actually [REC approval is] an arbitrary milestone and actually it's unhelpful because people are running towards it, putting in poor quality [research], which means that further downstream there are blockages. So, what we want to do is try and allow there to be [fewer] blockages downstream by improving the quality upstream and by providing support upstream, and along the way we should be able to help with that.
>
> [...]

---

[44] Adapted from Graeme Laurie and others, 'Charting Regulatory Stewardship in Health Research: Making the Invisible Visible?' (2018) 27 Cambridge Quarterly of Healthcare Ethics 333.

Medical research is hard. We see 6000 applications a year for medical research; it is hard, and we need to be helping these people realize their ideas rather than just being what's seen as a bureaucratic block at the beginning of something that is a very long process. Also, I guess there's the obligation there again not to waste money by blocking things, not to stop things because they are illegal. Obviously, we can't let them go through, but it's providing the support to enable people to realize their goals on an ongoing basis. But again, I think it's working in partnership with other people. (P2)

The HRA's role as a regulatory steward is manifest at varying levels. At a high level, there is guidance on the HRA website for researchers, in terms of best practices, policies, and regulations. HRA interlocutors told me they aimed to provide researchers and sponsors with as much information as they could upfront so that when an application came to the REC, it was as good as it could be at that point in time. At a more granular level, the HRA in the past has, on an interim basis, created 'Application Managers', who helped researchers navigate through complex cases that straddled regulatory regimes, such as those involving multiple domains (e.g. data, tissue, and devices), and piloted an 'Ethics Officer' role, which will be discussed briefly below. In Chapter 6, I argue that in embedding regulatory stewardship into the regulatory framework, there is room for the HRA to further improve their practices.

Regulatory stewardship also is manifest in the REC itself. REC members, individually and as a group, saw themselves as providing a kind of upstream pastoral support to researchers. They serve to protect the rights, interests, and welfare of research participants, but equally, they felt as though they serve to promote ethical research by *working with* researchers. RECs are removed from the 'real happening' of research, but in any event, their role is not to monitor the day-to-day practice of research. There is a distinction to make here between a steward and a gatekeeper. A gatekeeper monitors and may also enforce and sanction. A steward, however, helps others navigate difficult terrain and inculcates values and principles that are embodied and instantiated in everyday practices. A REC's role is to evaluate the ethical acceptability of a research project and to help researchers (and to some degree, sponsors) navigate complex regulatory terrain, insofar as that regulation is of an ethical nature, though we have seen that this necessarily overlaps with science and law. It is also a REC's role to encourage researchers to comply with appropriate regulatory and professional standards in the way they conduct themselves as researchers. Researchers are in a position to inform RECs of the latest trends and issues in research, as well as to report back to them their experiences in working through ethics reviews and other regulatory processes. Viewed together, this dynamic is mutually reinforcing.

To be clear, the stewardship practised by REC members is not necessarily direct and deliberate (and indeed RECs cannot write an application or protocol for a researcher), but through nudges, comments, and responses to queries, members help assuage or even persuade research applicants to improve the quality of their research design or work around a false roadblock in law (e.g. a misinterpretation that data protection law or adults with incapacity law is stricter than it really is regarding research). Even though a few REC members and Managers were hesitant to view RECs as promoting research or serving as advisers to researchers ('we're not there to spoon-feed the researchers on how to do their job', one Manager told me), in practice, across all five RECs I observed instances of a stewardship function at every meeting. From this I gathered that for some members, research promotion is an unconscious role that is wrapped up in the process of their review. Ethics review is not a static event of compliance with a checklist of standards (though three members complained that it can feel as such with the HRA Ethical Review Form). Instead, it is a dynamic process whereby researchers, the application, and protocol are carried across thresholds by various actors, including the REC, who suggest 'better ways' to devise a project and thereby shepherd it forward.

A few examples from my observations illustrate this finding. Scotland A REC members reminded researchers that if they asked participants for consent to follow-up their medical records, it would allow them five years of follow-up without any additional cost. Not infrequently, other RECs offered suggestions to improve recruitment numbers for a project, pleasantly surprising the attending researchers. 'Not a question, but a suggestion,' a statistician remarked to one group of researchers. 'Speak with a local statistician and mention "case control" to them. What you're doing isn't wrong, but you may be able to get more out of what you're doing.' During a face-to-face encounter with a researcher proposing a substantial amendment to a genetic research project, the researcher explained that her original protocol and PIS stated that all data related to the participant would be destroyed if the participant chose to withdraw. A REC member intervened at this point and encouraged the researcher to think about modifying the documents, should she want to retain the data collected and analyse the data up to the point of participant withdrawal. The researcher, unaware of this possibility, thanked the REC member for this suggestion, but then wondered whether this approach would properly constitute withdrawal and would respect the participants. The REC Chair replied that 'there's no clear answer' but thought withdrawal would be unlikely anyway. He encouraged the researcher to 'think about it'.

Face-to-face interactions with researchers also illustrate this steward-ship role. A Scotland A REC member relayed a story about the fluid ontological boundary between 'research' and 'audit' in contrast to its strict regulatory boundary:

> We had one very interesting study from [England] that was […] wanting to study care homes, and it was just going to be … it was a sociological study, and of course in the care homes were the people with incapacity. And we advised them that in Scotland, if they did this as an audit of what was going on in care homes, it would be very appropriate to go ahead. If they did it as research, then they couldn't look at patients in the care home who had … lacked capacity, because what they were trying to study had nothing to do with their disease. It took about four letters to the committee, to the researchers. So, we gave them a solution. All they insisted on saying was, yes, they agree, we'll do this as an audit on one care home in Scotland, but because in their perception it had to be seen as being research, to get the funding or to get validated or whatever it was down south, they didn't grasp that we were trying to open up the way to let them do it, it wasn't actually going to involve any interventions in patients that were in the care home. But they just couldn't actually do it without getting consent from everyone if they did it as a research study. (P18)

REC members were encouraging of regulatory stewardship at different levels, from the more complex cases involving interpretations of law, to simpler instances of ensuring an IRAS application is correctly filled in. One member considered it useful to 'triage' the application before it came to the REC (perhaps in coordination with sponsors, R&D offices, or others), looking at mundane issues such as grammar but also regula-tory and ethical issues. This suggests a need for stewardship at an earlier stage of research design and approval and, indeed, throughout the research lifecycle. Better triaged applications would lead to higher quality, more error-free applications at REC meetings, allowing RECs to focus their time on substantive issues. Instances of why this would be useful were observed in REC meetings. During one, the REC Manager explained to the REC that the researcher ticked a certain box in the IRAS project filter, which opens up certain questions for the IRAS ethics application form. Had the researcher clicked 'basic science' instead, it would have been much clearer for everyone when it came to performing the ethics review. The REC Manager further explained the application was transferred from one HRA Regional Office to another, which caused it to fall through the cracks. Neither a REC Manager nor HRA Regional Manager went back to the researcher to support her before she submitted the application, and the application was accepted in the early round of the validation process. 'It has snuck through validation, unfortunately,' the REC Chair sighed.

Though the REC itself can serve as steward, regulatory stewardship is evidenced most clearly in the work of actors in greater positions of authority or influence within a committee, namely Scientific Officers and the REC Chair and Manager, all of whom have closer contact with researchers. Between the monthly full committee meetings, REC Chairs receive a volume of correspondence from researchers asking for advice. REC Chairs told me they were happy to provide support because 'it helps to create the right environment' and achieves the shared end goal of 'high quality good research that's going to make a difference to people's lives' (P3). Through this support service, REC Chairs saw themselves as 'promoting research. I think the committee, as the committee's representative, I am promoting research in the UK and encouraging it, and trying to get it started as quickly as possible' (P3). Similarly, REC Managers saw their role as stewarding researchers through the application process:

> I'm here to try and help the researcher really to make sure that their information gets put across as well as possible. […] Part of my role is almost trying to pre-empt the questions that the committee will be raising as well. So, something obvious that's missing and I know the committee will look for, I can ask the researcher beforehand and that's to try and facilitate to try and get the application through for them as smoothly as possible. (P25)

Throughout my year-long observations and interviews, the four Scientific Officers in Scotland's RES were universally praised for their role in providing educational and regulatory support to RECs, researchers, and sponsors alike.[45] The CSO created the position in 2008 in response to the 2004 Lord Warner Report's recommendation.[46] Appointing one Scientific Officer in each of Scotland's four main regions was seen as a way to: (1) have Scottish RECs conform to national standards across Scotland, rather than local Health Board standards; (2) allow for Scottish RECs to better link with the CSO to ensure best practices were disseminated and ensure RECs were using the same documentation, databases, rules, and guidelines; and (3) help researchers get their applications through more

---

[45]   Indeed, one Scientific Officer (P23) told me that it is not unusual for researchers in England who are submitting applications to an English REC to contact a Scientific Officer for advice.

[46]   See Chapter 3 for discussion of the Lord Warner Report.

efficiently and make Scotland an attractive destination within the UK to conduct research.

Scientific Officers sit side by side with REC Managers on a daily basis, which, unlike in England, allows for constant interaction and more efficient communication with researchers and sponsors. Their side-by-side interaction with RECs also helps prevent RECs from getting bogged down in unnecessary details, as one Scientific Officer explained to me:

> we [Scientific Officers] are appreciated by the committees—that we can kind of just protect them from just getting bogged down with too many queries and things. Where we absolutely come into our own is all the queries at the pre-application stage are completely directed towards us and nothing goes through to the committee members or Chairs at that stage. And I think that makes a big difference. (P24)

Scientific Officers provide researchers and sponsors with guidance and support on a variety of matters, including compliance with correct documentation and conformity with legal requirements, all of which could impact the success of their research application and their research as a whole. At the same time, Scientific Officers help guide REC members in evaluating research applications, particularly when it comes to understanding the regulatory context of a given application:

> the other part was making clear that the committees are not just there to be a gatekeeper, but they're also there to try and facilitate research. So we should be talking to ... the Scientific Officers should be talking to researchers about how to do research, especially to sponsors about what the committee expects to see, and also to the members to explain that if you get a difficult application or an application that mentions previous ones, we should be helping the committee understand what's going on with applications, and keeping committees, committee members up to date with training. (P16)

Scientific Officers not only help researchers with the ethics component of their application; they can also help guide them to other regulatory steps needed for approval:

> The other thing is to remind [researchers] that ethics isn't the be-all and end-all. You're going to need R&D approval; that's going to take roughly this amount of time. And part of our job, which I might come back to, is because we have interactions with those people, we give researchers some guidance. [...] If I give advice to somebody, they might say, it's nothing to do with ethics. And so, I'm not doing this from an ethics point of view, I'm doing this as it facilitates research point of view, because I know that R&D will ask for this. [...] [Researchers] forget that part of [our] job is a facilitatory role and

it's not just ... it's not trying to catch people out who are doing the wrong things. (P16)

A Scientific Officer (P24) explained that if RECs see a local university consistently submitting applications that 'aren't up to scratch for different reasons', then they look to identify what the specific problem areas are and work with the university to remedy them for improved future applications. Another Scientific Officer (P27) distinguished the REC's task of ethics *review* (which, in her mind, is focused more on compliance with standards) from the 'office' in which she sat, which focuses more on science and serves as an ethics *advice service*, with researchers viewed as 'clients':

> There's the committee and there's the office. And I think in the office we perceive the applicant, as it were, like our clients. So, you do all that you can to help them get through the process so that you're not blocking that application. So, we're quite ... we're trying to be very friendly and, you know, trying to tell them the information that they need to give us. But sometimes it is a bit like Chinese ... you know ... well not quite Chinese whispers, but, you know, you're trying to help them through the process, so we have that strong feeling. (P27)

England has not gone the route of Scientific Officers, but the HRA has been equally keen to support researchers. Unlike Scotland, however, embedding regulatory stewardship within a specific actor equivalent to a Scientific Officer has presented challenges. As explained to me by an HRA regulator, the HRA conducted an 'Ethics Officer' pilot in 2012 as a potential avenue for supporting researchers through the application stage by providing them with advice on preparing for attendance at the REC meeting following submission of their application. According to the regulator, it was not a success. REC Chairs, who took the lead as Ethics Officers, attended *other* REC meetings as supporters of researchers. REC members apparently felt uneasy or even threatened by having an 'outsider' REC Chair attend their meeting and comment on an application, which they felt was their responsibility (and considering the above discussion about black boxes between RECs and an ethics of space, we come to understand why). More recently, the HRA contemplated rolling out a 'REC Application Review and Advice Service' that encouraged REC Managers to conduct an 'enhanced check' on an application submitted to their REC. This would have involved looking at the project-specific documents and thinking about potential administrative issues that needed fixing. One HRA regulator explained that an example would be if a REC Manager knew that their committee were likely to ask for a certain aspect of the information sheet to be changed, [...] they would pick that up with the applicant and say you're likely to be asked to change this, you can either change it now before the meeting, but you may still be asked to make extra changes after the meeting depending on what the committee say in their review. (P26)

Of course, this role differs from what Scientific Officers do, as the latter also provide help on matters of scientific design and legal interpretation. A further twist is that with the introduction of HRA Approval in England, HRA Assessors are picking up administrative discrepancies and inconsistencies as well. If, for example, the protocol said one thing but it was described differently in the PIS, both HRA Assessors and REC Managers would be picking this up. Due to the duplication 'between the two teams' (P26) and the concern that it could cause more confusion for applicants in terms of being contacted by two different people for two sets of issues, the HRA has scaled back on REC Managers conducting enhanced checks, such that this is only now done for Phase 1 CTIMPS with healthy volunteers, which are not eligible for HRA Approval and thus not looked at by an HRA Assessor. Regardless, my impression of HRA Approval is that it is more of a 'compliance check' process than an opportunity for stewardship whereby actors within the HRA not only remove barriers, but also help facilitate better research. Stewardship, to the extent it operates currently within the HRA, will be found in other processes carried out by other actors.

To this end, the HRA now encourages: (1) researchers to consult the HRA's online decisional 'toolkits'; (2) researchers to email queries to HRA staff; and (3) REC Managers to look carefully at the research applications before the REC meetings and 'think about what ethical guidance they might want to point their committees in the direction of' before the meeting (P26). The HRA also wants to 'empower' REC Managers to think about what laws and ethical guidance the REC might want to take into consideration when reviewing applications so that the discussion is 'focused more on the ethical issues' (P26), and so that in the opinion letters, there is more explicit reference to guidance to explain the REC's reasons for why they are requesting changes to the application or rendering a provisional or unfavourable opinion.

Whether this is a role that REC Managers can successfully take on, given their competing demands, remains to be seen. The Scientific Officers I spoke with contrasted their roles with REC Managers on numerous grounds, including the educational differences between them. Scientific Officers have tended to hold PhDs in a scientific field; REC

Managers may or may not hold university undergraduate degrees. Because of this, REC Managers may be unable to read an application as expertly to understand the ethical, scientific, and legal issues at play. Regardless of these challenges in England, the HRA is committed to providing a robust ethics guidance and support service to researchers. As I will argue in the next chapter, however, more can be done to embed regulatory stewardship in the health research regulatory framework, and the HRA is positioned to take a leading role here.

III. CONCLUSION

Informed by anthropology of regulation methodology, this chapter examined the ways in which practices, people, and entities are structured in and by health research regulation, and vice versa. The findings reveal a critical understanding of REC practices and the form and function of health research regulation. The findings also reveal a processual and experiential understanding of RECs and the ways in which they affect and are affected by regulation.

The data suggest that modifications to the health research regulatory space at the levels of statutory law and central regulatory authorities have not so much 'trickled down' to the day-to-day practices of RECs, as the day-to-day practices have long reflected what has only recently been enacted in law. RECs, the HRA, and researchers share a common goal of promoting research that is safe and of high quality. They carry similar interests and shared responsibilities, helping each other to cross boundaries and deal with major moments of transition in the research lifecycle. However, a concern that emerges from the research, and which I address in Chapter 6, is that the respective roles, competencies, and influences among the actors are not always clear, and the regulatory conversations are sporadic and at times weak between regulators (the HRA and RECs), though relatively strong between regulators (RECs) and regulatees (researchers). Consequently, spaces can appear *within* the health research regulatory space where hazards may occur.

In the next chapter, I suggest a normative model of what a new regulatory framework, informed by these empirical findings, ought to look like. The empirical data suggest that the REC's stewardship role has the potential to reach *beyond* the *ex ante* stage of research, that is, before the research project begins. The hybrid protectionist-promotionist model that operates in practice fosters an environment that both protects research participants *and also facilitates* responsible health research in the country through proportionate regulation and coordinated alignment of ethics review and other regulatory processes. This can be operational-ized not only at the initial stage(s) of the research lifecycle, at the moment of research design and initial application, but also, I will argue, throughout the lifecycle—importantly in partnership with other regula-tory actors—where ongoing opportunities for 'regulatory play' can emerge.

Thus, in Chapter 6, I argue that, in the absence of an expressed theory of how the objectives of research promotion and participant protection should be achieved, a theory (or decision framework) should be crafted that may not invariably hinge on the mechanism of balance. If we envision RECs as evaluating research projects in stages and acting as gatekeepers and stewards at several thresholds, how can health research regulation, including at the level of legal architecture, take up the insights from liminality to provide a suitable space to capture these stages of dual commitment and realms of possibility? How might a regulatory frame-work, which legally must be 'proportionate',[47] enable regulatory stewards to take charge in accommodating potential harms and maximizing research outcomes? And how can law help create a space within which there is more room to protect and promote, a space for more epistemic latitude—a realm of possibility—for RECs to 'roam in' and experiment together with other actors, including those who may have cross-cutting motives? We now turn to see how the empirical findings from an anthropology of regulation may help build such a regulatory framework for stewardship to flourish.

---

[47]   Care Act 2014, s 111(3) and Department for Business, Innovation and Skills, *Regulators' Code* (UK Government 2014).

6. Charting a framework for regulatory stewardship

I. INTRODUCTION

In the previous chapter, I examined the ways in which certain actors in health research—particularly RECs—are affected by regulation, and similarly, the ways in which they can affect regulation. The findings revealed that research ethics review is an essential component of health research regulation and the ethics review system overall appears to be operating relatively smoothly, at least in comparison to previous decades. At the same time, though, the evidence suggests that several regulatory components can be refined.

In this chapter, I unpack further the significance of the liminality of RECs and the ability of actors within the health research regulatory space to serve as 'regulatory stewards'. I do so by taking up the normative dimension of anthropology of regulation, suggesting a model of what a regulatory framework for health research oversight ought to look like if it were to incorporate the findings from this empirical investigation. This would include explicit endorsement of regulatory stewardship and a charting of how protection and promotion can and should work together in regulatory design and practice.

This proposed framework has application at two levels, which can be seen as both top-down and bottom-up: (1) the government and managing regulators (e.g. Department of Health and Social Care, HRA), and (2) RECs and regulatees (e.g. researchers, sponsors, institutions). As the evidence in Chapter 5 indicates, RECs are embedded in multiple overlapping, interconnecting regulatory spaces, yet their roles and the roles of other actors are not always manifest in regulation. Further, the conversations between regulators, namely between RECs and the HRA, can be sporadic and at times less effective as compared to the conversations between regulators and regulatees (here, being RECs and researchers). This can cause disconnected spaces to appear *within* a given regulatory space where hazards may occur. A reformulated framework could work to improve regulatory conversations between actors, provide ongoing opportunities for 'regulatory play' to emerge, and shift the burden and emphasis away from procedural work and towards flexibility and experimentation in ethics review. What I suggest, in other words, is a refinement of the existing framework, not wholesale change. Nonetheless, this is a refinement that can be worth exploring to reveal the full range and weight of the impact of RECs within and throughout regulatory practices in health research regulation.

In what follows, first, I expand on the significance of the liminality of RECs and unpack the concept of regulatory stewardship. I argue that regulatory stewardship serves as a manifestation of liminality and deserves greater instantiation in regulation. I draw on extant examples within the UK's RESs that demonstrate how regulatory stewardship can play a vital role for researchers in navigating complex regulatory terrain. Then, I consider what should happen when a proposed research project involves a conflict of principles or values—in this context, the potential for protection *versus* promotion. I then conclude with a proposal for a more *processual* regulatory framework that enables regulatory stewards to assist in accommodating potential harms and maximizing research outcomes, and that creates a regulatory space within which there is more room for regulators to protect *and* promote, including room to experiment in working through these principles together with other actors.

II. THE LIMINALITY OF RECs—REGULATORY STEWARDSHIP

From what I observed over the course of a year, ethics review is less an administrative process, where ethical considerations of proposed research end once a favourable opinion is given by a REC, than it is a process of ongoing support, dialogue, and education. If we accept Bobbie Farsides's claim that '[t]he goal of an ethics committee is to facilitate ethically sound practice, and to encourage researchers to honour their moral responsibilities towards participants',[1] we should further accept that this cannot be adequately accomplished within a regulatory framework that charges ethics committees to engage merely in regulatory verification of ethical standards, scientific value, and accordance with law.

Facilitation of ethically sound practice and inculcation of moral responsibilities in researchers necessitates a framework of regulatory

---

[1] Calliope (Bobbie) Farsides, 'The Ethics of Clinical Research' in Sue Eckstein (ed), *Manual for Research Ethics Committees* (6th edn, CUP 2003) 13.

stewardship (the prudent guidance of one or more actors across regulatory thresholds), whereby a range of actors, including RECs, work with researchers, sponsors, and others not just to achieve regulatory compliance, but also to work *through* stages in the research lifecycle, all the while instilling ethical norms of good scientific conduct. Thus, stewardship is a stand-alone regulatory role and collective responsibility that should be assumed by different actors at multiple stages. For their part, RECs should have an expanded role to play in the research lifecycle, but as I will discuss, they cannot and should not cover each and every stage. As regulatory stewardship permeates health research, all actors should view each other as crucial links in a chain that moves ethical research from design to approval to recruitment and action, and ultimately, to health improvement. With different actors embodying roles at different stages, connected by communicative channels that allow for a 'passing of the mantle', stewardship helps us think differently about what is going on in research and how each link connects to the other.

Chapter 5 illustrated in several ways how RECs are liminal actors. Relative to each other and to much of the public, RECs are black boxes, existing in multiple spaces, despite exhibiting a surprising degree of group homogeneity in approach and rituals. RECs engage in various mechanisms to evaluate research applications (e.g. balance, ranking, negotiation) that manifest themselves at a lower level of abstraction— 'good research design', 'competent investigator', 'favourable balance of harm and benefit', 'adequate informed consent'—which in turn yield 'ethical' judgements. Embodying a liberal approach that aims to eschew a paternalistic stance towards participants, RECs adopt a pragmatic ethics that is informed by members' intuition, feeling, and experience.

RECs do not fit the mould of a classic risk-based regulator. For example, we saw that they are also attuned to potential burdens as well as issues surrounding scientific design and law. Returning to the discussion first opened in Chapter 2, we saw that RECs' operative ethical deliberation is the facilitation of a context in which a *fair choice* is offered to participants whereby they can decide whether to participate in a project that presents ethically acceptable risks and burdens and is likely to answer, or at least contribute to, the research question it purports to address. Members adopt rituals in undertaking the process of ethics review that work best for them as individuals and as a committee. Through teamwork and consensus, they render an opinion that mediates the demands of science and society and achieves a kind of optimization of the similarly appreciated values of protection and promotion. The opinion allows a research protocol to transition, as colleagues and I have written elsewhere, *'from a mere proposition of involvement with partici-pants to an actual plan of action with participants.* This implicates a range of actors, and importantly, it further transforms individuals (be they healthy "volunteers" or patients) into active research participants'.[2]

Given the fluid jurisdiction between ethics, science, and law, and given their active role in steering behaviour, what kind of regulators are RECs? Can we accurately label them 'ethics committees'? As RECs become institutionalized and professionalized, acting as multi-faceted and multi-disciplinary regulators of health research (concerned with, for example, minimizing risks and ensuring scientific and social value), and as more national and international regulations come into force that impact health research, RECs might be expected to act more as 'health research regulatory committees'. Indeed, the empirical research suggests that RECs are not mere ethics consultation groups. They do certainly engage in some form of ethics deliberation and discussion, but much more *regulatory* work is also being performed alongside other actors, including researchers. 'Health research regulatory committees' may well be a more accurate name to reflect what they do.[3] And, if we do treat RECs more as health research regulatory committees, we would be well served to rethink their roles and the regulatory frameworks that govern them to better incorporate the regulatory processes they undertake.

What can we make of Deryck Beyleveld's claim that a 'dog cannot serve two masters, and the role of RECs, in fact, is solely to try to prevent unethical research. The facilitation of research is the role of other bodies'?[4] Let us recall that liminality draws our attention to how actors experience and react to change, and that the evidence from Chapter 5 suggests that, if anything, recent changes in the law reflect already-existing practices of RECs. RECs, managing regulators, and researchers share a common and desired goal of promoting research that is safe and of high quality.[5] Actors in these regulatory spaces carry similar interests

---

[2]   Agomoni Ganguli-Mitra and others, 'Reconfiguring Social Value in Health Research Through the Lens of Liminality' (2016) 31 Bioethics 87, 89 (emphasis in original).

[3]   See also Sheelagh McGuinness, 'Research Ethics Committees: The Role of Ethics in a Regulatory Authority' (2008) 34 Journal of Medical Ethics 695 ('RECs act as regulatory authorities with concerns beyond those of ethical deliberation. I argue that RECs are regulatory rather than advisory').

[4]   Deryck Beyleveld, 'Law, Ethics and Research Ethics Committees' (2002) 21 Medicine and Law 57, 73.

[5]   Such a finding accords with Adam Hedgecoe's empirical research, which found that NHS RECs can proactively promote research. See Adam Hedgecoe,

and shared responsibilities, helping each other to cross boundaries and deal with major moments of transition in the research lifecycle. My investigation has not indicated that RECs are guided by a single principle of participant protection. Research promotion is also very much present and at play—and welcomed—in their functions.

As we saw, regulators in this space can have a problematic relationship between each other, much more so than between regulators and regulatees. The HRA strives to chart a regulatory environment that enables researchers to bring a research project to light in a smooth and efficient manner; a critical component of this charting involves interactions with RECs. The relationship between the HRA and RECs can be politically fraught, though, drawing RECs into struggles for power with their managing regulatory authority. There is a strong desire by RECs, including REC Chairs and Managers, to preserve the sanctity of *their* black box and ethics of space. RECs simultaneously want more guidance from the HRA on regulatory developments (such as, during the time of my investigation, HRA Approval) and limited imposition on their everyday workings. That possible imposition of power is exemplified in the HRA's Ethical Review Form, which influences the processes of ethics review. The 'balance' managing regulators must achieve between sound coordination and overreaching diktat is a difficult one, particularly in a country with devolved administrations. The relatively limited communication channels with the HRA generally are viewed not as problematic per se; indeed, they may be beneficial. The HRA sees itself as providing a steering (i.e. catalysing), not controlling, role for RECs. For many REC members, that relatively light-touch approach is a value that reinforces the RECs' independence (or phrased somewhat differently, preserves their autonomy) and ability to reach decisions without fear of external pressure or loss of power over their domains of control.

More profoundly, the interactions between RECs and their managing regulators suggest that regulation is increasingly 'centred' where the state, through the Department of Health and Social Care, the HRA, and equivalent bodies in Wales, Northern Ireland, and Scotland, is exercising growing influence, but not necessarily control. There is also evidence, though, that the resources relevant to holding regulatory power and exercising capacities in research involving humans are dispersed. Never have the resources in this space been restricted to formal, state authority derived from legislation. Historically, and continuing through the present,

'Research Ethics Review and the Sociological Research Relationship' (2008) 42 Sociology 873.

those resources have included expertise and organizational capacities shared between state and non-state bodies, including sponsors and funders.

RECs do serve to control access to the potentiality of research involving humans, but controlled access through their 'event licensing' system is buttressed by a facilitative ideology set within an 'ethics of space'—a conscious desire to promote research and, in turn, advance human health. And this, arguably, is the 'ethics' in the REC. Ethics is not about compliance or control, but rather about debate, reflection, values, argument, and justification. Legitimate and diverse disagreement can (and ought to) occur. As a matter of regulatory practice, then, an ethics of space must accommodate diversity, disagreement, and dissent across applications and across time. This in turn suggests that, by their nature, liminal regulatory spaces must be provided for RECs and applicants alike to explore and deliberate on the 'ethics'. Unsurprisingly, a substantial majority of REC members I interviewed and observed did not view protection and promotion as creating a conflict. Rather, their practice of working through both seems to instantiate the Declaration of Helsinki's Paragraph 23 recommendation to not only consider, comment on, and potentially approve a research protocol, but to offer 'guidance' on it as well.[6]

More questionable, though, is whether this practice instantiates Paragraph 8 of the Declaration of Helsinki and the GAfREC guidance, that is, that the goals of research and the researcher, while important, should always be secondary to the dignity, rights, and well-being of the research participant. Certainly, the dignity, rights, and well-being of research participants were always considered and respected in the REC meetings I observed, but it cannot be said that the interests of researchers and research were 'always' treated as 'secondary to the dignity, rights, safety and well-being of people taking part in research'.[7] Instead, the interests of researchers, research, and participants were often treated as aligned or even merged. Some REC members and regulators actively questioned the absolutist position taken in ethical guidelines that prioritize the individual over society. REC practices demonstrate that to protect *is* to promote. The blurring of the role hierarchy, or this long-standing ambiguity of role hierarchy in the UK if we consider the Royal College of Physicians Guidelines dating back to 1984, reflects, as with the fluidity of science

---

[6] World Medical Association, *Declaration of Helsinki* (World Medical Association 2013) para 23.

[7] GAfREC para 3.2.2.

and ethics review, an incongruence between certain regulatory strategies and general practices that the HRA and other managing regulators may need to reassess.

Does this finding of regulatory connectivity impact the overall quality and effectiveness of health research regulation? Not in terms of REC practices, I would argue, but it does invite questions about the role RECs and other actors can play if provided more room to 'roam' throughout the regulatory space. RECs, I would argue, engage in a pragmatic form of instantiated regulation, translating written regulatory guidance from the HRA and other managing regulators into practical action that capitalizes on the relative interpretative flexibility of their regulatory texts.[8] They enact situationally specific ways to implement the regulations (from the SOPs, GAfREC, and so on) that govern their practice in determining the ethical acceptability of research applications. And, their role as regulatory steward reflects a collectively negotiated, practical, doable solution that satisfies the spirit of the regulations. RECs indeed have more regulatory flexibility than first appears and part of this flexibility is based on 'interpersonal trust in instantiating and maintaining system trust'.[9] Even so, in this chapter I want to argue that more flexibility should be provided in the regulatory framework to enable specific actors to engage in this stewardship role and experiment with different ways of working through the stages of the research lifecycle. Liminality can help us to both recognize uncertainties that may arise across the research lifecycle, embrace them to a certain extent, potentially even exploit them, and pay attention to what is required to work through them.

I want to argue for regulatory stewardship's embeddedness in the regulatory framework because the empirical data suggest that RECs' knowledge control and gatekeeping activities have the potential to reach beyond the *ex ante* stage. The hybrid protectionist-promotionist model that operates in practice fosters an environment that both protects research participants *and also facilitates* responsible health research through proportionate regulation and coordinated alignment of ethics review and other regulatory processes. This can be operationalized not only at the early stage(s) of the research lifecycle, at the moment of research design and initial application, but also throughout the lifecycle in partnership with other regulatory actors where ongoing opportunities for 'regulatory play' can emerge. Crucial to this argument are the

---

[8] Neil Stephens and others, 'Documenting the Doable and Doing the Documented: Bridging Strategies at the UK Stem Cell Bank' (2011) 41 Social Studies of Science 791.

[9] ibid 808.

research findings that suggest that the currently existing arm's-length approach from *law* is beneficial. By avoiding clearly defined roles of RECs and their procedural and substantive aspects, the law is actually helpful in promoting the normative behaviours that I recommend.

In what follows, I propose modifications to the existing regulatory framework by suggesting elements of regulatory stewardship that allow RECs to act as 'work groups' with their managing regulators, as well as regulatees. In so doing, I contend that if the 'regulatory conversations'[10] that RECs engage in with other actors are structured well (e.g. steps are enacted to avoid regulatory capture or inequity), one can mitigate the concerns about co-constructed 'organisational deviance' that Hedgecoe warned about in his discussion of the TGN1412 drug trial scandal at Northwick Park Hospital.[11] Embedding regulatory stewardship, I contend, allows RECs to better engage with the processual and experiential dynamics of health research and instantiate a processual-oriented mode of regulation.

First, however, I propose a framework for working through protection and promotion, namely a deliberative and accommodating mode supported by a looping mechanism of transition for a research protocol that transforms it into something 'ethical' within a given moment of time and within particular spaces. Research passes through multiple liminal phases; ethicality is not guaranteed across each stage. As different actors and regulatory and ethical implications arise with each stage, RECs and others can play a crucial role in helping research and researchers follow these processes through each stage. Of course, stewardship is only as good as its weakest link in the chain. As different actors come into the fold across the research lifecycle, the mantle of stewardship through each of these stages must be passed smoothly and efficiently. Key to this is an effective regulatory design that enables robust and dynamic communication among all actors.

III. WORKING THROUGH PROTECTION AND PROMOTION

We have seen that REC members can utilize several different mechanisms to work through protection and promotion. As the bioethicist

---

[10]   See Julia Black, 'Talking About Regulation' [1998] Public Law 77.

[11]   Adam Hedgecoe, 'A Deviation from Standard Design? Clinical Trials, Research Ethics Committees, and the Regulatory Co-Construction of Organizational Deviance' (2014) 44 Social Studies of Science 59.

Michael Dunn writes, 'aligning normative justification with policy and practice in research ethics is likely to require the introduction of novel governance frameworks that support an ethics committee's adjudication between general principles upon which people can reasonably disagree'.[12] In the context of this book, the absence of an expressed theory of how the objectives of protection and promotion should be achieved necessitates the crafting of at least the outline of one.

The physician Simon Whitney argues that there are 'two major moral considerations in research with human subjects' that ethics committees must 'balance': the rights and welfare of research subjects and the 'shared interest in better treatments for disease'.[13] My concern with this argument is that Whitney assumes that 'balance' is the correct (or best) operative mechanism to adequately reconcile the objectives of participant protection and research promotion. 'Balance', I argue, is both an ambiguous metaphor (for a scale of measurement) that is cognitively suspect in health research and also a mechanism that wrongly antagonizes the values at stake.

There is no mechanism within 'balance' that enables one to weigh competing claims. As the communication studies scholars Robert Patterson and Ronald Lee write: 'On the one hand, "balance" evokes the precision of the objective scale; on the other, it evokes the democratic value of equity. As a result, "balance" connotes a process that is simultaneously precise and fair.'[14] If there is no agency of balance, balance becomes a rhetorical construction of fairness and (pseudo-)-objectivity. At most, one can trust that individuals and groups inter-subjectively reach an *acceptable* balance between protection and promotion, whereby acceptability reflects a range of ethical acceptability. Moreover, the empirical research suggests that protection and promotion are not seen as oppositional values. 'Balance' would fail to capture the iterative, communicative, and fluid nature of ethical deliberations that seek to have protection and promotion work together. In sum, balance may not be the correct (or best) mechanism. The values of protection and promotion are unsuitable for a utilitarian calculus that positions them as oppositional. And, to the extent this 'balance' currently happens, it may

---

[12] Michael Dunn, 'Getting the Justification for Research Ethics Review Right' (2013) 39 Journal of Medical Ethics 527, 528.

[13] Simon Whitney, *Balanced Ethics Review: A Guide for Institutional Review Board Members* (Springer 2016) vii.

[14] Robert Patterson and Ronald Lee, 'The Environmental Rhetoric of "Balance": A Case Study of Regulatory Discourse and the Colonization of the Public' (1997) 6 Technical Communication Quarterly 25, 35.

well suffer from the same flaws or weaknesses as the risk-benefit calculus noted by several scholars.[15]

Thus, I advocate instead an iterative view of protection and promotion defined by process and tolerance, where both protection and promotion are generally treated simultaneously and relationally. Specifically, protection and promotion *should* be treated as twin objectives for regulators. The liminality of RECs suggests that there is a need for a deliberative space within which RECs can both negotiate the risks relevant to a research application and work with researchers to get to a point where the application can be deemed ethically acceptable. This deliberative space ought to be protected to capture and promote the fluid, processual nature of those deliberations. Tolerance indicates that, within this space, REC members should feel comfortable debating the strengths and weaknesses of a research project, and achieving some consensus position on how much risk they are willing to tolerate. This risk toleration, in turn, needs to be considered relative to the notion of research promotion. Thus, rather than viewing protection as a bright-line test, tolerance accommodates the fluid nature of ethics deliberation and the relative nature of risk, that is, a higher tolerance of greater risk if it is seen as reasonable in relation to the benefits to participants and society.

Moreover, I claim this approach should be iterative as RECs' regulatory roles should manifest themselves not only at the singular stage of ethics review, but also before and after in the research lifecycle. An ethically approved research project does not necessarily remain ethical throughout its duration. Both time and space can impact this judgement and liminality encourages actors to follow processes through their stages of transition. 'Ethical research', as determined by achievement of protection and promotion, must continually be created and re-evaluated as a research project progresses. Feedback loops (i.e. opportunities for, and various channels of, communication, dialogue, and negotiation) should be built into the regulatory framework to prevent a static and putatively binding approach to 'ethical research', thereby encouraging greater regulatory conversations that allow RECs to continually ensure research

---

[15]   See e.g. Annette Rid, 'Rethinking Risk–Benefit Evaluations in Biomedical Research' in Daniel Strech and Marcel Mertz (eds), *Ethics and Governance of Biomedical Research* (Springer 2016) 153; Michelle Meyer, 'Three Challenges for Risk-Based (Research) Regulation: Heterogeneity Among Regulated Activities, Regulator Bias, and Stakeholder Heterogeneity' in I Glenn Cohen and Holly Fernandez Lynch (eds), *Human Subjects Research Regulation: Perspectives on the Future* (MIT Press 2014).

is ethical—which is to say, protecting participants and optimizing the research project's social and scientific value as it evolves.

Such an iterative view of protection and promotion would better recognize the liminal and thus processual enterprise of health research. It would also operationalize the language already contained in the Care Act 2014,[16] the latest edition of the Royal College of Physicians Guidelines,[17] and HRA guidance for REC members.[18] Further, it would reinforce the Declaration of Helsinki's Paragraph 8: 'While the primary purpose of medical research is to generate new knowledge, this goal can never take precedence over the rights and interests of individual research subjects.'[19] A couple of REC members expressed concern that this statement might imply the interests of science and society should not be considered in *any* assessment. As a REC Chair told me, 'you may attach less weight to them, but you need to attach some sort of weight to them' (P10). But if this assessment were treated as a weighing (i.e. balancing) of interests, undoubtedly they would always be weighed in favour of 'individual research subjects'. Thus, the problem is that balancing would fail to reflect the REC's role as not merely internally consultative— deliberations among themselves as to whether participants are adequately protected—but also as a *promoter* of ethical best practice that necessitates ongoing dialogue with other actors, foremost research-ers themselves.

Such an approach to protection and promotion would work to avoid a 'bureaucratization of ethics', where research ethics is treated as equiva-lent to REC processes (and in particular, approval of consent forms and information sheets) and the scope of ethical concerns is narrowed to the front end of approvals of research proposals. Coupling this approach with regulatory stewardship allows for smoother navigation of spaces that emerge in-between actors and between stages in the research lifecycle.

---

[16] Care Act 2014, s 110(2), stating that one of the HRA's objectives is 'to promote the interests of those participants and potential participants and the general public by facilitating the conduct of *research that is safe and ethical*' (emphasis added).

[17] Royal College of Physicians, *Guidelines on the Practice of Ethics Com-mittees in Medical Research with Human Participants* (4th edn, Royal College of Physicians 2007) 4 ('RECs have a duty to encourage important ethical research').

[18] Health Research Authority, 'Information for Potential Research Ethics Service Committee Members' <www.hra.nhs.uk/documents/1025/standard-application-pack-rec-members.pdf> accessed 22 October 2019 ('The key duty of a REC is to protect the interests of research participants whilst at the same time facilitating ethical research').

[19] *Declaration of Helsinki* (n 6) para 8.

An iterative view allows RECs to escape the institutionally delineated time-space trap where their work is fixated on a specific moment in time and within a specific space of the committee meeting, and thereby possibly avoid a 'permanent liminality—where uncertainties and anti-structures prevail'.[20] RECs, along with other actors, may instead come to be seen as stewards that help guide health research through multiple thresholds: from research design, to ethics approval, to participant recruitment and consent, to data generation, to data analysis, to knowledge translation, and so on.

Having set out to offer a framework of working through protection and promotion that incorporates liminality as an analytic and normative frame, I now turn to suggest a normative model of what a regulatory framework for health research oversight ought to look like if it were to explicitly endorse regulatory stewardship and chart how protection and promotion can work together. As Chapter 5 explained, regulatory stewardship can be defined as the prudent guidance of one or more actors across regulatory thresholds—without which there is risk of failure, impairment, or harm—with a view to fulfilment of regulatory objectives and collective betterment.[21] While stewardship is a somewhat well-known concept,[22] *regulatory* stewardship is not. I argue that it can demonstrate considerable added value for all actors implicated in the network of health research ethics oversight in delivering and benefiting from efficient and effective navigation of regulatory landscapes. In so doing, I also chart the nature of regulatory stewardship's features and functions, and the different types of stewards that can exist to take on different functions.

---

[20] Samuel Taylor-Alexander and others, 'Beyond Regulatory Compression: Confronting the Liminal Spaces of Health Research Regulation' (2016) 8 Law, Innovation and Technology 149, 174.

[21] Adapted from Graeme Laurie and others, 'Charting Regulatory Stewardship in Health Research: Making the Invisible Visible?' (2018) 27 Cambridge Quarterly of Healthcare Ethics 333.

[22] See e.g. World Health Organization, 'Stewardship' <www.who.int/health systems/stewardship/en/> accessed 22 October 2019; Lynn Jansen, 'Between Beneficence and Justice: The Ethics of Stewardship in Medicine' (2013) 38 Journal of Medicine & Philosophy 50.

IV. CHARTING A FRAMEWORK FOR REGULATORY STEWARDSHIP

In what follows, I propose three elements (some with sub-parts) to improve the current regulatory framework for oversight of health research involving human participants. These elements flow naturally from the empirical results and as such should be charted. I begin with the element that imposes the least transaction cost and reflects most accurately what already occurs in practice, based on my research, and thus requires minimal regulatory change. I end with the element that may be more potentially disruptive to the current system and thus requires more extensive reform. The elements are proposed with a view towards a realistic, practical view of current resource constraints, both within the NHS and within RECs themselves. It is clear that RECs must be properly resourced to fulfil the roles expected of and practised by them. Moreover, regulatory administration must be in lockstep with research growth: to the extent the UK's research environment is in good health, so too must be the regulatory actors responsible for regulating research. The overall approach taken here is one that encourages greater cooperation among and integration of regulators and regulatees.

4.1 Flexibility

As this book has argued, RECs operate within a hybrid regulatory design: social control of research is divided between state-based actors (e.g. HRA, MHRA) and non-state actors (e.g. volunteer REC members, sponsors). Decision-making combines central and regional or local controls, and a multiplicity of actors are engaged in regulatory policy-making. Hybrid design is seen as fostering greater regulatory flexibility, but we have also seen that, within the health research regulatory space, RECs are increasingly tacking towards the state; a 'centring' regulation is occurring that may limit the potential for regulatory flexibility. RECs may feel curtailed in their ability to adapt ethical frameworks or standards to a given research project when faced with the threat of sanction from above. As I have argued, an ethics of space must accommodate diversity, disagreement, and dissent across applications and across time. Likewise, researchers may feel curtailed in their ability to adapt their research as it develops, still within reasonable ethical bound-aries, out of fear of falling foul of an already-approved protocol. In both instances, a culture of caution and rigidity can come to dominate decision-making. RECs and researchers therefore should be enabled to decide and act on matters within a range of reasonableness. Not only will this allow the flourishing of sound and ethical health research grounded in conscience rather than compliance, it will allow RECs and researchers to adapt regulatory responses to changing environments (both within a specific research project and across types of research).

For example, REC SOPs have served to greatly improve clarity and consistency in structure and processes, but positivistic rule-following is not the only value at stake in ethics review; 'responsible conduct often runs obliquely to compliance with rules'.[23] The length of REC SOPs have become colossal (a document now running to over 300 pages), and one wonders if something—flexibility and an opportunity to innovate—is getting lost in the drive to conform to such numerous standards. Through issuance of guidance with best practices, RECs should be encouraged to act with greater discretion to enable them to develop more innovative, experimental, and strategic approaches to their reviews. To this end, Annette Rid has called for a comprehensive and detailed ethical framework for risk-benefit evaluations centred on social and scientific value.[24] I support this call, provided, however, that such a detailed ethical framework allows RECs some interpretive flexibility in how they undertake such evaluations. A rigid application of a framework, especially one that is comprehensive, may well lead to pushback or failure. As another example, managing regulators such as the HRA should be wary of prescribing procedural requirements that restrict what RECs can accomplish in conducting reviews both within and outwith scheduled monthly full committee meetings (such as rushing to get through six research ethics applications in three hours). Checklists should be treated as aide-memoires, not rigid forms to judge REC performance. As the bioethicist Linus Johnsson and colleagues write: 'If ethical guidelines are to actually inspire researchers to make better decisions, they must have a sufficiently high level of abstraction to give room for deliberation. They must never be allowed to degenerate into checklists.'[25]

Perhaps the best example of enhanced regulatory flexibility, though, is greater tolerance for an ethics of space that encourages deliberation and debate regarding protection and promotion.

---

[23]   Linus Johnsson and others, 'Making Researchers Moral: Why Trustworthiness Requires More Than Ethics Guidelines and Review' (2014) 10 Research Ethics 29, 40.

[24]   Rid (n 15).

[25]   Johnsson and others (n 23) 42.

4.1.1   An ethics of space

The empirical research suggests that REC members treat participant protection and research promotion as intertwined values that manifest themselves through the process of their review and in the course of their deliberations at REC meetings. In some cases it may be possible for RECs to focus first on protection and only thereafter on promotion, but for the majority of research ethics applications, an ethics of space requires room for deliberation and fluidity in the assessment of risks, benefits, and social and scientific value. Little change would need to occur in the extant regulatory framework to acknowledge the importance of 'tolerances' (as opposed to bright lines or thresholds) in REC deliberation regarding whether participants are adequately protected and the ways in which research can be improved. Regulations could be more explicit in delineating the functions of RECs to protect and promote. While the GAfREC suggest that RECs have a primary role of participant protection and a secondary role of promoting the interests of research, researchers, and the public, a clearer charting of functions—treating these not as primary and secondary per se, but rather as relational values that are deliberated in a fluid manner—would likely improve inter-regulator relations as well as researchers' (and publics') understanding of what RECs do. RECs, it is suggested, have the twin role of participant protection and research promotion, but they also have an educational role in increasing knowledge and awareness of ethical issues and regulations; an advisory role in guiding researchers, sponsors, and institutions; as well as a conciliatory role in helping adjudicate potential conflicts between researchers and participants.[26]

Feedback loops can be further developed in the regulatory framework. These are closely connected to 'regulatory conversations' as discussed below. A processual-oriented mode of regulation (1) recognizes the inherent flexibility and fluidity (and indeed uncertainty) in health research, (2) enables adaptive responses to changes in law and regulation, and (3) helps guide actors through the research process.[27] Currently, there is weak association between rendering an ethics opinion and learning about its outcome. As I have indicated already, 'ethical research' is not a static concept; feedback loops in the form of electronic communication and face-to-face meetings should be strengthened to encourage RECs to

---

[26]   See HSE Research Ethics Committees Review Group, *Review of Research Ethics Committees & Processes in Republic of Ireland* (Health Service Executive 2008) 7.

[27]   Taylor-Alexander and others (n 20) 158.

engage in dialogue with researchers, sponsors, and others to continually ensure research is ethical. That is, they can help sustain an environment where participants are adequately protected and research optimizes social and scientific value. Mechanisms also should be developed to foster feedback loops where researchers can re-engage in discussions with RECs and the HRA so as to adapt regulatory processes—leading to ongoing improvement and an evidence-based framework. This would help ensure regulatory processes are effective and cost-justified, and also increase expertise in decision-making. A more evidence-based framework would not only enable REC members to improve their ability to make good decisions, it would also make the process more transparent and enable (managing) regulators and publics alike to evaluate the effect-iveness of REC decisions in protecting participants and promoting research.

4.1.2   Enhanced regulatory connectivity
We saw in Chapter 5 that regulations such as the GAfREC are ambiguous in delineating the relationship of science and law to ethics review, and fail to capture the inherent connections between these regulatory spaces. A relatively minor amendment to the regulatory framework would be to revise the GAfREC and other regulations to account for regulatory connectivity that occurs in practice. The REC's opinion is not a legal opinion, but it is necessarily informed by the law. Likewise, an ethics opinion cannot be achieved without an adequate investigation of and satisfaction with the science. Regulations also should not encourage delegation to other regulatory bodies out of concern for potential overlap; such overlaps tend to occur inevitably. Rather, regulations should encour-age greater synergy, not to mention greater efficiencies, among RECs and other bodies such as the MHRA, data monitoring committees, and data access committees.

4.2   Conversations

To foster regulatory responsiveness, RECs should be encouraged to engage in discussions and negotiations with researchers, sponsors, and other actors before an application is submitted to the REC, as well as after a proposal has received a favourable opinion. These conversations may revolve around ethical concerns that have arisen during the course of the project, but they may also go beyond this. Figure 6.1 represents where opportunities arise for RECs and other actors to engage in

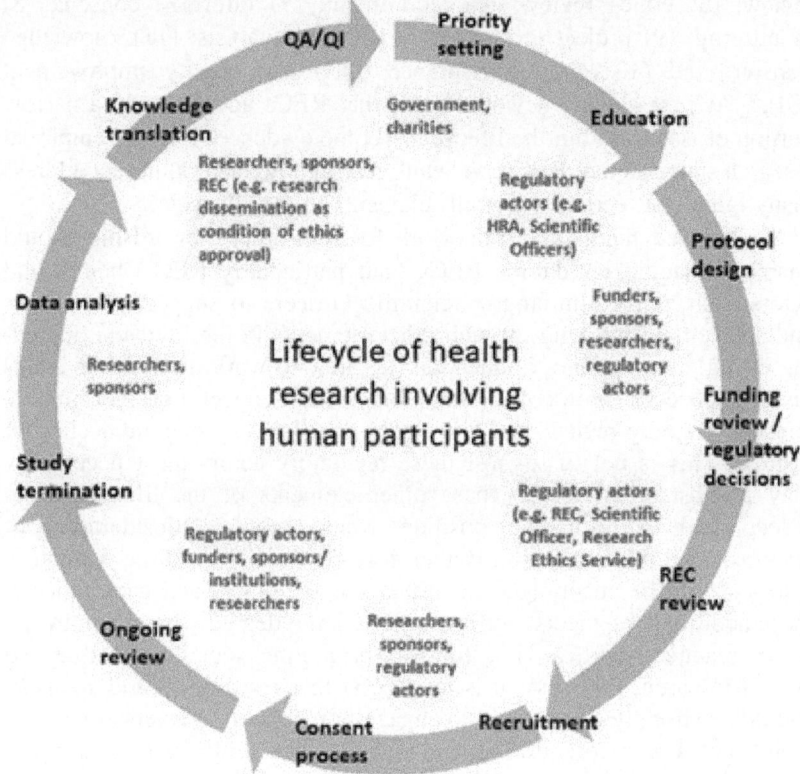

Note: QA/QI = quality assurance/quality improvement

*Figure 6.1   Lifecycle of health research involving human participants,
with proposed augmented roles for actors to engage in
'regulatory conversations' across different elements of the
lifecycle[28]*

'regulatory conversations'[29] with researchers, sponsors, and institutions
across the lifecycle.

James Anderson and colleagues identify 12 elements in the lifecycle
of health research involving human participants: (1) priority setting;
(2) education—scientific and ethical; (3) protocol design; (4) funding

---

[28]   Figure adapted from James Anderson and others, 'Research Ethics Broadly
Writ: Beyond REB Review' (2011) 19 Health Law Review 12.
[29]   See Black (n 10).

review; (5) ethics review; (6) recruitment; (7) informed consent; (8) monitoring; (9) project termination; (10) data analysis; (11) knowledge transfer; and (12) quality assurance (QA) and quality improvement (QI).[30] At first glance, it would seem that RECs address only a narrow portion of issues within the lifecycle. Yet the evidence from the empirical research suggests that RECs, as health research regulators, in fact address many other (but certainly not all) elements in the lifecycle.

A revamped regulatory framework for regulatory stewardship should enable managing regulators, RECs (and particularly REC Chairs), and actors such as (or similar to) Scientific Officers to support researchers and sponsors in working through other elements in the lifecycle, including ethical and regulatory education (i.e. how to work through the ethics review process), protocol design, and issues concerning recruitment, consent, ongoing review, and knowledge transfer (e.g. communication of results). This is not to suggest these regulatory actors must necessarily play a substantive role in these other elements of the lifecycle (and indeed such a normative position would require consideration of resources and infrastructure). Rather, it is to suggest that these regulatory actors should be encouraged to further engage others and each other in these additional elements—reflecting to a large degree what they already do in practice—with a view towards promoting socially valuable and ethical research. Likewise, it is to suggest that researchers and sponsors should be strongly encouraged to engage in regulatory conversations with their regulators, before, during, and after the launch of a research project.

4.2.1 Sounding board and discourse ethics

We saw in Chapters 2 and 3 that a common past criticism of RECs has been that they engage in a 'tick-box' bureaucratic ethics rather than a deliberative ethics. If research ethics is to be seen as more than rigid application of rules and standards, it must be allowed to flourish through discourse.[31] Linus Johnsson and colleagues argue that ethics review should be 'an arena for researchers to discuss their research, receive advice, and practise their ethics skills, and guidelines to be generally applicable, value-based and inspirational rather than specific, rule-based and regulative'[32] (if we take the term 'regulative' to mean controlling and

---

[30] ibid 13–14.

[31] This argument is advanced more fully in David Townend and Edward Dove, 'Approaching Ethics Review Equivalency Through Natural Justice and a "Sounding Board" Model for Research Ethics Committees' (2017) 36 Medicine and Law 61.

[32] Johnsson and others (n 23) 43.

compliance-driven). Regulatory actors such as the HRA, RECs, and Scientific Officers should be encouraged to engage in informal dialogue with researchers (as well as institutions and sponsors) to offer them guidance through regulatory pathways.[33] Similarly, researchers and sponsors should be encouraged to speak with regulatory actors to provide them with on-the-ground information regarding a research project: how it is developing, whether any roadblocks or surprises have emerged, or whether there has been any deviation between the approved protocol and the actual conduct of the research.

In-person REC meeting attendance by researchers should continue to be strongly recommended, but not required. Researchers should be made aware that deliberations can be unpredictable (a REC that favourably approves an application upon internal deliberation will not need to then speak with the researcher, and thus a researcher may risk 'wasting' resources in attending). A face-to-face meeting will not guarantee a certain outcome, but it may increase the chance that a REC will render a provisional opinion as opposed to an unfavourable opinion.[34] Thus, a recommendation for face-to-face meetings should clarify the benefits that may accrue: not only a decreased risk of an unfavourable opinion, but an opportunity to engage with a REC to protect participants and promote ethical research through a dynamic, nuanced ethical discourse. Ideally, this encounter should be in person, but if not, managing regulators should ensure there are proper resources for RECs to engage in reliable telecommunication (e.g. video or teleconference) with researchers.

4.3 Stewardship

Regulatory stewardship involves different actors helping researchers, sponsors, and institutions navigate complex regulatory pathways and work through the thresholds of regulatory approvals. Collective responsibility also defines regulatory stewardship. In the case of health research, collective responsibility involves regulators and regulatees alike working together to design and conduct research that is ethical and socially and scientifically valuable, and that ultimately aims to improve human health. This can only be accomplished if regulators and regulatees communicate

---

[33] Robert Klitzman refers to this as 'curbside consults' with researchers. See Robert Klitzman, *The Ethics Police? The Struggle to Make Human Research Safe* (OUP 2015) 330–31.

[34] Peter Heasman and others, 'Does Researchers' Attendance at Meetings Affect the Initial Opinions of Research Ethics Committees?' (2008) 4 Research Ethics Review 56.

with one another and make clear who has what responsibility and role to be played (if any) at each stage in the research lifecycle.

To be clear, then, regulatory stewardship involves different actors serving not in a protecting capacity alone, but also in a capacity to promote the pursuit of clearly identified ends, including ethically robust, scientifically sound research. In so doing, stewards can help reduce regulatory burdens and achieve proportionality in research ethics review and oversight. While this function is performed currently by different non-REC actors relatively well (e.g. NHS R&D Forum,[35] MRC Regulatory Support Centre,[36] institutions that may create regulatory knowledge and support programmes to support their researchers[37]), more stewardship support can and should be provided by RECs and managing regulators such as the HRA. Indeed, a key feature of regulatory stewardship is that it may be practised as much by non-state actors as by state actors charged with formally prescribing and proscribing actions under the law. Here, opportunities are present for several regulatory actors to assist researchers, sponsors, and others in manoeuvring complex regulatory regimes. For example, we have seen that the four Scientific Officers in Scotland provide an immense amount of support to RECs, researchers, and sponsors alike. There is no Scientific Officer equivalent in the other three nations. Here, the HRA may consider creating equivalent positions in England. To do so, it may not need to create multiple Scientific Officers in each of the HRA's Regional Offices. Instead, it can revive its effort to create a REC Application Review and Advice Service staffed by independent experts who may have had previous experience in chairing or managing RECs, as well as experience in health research and regulation.

Regulation should more clearly provide channels for RECs and managing regulators to engage with researchers and sponsors in improving the quality of research protocols and applications and in working through law, regulation, and regulatory approvals. These channels could include enhanced online toolkits provided by the HRA coupled with online support or through meetings in HRA Regional Offices.

---

[35]   NHS Research & Development Forum <www.rdforum.nhs.uk/content/> accessed 22 October 2019.

[36]   MRC Regulatory Support Centre <www.mrc.ac.uk/research/facilities-and-resources-for-researchers/regulatory-support-centre/> accessed 22 October 2019.

[37]   See e.g. University of Edinburgh, 'Academic and Clinical Central Office for Research and Development' <www.accord.ed.ac.uk/> accessed 22 October 2019.

Regulatory stewardship also could be put on a legal basis. For example, in New Zealand, one of the purposes of the State Sector Act 1988, as amended, 'is to promote and uphold a State sector system that [...] fosters a culture of stewardship'.[38] The Act defines 'stewardship' as the 'active planning and management of medium- and long-term interests, along with associated advice'.[39] The Care Act 2014 goes to some length to enact stewardship by confirming as a matter of law that health research regulatory agencies have responsibilities not just to protect research participants' interests, but also to promote ethical and safe research. Yet further legal footing can be provided by declaring through statutory regulation, guidance, or otherwise that health research regulatory agencies are expected to bring a more systematic, comprehensive, lifecycle approach to the management of existing regulation, which in this context, would mean ensuring that regulations are: (1) proportionate; (2) fit for purpose; (3) enabling for stewards to work with researchers and others in achieving their desired ends; and (4) enabling for regulators to articulate how the public interest will be promoted through research. Such a legal footing would clarify the value of different actors in enacting regulatory stewardship across the research lifecycle, and also avoid constricting the roles and procedural and substantive aspects of actors in rigid law that can be counterproductive to the value of flexibility that is inherent in liminality.

Stewardship is a heterogeneous concept. Given the various actors who can serve in a stewardship capacity, regulation should be designed to promote specific (but not necessarily narrow) tasks for different actors. Depending on the context, these different actors could be labelled as state stewards (e.g. the Department of Health and Social Care and the HRA must act in a manner deemed to contribute to the public interest, for example as established by law), operational stewards (e.g. REC Managers or Scientific Officers who help usher researchers through the complexity of established procedures such as ethics application processes), and ethics stewards (e.g. RECs that act to protect participants and promote research). At the same time, as I and colleagues have argued elsewhere:

> It would follow also from this that researchers must be trained in, and made aware of, this central role in making (good) research happen. As a minimum, this would require researchers to acknowledge their role in contributing to

---

[38] State Sector Act 1988, as amended 2013 [NZ], s 1A.
[39] ibid s 32.

streamlined regulation by responsible discharge of duties to work with regulators effectively.[40]

By stating clearly what roles each actor should play at the different stages in the research lifecycle, and how each actor should work with others to move from one stage to the next (i.e. how and when 'the mantle should be passed'), health research regulation could achieve more robustly the twin aims of participant protection and research promotion.

V. CONCLUSION

In this chapter, I further unpacked the significance of the liminality of RECs and the ability of actors within the health research regulatory space to serve as regulatory stewards. I did so by charting how protection and promotion can and should work together, and by suggesting a normative model of what a new regulatory framework for health research oversight ought to look like if it were to explicitly endorse regulatory flexibility, conversations, and stewardship. I suggested that an iterative view of protection and promotion defined by tolerance for fluidity would better recognize the liminal and thus processual enterprise of health research. I also argued that regulation would be well served if it accounted for the roles that RECs and other actors (such as Scientific Officers) can play across the lifecycle of research by engaging in 'conversations' with researchers and sponsors (among other actors, such as funders). Providing such a space for flexibility and experimentation across the research lifecycle would allow for greater opportunities for 'regulatory play' to emerge, and in so doing foster an environment that both protects research participants *and also facilitates* responsible health research through proportionate regulation and coordinated alignment of ethics review and other regulatory processes.

In the concluding Chapter 7, I recap the arguments of this book, my main research findings, and possible future directions for research.

---

[40]   Laurie and others (n 21).

7. Conclusion

I. INTRODUCTION

This book has provided insight into the everyday workings of RECs and other regulatory actors in light of 'next-generation' health research regulation that seeks to both protect participants and promote research. It has done so through an empirical investigation—set within an anthropology of regulation—of the nature of health research regulation and of the behaviours and experiences of actors within regulatory spaces, and the ways in which they themselves affect and are affected by processes of regulation. Further, it has positioned liminality and regulatory stewardship as key components in a regulatory framework for health research.

The research set out to explore how and why RECs make the decisions they do, and how the dynamics of RECs and central 'managing' regulators play into decisions in an emerging regulatory backdrop of twinned 'protection and promotion'. It also set out to go inside RECs to ask and examine how they, as individual members and as a collective body, see themselves in a changing regulatory environment. In addition, perspectives were gathered on the roles of RECs and the relationship between the HRA and RECs. In so doing, I queried the precise nature of the interaction between central regulators and RECs, and queried the functional operations and deliberative processes of RECs in an era of twinned regulatory objectives of participant protection and research promotion. To date, this topic has received little coverage in the literature despite its significance, much less through a qualitative study from a regulatory perspective.

This final chapter draws together the findings from this body of work. First, I recap the key research findings. Second, I consider possible next steps for the research.

II. RECAP OF THE BOOK

2.1   Context-Setting Chapters

I began this book by providing a conceptual framework and historical regulatory tracing of RECs. Chapter 2 argued that RECs have been central in regulating the ethical acceptability of health research—and by extension, much of health research's very existence—since the late 1960s. They serve as gatekeepers that determine whether a proposed research project is ethically acceptable and therefore may proceed. Since its formation in late 2011, the HRA has been tasked with both protecting research participants from harm *and* also facilitating a productive research environment by streamlining health research regulation. The HRA is a central regulatory body that is seen to help make the UK once again an attractive place to conduct health research such as clinical trials. The HRA, particularly through its RES, and equivalent bodies such as the CSO in Scotland, is working to make REC processes more effective and efficient. I therefore raised the question of whether the roles and practices of RECs are shifting in response to 'next-generation' regulation such as the Care Act 2014, and whether modifications to the health research regulatory space at the levels of statutory law and central regulatory authorities 'trickle down' to the day-to-day practices of RECs.

Chapter 3 traced the regulatory development of RECs and health research regulation within the UK, with a view to demonstrating both the growth of health research regulation and the increasingly central role that RECs play in regulating health research. Tracing history over the past half-century, we saw that as health research gained prominence in the UK as both a driver of scientific knowledge and economic development, self-regulation of health research—ad hoc peer review by fellow scientists based on professional norms and local customs—gradually gave way to stricter, stronger, more centralized forms of regulation, particularly through policies and guidelines set by the UK's constituent governments. The central claim I made is that while, to a certain degree, research promotion has always been embedded in the regulatory techniques of RECs, it has not until now been instantiated in law with the creation of the HRA and rules promulgated under the Care Act 2014. Participant protection and research promotion have had an uneasy, unequal, but sustained marriage across the RECs' lifespan. And along the way, REC members have faced the challenging task of working in regulatory spaces that demand that they work with various regulatory actors and that they not only operate within the (shifting) regulatory spaces' confines, but also help shape their contours. It is this finding that led me to query whether this instantiation of research promotion in law has a (hitherto absent) trickle-down effect that impacts the day-to-day practices of RECs, and if so, how, or indeed, whether the law is only now coming to reflect an everyday practice that has long existed.

2.2   Anthropology of Regulation

In Chapter 4, I explained the research approach, theoretical under-pinnings, and analytical concepts that drove the empirical investigation. I proposed an anthropology of regulation that blends the theoretical with the empirical, and which affords critical methodological improvements to common research approaches. As anthropology of regulation draws explicit attention to processes, passages, and change, I further drew on the anthropological concept of liminality, which served as a sensitizing concept, in addition to concepts provided by regulatory theory. Together with regulatory theory, liminality helped me to better understand the nature of transformations of actors within the regulatory space, the form of regulation in this space, as well as the behaviours and experiences of actors as they go through processes of change.

2.3   The Research Findings and Normative Implications

In Chapter 5, I presented three main themes from my findings: the 'black boxes' of ethics review; regulatory connectivity; and regulators as stewards. I found that RECs serve as liminal actors. Relative to each other and to publics, they are black boxes existing in multiple spaces, despite a surprising degree of group homogeneity in approach and rituals. Significantly, I also found that RECs and other actors can serve as 'regulatory stewards' in helping researchers and others navigate difficult regulatory spaces and improve the overall quality of research. They can play a critical role in assisting researchers navigate the demands of putting an application and protocol together; as regulatory stewards, they can help researchers cross thresholds—serving as 'ethical research promoters'.

Contrary to my early expectations, and critically for the purposes of this book, the empirical data suggest that modifications to the health research regulatory space at the levels of statutory law and central regulatory authorities have not so much 'trickled down' to the day-to-day practices of RECs, as the day-to-day practices have long reflected what has only recently been enacted in law. The data also suggest that RECs, managing regulators, and researchers share a common goal of promoting research that is safe and of high quality. Actors in these regulatory spaces carry similar interests and shared responsibilities, helping each other to cross boundaries and deal with major moments of transition in the research lifecycle. This led me to further investigate how, normatively speaking, protection and promotion ought to be worked through, as practised by RECs, the HRA, and other actors, and what a model of a new regulatory framework for health research oversight ought to look like if it were to explicitly endorse regulatory stewardship.

Chapter 6 unpacked the significance of the liminality of RECs and the ability of actors within the health research regulatory space to serve as 'regulatory stewards'. I charted how protection and promotion can and should work together. Specifically, I argued that protection and promotion *should* be treated as twin objectives for regulators. The liminality of RECs suggests that there is a need for a deliberative space within which RECs can both negotiate the risks relevant to a research application and also work with researchers to get to a point where the application can be deemed ethically acceptable. This deliberative space ought to be protected to capture and promote the fluid, processual nature of those deliberations. Within this space, REC members should feel comfortable debating the strengths and weaknesses of a research project, and achieving a consensual position on how much risk they are willing to tolerate. This risk toleration, in turn, needs to be considered relative to the notion of research promotion. Thus, rather than viewing protection as a bright-line test, a tolerance perspective accommodates the fluid nature of ethics deliberation and the relative nature of risk, that is, a higher tolerance of greater risk if it is seen as reasonable in relation to the benefits to participants and society.

I concluded that a reformulated regulatory framework could work to improve regulatory conversations between actors, provide ongoing opportunities for 'regulatory play' to emerge, and shift the burden and emphasis away from more procedural work and towards flexibility and experimentation in ethics review. Three principal elements, flowing from the empirical research, were offered to improve the extant framework and were organized by starting with those less potentially disruptive to the current system:

- **Flexibility**
  I argued that the regulatory framework should provide RECs with sufficient room to roam in an ethics of space that accommodates diversity, disagreement, and dissent across applications and across time. This requires little change to the current system, as RECs are already permitted to protect and promote. However, room for improvement is called for in two areas, namely feedback loops and

enhanced connectivity between the regulatory spaces of law, science, and ethics.

- **Conversations**

  I argued that, to foster greater regulatory responsiveness, RECs should be encouraged to engage in discussions and negotiations with researchers, sponsors, and other actors before submission to the REC as well as after a proposal has received a favourable opinion. These conversations may revolve around ethical concerns that have arisen during the course of the project, but they may also go beyond this. RECs are not expected to play a role in each element of the research lifecycle. Rather, I suggested that RECs, along with other actors, should be encouraged to engage in regulatory conversations with each other, before, during, and after the launch of a research project, clarifying both their respective roles and when they should intervene to assist in helping move research across the stages of the lifecycle.

- **Stewardship**

  I argued that regulatory stewardship involves different actors helping researchers and sponsors navigate complex regulatory pathways and work through the thresholds of regulatory approvals. Collective responsibility, as a component of regulatory stewardship, requires relevant actors to work together to design and conduct research that is ethical and socially and scientifically valuable and that ultimately aims to improve human health. This can only be accomplished if a framework delineates how and when regulators and regulatees should communicate with one another and makes clear who has what responsibility and role to be played (if any) at each stage in the research lifecycle. To this end, I suggested that a regulatory framework for health research could chart different kinds of regulatory stewards, such as operational stewards (e.g. REC Managers or Scientific Officers that help usher researchers through the complexity of established procedures such as ethics application processes) and ethics stewards (e.g. RECs that deliberate in an ethics of space to protect participants and promote research).

Summarizing the research findings, while there has been reform in the health research regulatory space at the level of legal architecture to foster an environment that promotes health research in addition to protecting participants (particularly through the method of streamlining perceived regulatory barriers), there has not been a consequential change in how RECs act among themselves. Legal reform such as the Care Act 2014 reflects already-existing, everyday workings of RECs. RECs are remarkably similar to each other in terms of demographics and practices, yet they are relatively black-boxed to each other; they operate in fairly splendid isolation despite having a fair degree of homogeneity in culture. This said, an area of concern in light of recent regulatory reform is the nature of the interaction between RECs and their managing regulators, namely the HRA. Perhaps because of their homogeneity in culture, there is a strong desire by RECs, including REC Managers, to preserve the sanctity of *their* black box and ethics of space. Initiatives by the HRA that try to improve the regulatory pathways for researchers can backfire if there is improper consultation with RECs. As we saw, regulatory tension or failures are more likely to exist between regulators than between regulators and regulatees.

We can also say that, while the bond of research and ethics remains strong, there is some room for improving the regulatory framework. RECs, managing regulators, and researchers share a common goal of promoting research that is safe and of high quality. Actors in this health research regulatory space carry similar interests and shared responsibilities, helping each other to cross boundaries and deal with major moments of transition in the research lifecycle. The respective roles, competencies, and influences among the actors in these spaces are not always clear, and the regulatory conversations are sporadic and at times weak between regulators, though relatively strong between regulators and regulatees. To avoid dangerous spaces from appearing *within* the health research regulatory space where hazards may occur, in Chapter 6 I suggested several elements to improve the regulatory framework and prevent these spaces from appearing or opening too widely or disjointedly.

III. FUTURE DIRECTIONS FOR RESEARCH

Having considered the core contribution which this book makes, a final task lies in considering how this work can be further developed. Areas for future investigation include:

- evaluation of the added value Scientific Officers bring to health research regulation and consideration of how they can be brought into the RESs in the three other nations;

- assessment of how NHS R&D offices are coping in light of HRA Approval (e.g. how do R&D officers now see their role; what is their relationship with HRA Assessors and other regulatory actors?);
- cross-jurisdictional comparisons of health research regulation to evaluate similarities and differences among RECs, managing regulators, and other actors. Such an assessment may lead to formulation of best practices for health research ethics oversight;
- horizon-scanning to assess the potential impact of 'Brexit' on UK regulatory flexibility (i.e. will a formal de-coupling from EU regulation lead to regulatory fragmentation, harmonization, or something else?);
- how regulatory flexibility might afford opportunities for 'regulatory play', that is, opportunities to think beyond rules and engage in innovation and experimentation ('sandboxes' to design and experiment without fear of falling foul of regulatory infraction);
- deeper understanding, through empirical investigation, of the actual blockages and perceived impediments to health research so as to promote a culture of confidence and proportionate regulatory practices; and
- charting a path for collective responsibility for the (co-)design and delivery of health research and health improvements therefrom. Such investigation may explore how actors other than regulators (e.g. researchers, sponsors, publics) can view themselves as responsible for designing and delivering ethical and scientifically robust health research.

In each of these areas, anthropology of regulation can play an invaluable role in investigating empirically the form and function of regulation across different contexts (e.g. locales, cultures, time periods). It allows us to uncover the experiences and practices of regulators and regulatees and the ways in which they understand themselves and their roles. In so doing, it can also problematize the notion of regulation, challenging us to consider the multiple phenomena that it may constitute and the ways in which it manifests and shapes behaviours. Anthropology of regulation, underpinned by regulatory theory and liminality, helps us make sense of the nature of regulation as a form of social control (an ontological concern), as well as how regulation structures our living in the everyday and in the in-between (a functional concern). Analytically, it has the potential to contribute to deeper understandings of local dynamics and contexts, as well as the multiple roles regulation plays in a complex world as a form of social control. Finally, it can offer normative prescriptions that are developed from the empirical investigation to guide actors in achieving regulatory goals.

Undoubtedly, there are numerous further lines of enquiry that flow from this book. The findings from the empirical research demonstrate a wide applicability to a diverse array of settings. While such enquiries are left for the future, it is my hope that this book has in its own right contributed to a deeper theoretical and practical understanding of the precise nature of health research regulation; the roles of actors within regulatory spaces; and the processual, iterative realization of the public interest aim of health research oversight—namely to protect the rights, interests, and welfare of research participants *and* to promote valuable research that advances human health for the benefit of the public.

Appendix 1: Research methods—steps, techniques, and tools

In this appendix, I describe the research methods undertaken for my empirical work and which define an anthropology of regulation, including the justification for undertaking a 'research trinity' of document analysis, semi-structured interviews, and naturalistic observation. Specifically, I link anthropology of regulation methodology with its methods by discussing procedural aspects such as recruitment strategy, interview topic design, data analysis, ethical considerations, and potential limitations to my methods.

Data Sources, Types, and Forms

As regards the first arm of the research trinity, I undertook a literature review that centred on qualitative document analysis of legal rules and academic and grey literature from different disciplinary fields—primarily law, anthropology, sociology, and biomedical science—as well as 'human subjects' research regulations. These texts were examined both for substance and context through thematic analysis. This document analysis was coupled with obtaining primary data in word and visual form (through interviews and observations) from individuals and groups in natural and semi-natural settings, as I explain below.

I observed REC meetings to gather data on actual behaviours and practices and develop a detailed description of how RECs operate and make decisions. By observing RECs, I aimed to witness what members of these committees do in their natural settings.[1] This meant that I observed not only REC members, but also a fluctuating array of other actors that form part of the ethics review system, for example, REC Managers, REC Assistants, investigators, patient advocates, and others. Some of these other actors varied from one meeting to another for different reasons. Individual REC members could be absent for a meeting due to illness or scheduling conflict, investigators and patient advocates

---

[1] Yvonna Lincoln and Egon Guba, *Naturalistic Inquiry* (SAGE 1985).

would appear only for their specific application, REC Assistants and REC Managers occasionally would be replaced by a substitute, and observers generally would attend only one meeting. On one occasion, for example, the REC Chair was ill and a Chair from another REC in another city came in to replace him, creating an interesting dynamic with the other REC members. Observations took place at the site where full committee REC meetings occur; usually these are in hotel conference rooms, NHS Health Board buildings, or NHS hospital conference rooms. I collected, with permission, some social artefacts of RECs, such as the agendas of each meeting and, occasionally, a REC member's review of an application as written in the HRA Ethical Review Form.

I use the term 'naturalistic observation' in contradistinction to 'partici-pant observation', as the latter implies that the observer becomes *part* of the group being observed to get a deeper insight. As an 'observer' of RECs who was required to remain silent during the meetings, the term 'participant' seems inappropriate, even if I attended multiple REC meetings over one year. Moreover, naturalistic observation describes the technique of observing people in their natural environment, usually episodically rather than continuously (e.g. REC members at their monthly full committee meetings) without any manipulation by the observer, which more accurately describes the empirical research I conducted.

Selection of Data Sources: REC Observations

The sample size for interviews and observations was largely dictated by resource and time constraints. I determined that it would be sufficient to select four RECs across both England and Scotland for observation over the period of approximately one year, though as I explain below, this eventually increased to five RECs. I identified RECs on both sides of the border. This was not out of an explicit desire for a comparative approach, but rather, to collect data in different settings. Nonetheless, throughout my research, I intended to account for any perceivable cultural and regulatory differences between these two nations.

One REC was identified through a serendipitous encounter with an academic colleague who was a member of a REC in England. When chatting with her at a biobank conference in London a year prior, she suggested that I write to her REC Chair to see if it would be possible to observe it. Accepting her advice and invitation, I did so, and the Chair invited me to observe the REC over the course of the year. The other three RECs I purposively selected through browsing the HRA's online

REC directory:[2] I selected one REC in England and two RECs in Scotland. These RECs were deliberately chosen for their geographic differences and for their different 'committee flags', which is the term used by the HRA to denote specific areas of health research that RECs are authorized to review (e.g. gene therapy clinical trials, Phase 1 studies involving healthy volunteers). The fifth REC also was added serendipitously. I encountered it after an interviewee suggested I speak with the Chair of this REC; I then did so, and he invited me to observe his REC. I also was invited by two interviewees to observe two of the HRA's five offices in England: the Skipton House office in London and another in the North of England. A third interviewee (REC Manager) invited me to the NHS Scotland Health Board office where her REC meets to get a sense of how her job and the HARP system works.[3] Table A1.1 lists the five RECs observed.

Table A1.1   Attributes of RECs observed

REC pseudonym	Location	Committee type
REC 1	England	• RECs recognized to review CTIMPs in patients—type iii
REC 2	England	• RECs recognized to review CTIMPs in patients—type iii
REC 3	England	• RECs recognized to review CTIMPs in healthy volunteers—type i • RECs recognized to review CTIMPs in patients—type iii
REC 4	Scotland	• Authorized REC
Scotland A REC	Scotland	• RECs recognized to review CTIMPs in healthy volunteers—type i • RECs recognized to review CTIMPs in patients—type iii

---

[2]   Health Research Authority, 'Search RECs' <www.hra.nhs.uk/about-us/committees-and-services/res-and-recs/search-research-ethics-committees/> accessed 23 October 2019.

[3]   HRA Assessment Review Portal (HARP) <www.harp.org.uk/Account/Login> accessed 23 October 2019.

I agreed with the REC Chairs to not identify the observed RECs in any publications. However, I obtained explicit consent to identify one of the RECs, the Scotland A REC, which meets monthly in Edinburgh.[4] This was done because of the unique nature of this REC; indeed, it is the only REC in Scotland that is authorized to review 'Phase 1 studies in healthy volunteers' and 'research involving adults lacking capacity', as the HRA parlance terms it. Even a brief amount of description of the REC and its dynamic likely would enable someone to identify it. The Scotland A REC was specifically constituted by statutory regulation in 2002[5] following the enactment of the AWI Act. Uniquely, members of the Scotland A REC are appointed not by a Health Board, but by the Scottish Ministers.

Selection of Data Sources: Interviews

As to the third arm of my 'research trinity', I planned to approach targeted RECs and regulatory bodies to interview individuals situated within RECs (as members, Chairs, and Managers) and regulatory bodies (e.g. HRA), or straddling both (Scientific Officers). These were conducted as one-on-one, in-depth, semi-structured interviews. The interviews were conducted in a semi-natural setting, specifically in person at the individual's office or over Skype, to discuss the activities in which these individuals were engaged in their natural settings: REC(s) or regulatory authorities that oversee RECs.

My strategy for the (managing) regulator-associated interviewees was to accumulate names through snowball sampling. After initially identifying a couple of individuals based on recommendations to me from a Scientific Officer and the HRA's Head of RES (England), I asked interviewees who else they thought would be valuable to speak with, whether they be regulators or REC members. This strategy worked well in accumulating a list of names, including the Chair of the fifth REC I came to observe. My strategy for the REC-associated interviewees was to approach the Chairs of the two initially identified RECs in England to see if they would be willing to be interviewed. Both obliged. I also asked each Chair if they would be comfortable asking their members and the REC Managers to share their email addresses with me, so that I could

---

[4] Consent was obtained in the Scotland A REC meeting held on 19 January 2017.

[5] Adults with Incapacity (Ethics Committee) (Scotland) Regulations 2002, as amended 2007.

then contact those members who responded affirmatively. Again, the REC Chairs obliged with this request, the first one very early on in 2016. A somewhat different strategy was employed in Scotland, where the responsible Scientific Officer requested that I work through them and the REC Managers rather than directly contacting the REC Chairs. This difference signified to me quite early on the crucial gatekeeping role of the Scientific Officer in the Scottish RECs.

Remaining mindful of resource and time constraints, I intended to interview no more than 25 individuals, constituting a mix of REC members and regulators involved in health research ethics and RECs particularly. Ultimately, emails were sent to 30 individuals, some of whom were REC members that contacted me first after my email address and interview request were shared with their REC Chair. In the end, 28 individuals were interviewed across the year 2016 after two individuals failed to respond to follow-up emails after expressing initial interest. Of these 28 interview participants, 7 were affiliated with the HRA (1 was a member of the HRA's NREAP), and the rest were REC members or Scientific Officers.[6] This number exceeds what has been deemed by some scholars as necessary to achieve both 'code saturation' (i.e. adequate identification of the range of thematic issues) and 'meaning saturation' (i.e. adequate textured understanding of the issues).[7] Eleven of the participants were located in Scotland; the remainder were located in England. The average interview time was 65 minutes (ranging from 27 minutes to 99 minutes). I sought and obtained written consent (via email) and verbal consent (prior to the interview commencing) from each interview participant. Table A1.2 lists attributes of each of the interviews. As the chapters of this book indicate, I refer to each interview participant as P1, P2, and so on.

Interview Guides

As these interviews were semi-structured, two interview guides were designed, one for REC members (including Chairs and Managers) and another for the regulators at the HRA and Scientific Officers. The interview guides were formulated based on findings from the document analysis conducted in 2015 and were influenced by an anthropology of

---

[6]   Several of these participants emphasized to me that they were speaking in their individual capacity and not on behalf of their organization.

[7]   Monique Hennink and others, 'Code Saturation Versus Moneaning Saturation: How Many Interviews Are Enough?' (2017) 27 Qualitative Health Research 591.

Table A1.2   Attributes of interviews and interview participants

Interview participant ('P#')	Location of interview participant	Role of interview participant	Location of interview
P1	England	Regulator (HRA)	In person
P2	England	Regulator (HRA)	In person
P3	England	REC (Chair)	Skype
P4	England	Regulator (NREAP)	In person
P5	England	REC (member)	Skype
P6	England	REC (member)	Skype
P7	England	REC (Vice Chair)	Skype
P8	England	REC (member)	Skype
P9	England	REC (Vice Chair)	Skype
P10	England	REC (Chair)	Skype
P11	England	REC (Chair)	Skype
P12	Scotland	REC (member)	In person
P13	England	Regulator (HRA)	Skype
P14	England	REC (member)	Skype
P15	England	REC (Manager)	Skype
P16	Scotland	Scientific Officer	In person
P17	England	Regulator (HRA)	Skype
P18	Scotland	REC (member)	Skype
P19	Scotland	REC (member)	Skype
P20	Scotland	REC (member)	Skype
P21	Scotland	REC (member)	Skype
P22	Scotland	REC (member)	Skype
P23	Scotland	Scientific Officer	Skype
P24	Scotland	Scientific Officer	Skype
P25	Scotland	REC (Manager)	Skype
P26	England	Regulator (HRA)	Skype
P27	Scotland	Scientific Officer	Skype
P28	England	Regulator (HRA)	Skype

regulation methodology: many of the questions were crafted to draw out the experiences of REC members and regulators, and to understand the ways in which they themselves affect and are affected by processes of regulation. Though the structure of questioning was consistent (beginning with biographical background and ending with questions about overall satisfaction with the ethics review system), many of the specific questions were modified as the study progressed to iteratively explore themes that appeared to emerge in prior interviews. Likewise, though the interviews were semi-structured, they were also open-ended, leaving participants free to form and express multiple associations with the concepts of 'protection' and 'promotion' and how these twin regulatory demands were seen to be operationalized in everyday practice of RECs, again, if at all.

Regulatory Approvals

Following identification of the RECs I wished to observe and drawing up an initial list of interview participants, I made inquiries with the Research Governance and Quality Assurance Office at the University of Edinburgh concerning the regulatory approvals needed for the empirical research. The Office suggested that I contact one of the Scientific Officers responsible for the RECs in the South East Scotland area (which covers Edinburgh), who could advise on the regulatory approvals needed. The Scientific Officer replied stating that Edinburgh Law School's Research Ethics and Integrity Committee (REIC) would be appropriate and sufficient for ethics approval, and that NHS research ethics approval was unnecessary for my project. The Scientific Officer also informed me that I would need to obtain 'management' approval from the HRA, relevant Health Boards in Scotland, and the CSO since Scotland A REC members are appointed directly by the Scottish Ministers and the CSO runs the RES in Scotland. This necessitated completing the electronic IRAS Application Form (Parts A–D),[8] along with other documents, for review and approval by both the HRA and the Health Boards and CSO in Scotland.

Following the Scientific Officer's confirmation, and with the assistance of the Scientific Officer, I was put in contact with the HRA's Head of RES (England) to begin the process of obtaining HRA management approval to observe the RECs in England and interview individuals. She informed me that she could arrange my observation of REC meetings and interviewing of REC members in England if I let her know which RECs I was interested in; she also suggested that I approach REC members via the REC Chair or Manager, which she also could arrange, and that

---

[8] Integrated Research Application System (IRAS) <www.myresearchproject.org.uk/> accessed 23 October 2019.

ultimately it would be up to the individual REC members to decide whether to participate.

I then submitted a 'Level 2' ethics application form (and related documents, such as consent forms and interview topic guides) to Edinburgh Law School's REIC; approval was received in November 2015. I then drafted the IRAS application in consultation with the point person in the Research Governance and Quality Assurance Office at the University of Edinburgh, who commented on draft versions of the 29-page IRAS NHS R&D application form, and informed me of the relevant materials I would need to include with my submission, including a 'study protocol', interview topic guides, and consent forms. The Research Governance and Quality Assurance Office then signed off on my IRAS form,[9] which enabled me to submit it for review by the HRA and Health Boards. That same day, I received approval from the HRA's Head of RES (England) and the following day, received R&D acknowledgement from NHS Lothian Health Board in Scotland. Shortly thereafter, I received confirmation from the CSO that they had no objection to my approaching NHS RECs in Scotland for the purpose of my project, enabling me to commence the empirical research.

Data Collection and Timing

Data from the interviews were collected at one-off points in 2016, while data from the REC meeting observations were collected at multiple points in 2016 and early 2017.

RECs meet monthly at full committee meetings up to 11 times per year. Knowing that two of the identified RECs had overlapping meeting dates and that I had cross-competing academic commitments in my diary, I aimed to observe at least four meetings for each REC over 2016, though this would come to depend not only on my own schedule, but in the case of Scotland, unforeseen situations such as one of the RECs cancelling a meeting when no new applications were received. This would also depend on the ongoing need of approval from the REC Chairs via the Scientific Officer and REC Managers, which seemed to turn on whether other observers were already scheduled to attend a meeting (a reoccurring issue for the Scotland A REC), and thus eliminating my ability to do so. The concern was that REC Chairs did not want too many observers attending a meeting, which might distract the REC members

---

[9] IRAS ID 194243; Study title: 'The Changing Health Research Regulatory Environment and NHS RECs'. The University of Edinburgh was my project sponsor.

and/or the investigators attending in person. In total, I attended 24 REC meetings. The REC observation schedule is reflected in Table A1.3.

Table A1.3   Number of REC observations in 2016/17

REC	Times observed
REC 1	5
REC 2	6
REC 3	5
REC 4	5
Scotland A REC	3

Before each REC meeting commenced, I would greet the REC Chair and Manager, the latter of whom would sometimes hand me a standard HRA confidentiality agreement form (tailored only to state which REC it applied to), which I was asked to sign and date. (Other times, the REC Manager would email the form for me to sign and return by email in advance of the meeting.) The confidentiality agreement required me, as an 'observer' (a term discussed in the GAfREC and REC SOPs), to agree to treat in complete confidence all information disclosed to me either in the meeting documentation or matters discussed at the meeting. In addition, some of the Chairs would verbally inform each investigator who attended the meeting that I was an observer conducting research on RECs, and give the investigator an opportunity to object to my presence (if there was an objection, I would have been asked to leave the meeting room for the REC's face-to-face discussion with the investigator). No investigator ever objected to my presence; indeed, the most common reaction was one of casual indifference, focused as they were on soon being interrogated by the REC members. This action by the Chairs is recommended (phrased as a 'should') in the SOPs,[10] and indeed, it was not always followed. Some Chairs would never inform investigators of my presence as an observer; others would sometimes inform the first few that would appear at the meeting but then apparently forget my presence as the hours of the meeting progressed.

To ensure that the data were accurate and comprehensive, I audio-recorded the interviews with the permission of each participant. To record

---

[10] REC SOPS para 2.72.

behaviours, actions, and settings of the REC meetings, I wrote fieldnotes on a laptop computer. This was not an extraordinary sight; to reflect the increasing digital nature of ethics review, at each of the REC meetings, at least one member (and often several) would operate from a laptop.

Data Analysis

Digital files of the audio-recorded interviews were immediately uploaded securely and transcribed in intelligent verbatim by a digital audio transcription typing specialist company based in Scotland. Via written agreement, the company agreed to treat all transcribed interviews in confidence. Once the transcribed interviews were completed by the professional transcribers, I would compare the transcription with the audio recording to ensure accuracy. The transcripts and fieldnotes were then anonymized by removing all identifying information that enabled indirect or inferential identification. The audio file of the interviews would then be deleted both from my computer and the company's server within three months from the recording. Once both the interview transcripts and the majority of the fieldnotes were completed, I printed out hard copies of both and put them into binders. Coding was done manually and in multiple stages, with Microsoft Office Spreadsheet and Microsoft Word used as electronic aids (e.g. keeping tabs of codes, development of a systematic and iterative codebook), as I felt I could obtain a deeper connection with the data and see patterns more clearly than I could with qualitative research software, which, though a powerful tool to assist in data analysis, is more prone to overwhelm than enlighten me. Several scholars have noted that simple word processing and spreadsheet applications can be used effectively with qualitative data.[11] During the coding process, I took notes in a memo-style format by writing down words and thoughts I considered could be of use during the data analysis and serve as a reference for potential coding ideas.

The analysis was inductive (i.e. data-driven) in that I coded the data without attempting to fit them into a pre-existing coding frame or analytic pre-conceptions. This is not to say that I coded the data absent any theoretical and epistemological commitments, as anthropology of regulation, elaborated in Chapter 4, is underpinned by theoretical concepts drawn from regulatory theory and anthropology. However, I made a conscious effort to strongly link the identified themes discussed to the

---

[11]   Daniel Meyer and Leanne Avery, 'Excel as a Qualitative Data Analysis Tool' (2009) 21 Field Methods 91; Johnny Saldaña, *The Coding Manual for Qualitative Researchers* (3rd edn, SAGE 2016).

data themselves, rather than casually map or force the data onto any of my theoretical underpinnings or analytic interests in the area.

The data from both the interviews (transcripts) and observations (fieldnotes) were coded using qualitative thematic analysis. Thematic analysis is a popular qualitative analytic method for 'identifying, analysing and reporting patterns (themes) within data. It minimally organises and describes [the] data set in (rich) detail. However, frequently it goes further than this, and interprets various aspects of the research topic.'[12] Several scholars describe thematic analysis as a process for encoding qualitative data, rather than a theoretically informed model for research and analysis.[13] Indeed, thematic analysis is an analytic tool for making sense of the data, whereas anthropology of regulation is underpinned by sensitizing concepts that are brought to bear in the encoding process. The encoding requires explicit 'codes', which are 'a form of shorthand that researchers repeatedly use to identify conceptual reoccurrences and similarities in the patterns in the data',[14] and which are usually situated in a 'codebook', which is the compilation of the codes in a study. A theme is 'a pattern found in the information that at the minimum describes and organizes the possible observations or at the maximum interprets aspects of the phenomenon';[15] it 'captures something important about the data in relation to the research question and represents some level of patterned response or meaning within the data set'.[16] To facilitate coding and the generation (and interpretation) of themes in the data, the empirical investigation was theoretically informed by two key strands of literature that form the theoretical backbone of anthropology of regulation: regulatory theory and liminality.

The process was such that I generated initial codes by comparing each of the transcripts and fieldnotes. I started 'open coding' by reading each transcript and the fieldnotes (collated into five bundles for each observed REC) word by word and line by line. After completion of the open coding, I constructed initial codes that emerged from the text and then coded the remaining transcripts and fieldnotes with those codes. When I

---

[12] Virgina Braun and Victoria Clarke, 'Using Thematic Analysis in Psychology' (2006) 3 Qualitative Research in Psychology 79.

[13] Richard Boyatzis, *Transforming Qualitative Information: Thematic Analysis and Code Development* (SAGE 1998); Greg Guest and others, *Applied Thematic Analysis* (SAGE 2012).

[14] Melanie Birks and Jane Mills, *Grounded Theory: A Practical Guide* (2nd edn, SAGE 2015) 89.

[15] Boyatzis (n 13) 161.

[16] Braun and Clarke (n 12) 82.

encountered data that did not fit into an existing code, I added new codes (the total number of codes exceeded 250). I then grouped the similar codes and placed them into categories. These categories were reorganized into broader, higher order categories, then grouped, revised, and refined, and finally checked to determine whether the categories were mutually exclusive. At this point I formed final categories, identifying subthemes both within and across the categories, which were then organized into main themes.[17] This process of coding using qualitative thematic analysis enabled me to fulfil the goal of anthropology of regulation: to explain and understand the processual nature of regulation and the experiences of regulatory actors who both regulate and are regulated (i.e. how they understand their own actions), thereby providing larger theoretical insight into regulatory processes within a given space and within a given society.

Research Method Limitations, Challenges, and Successes

There are some limitations with my research design. Regarding the research strategy, analysis revealed from an inductive approach is limited in time and space—in my case, broad generalizations from research regarding RECs, the nature of ethics review, or health research regulation are not possible. I can only present themes and concepts that emerged from the data as situated in the locations under study and in the time period in which the data were collected. As Sally Falk Moore says, 'life in society should always be conceived in a time-conscious frame, as in process, as in motion, and as a conglomeration of diverse activities noted at a particular time'.[18] For anthropology of regulation to have methodological integrity and resonance with liminality, attention to time-conscious frames and processes are a sign of strength rather than weakness. Semi-structured interviews are also necessarily limited to capturing a moment in time. This does not mean, however, that the themes and normative findings discussed in this book cannot be abstracted beyond the RECs observed and individuals interviewed, nor that the findings cannot be situated in their larger political, social, and regulatory contexts (which themselves contain past and present stories).

---

[17] This inductive approach is adopted from Ji Young Cho and Eun-Hee Lee, 'Reducing Confusion About Grounded Theory and Qualitative Content Analysis: Similarities and Differences' (2014) 19 The Qualitative Report 1.

[18] Sally Falk Moore, 'An Unusual Career: Considering Political/Legal Orders and Unofficial Parallel Realities' (2015) 11 Annual Review of Law and Social Science 1, 2.

There are limitations to the naturalistic observations. First, I observed only a snippet of what happens in ethics review processes. The full REC meetings that occur monthly are but one of the many activities that RECs perform; for example, I have noted in this book that there is sub-committee work (e.g. Proportionate Review, substantial amendments) conducted 'by correspondence' (i.e. email), and there are multiple documents that circulate among the REC members that I never had access to, the most important of which were the research applications and attendant documents themselves. This limited my ability to understand the intricate details of the discussions during REC meetings; I could only surmise what REC members were talking about for a given research application as I never could see the documents themselves. Second, the observations do not constitute a representative sample of RECs across the UK and may not be reliable as variables cannot be controlled, which also means cause and effect relationships cannot be established (e.g. that the Care Act 2014 and the HRA's regulations *cause* RECs to instantiate research promotion in their practices). I did not perceive any pronounced observer effects, however. This was likely due to the fact that observers are a regular presence at REC meetings and I sat quietly either at a corner of the conference table, or in a chair in the corner of the room, taking notes by hand or on my tablet computer. Occasionally, REC members would make a joking remark to the effect of 'Are you recording that, Edward?', but my impression was that my presence did not impact the style and substance of meeting dynamics.

Reliability with thematic analysis causes some concern as a limitation (particularly for those within a positivist tradition) because of the wide variety of subjective interpretations that arise from the themes, as well as applying themes to large amounts of data (in my case, a daunting corpus of approximately 1000 pages of transcripts and fieldnotes). To increase reliability as much as possible, I monitored themes and code tables throughout the data analysis process through memos and detailed pro-gress tracking. Regarding limitations to the sampling strategy, it may both under- and over-represent particular groups (e.g. RECs and indi-viduals) within the sample. For instance, many of the REC member interviewees were members of the same REC in England; also, I interviewed only two REC Managers and three REC Chairs, which consequently may not provide a comprehensive portrait of these roles. Since the sample of interviewees and RECs was not chosen at random, there is an inherent selection bias such that the samples are unlikely to be representative of the target population of RECs, REC members, and regulators. Again, this can undermine my ability to make generalizations from my sample to RECs and health research regulation at large.

Nonetheless, purposive and snowball sampling afforded me relatively easy access in a short amount of time and yielded significant data that, in my firm belief, addressed the research questions.

One of the challenges anticipated was access to meetings. RECs are notoriously difficult to access for those wishing to make them the object of investigation.[19] Similarly, regulators can be difficult to access and may not speak forthrightly about their views. Yet, few access difficulties were encountered. Though I was expecting the HRA, the CSO, or a specific REC Chair to decline my requests, none did, and on the contrary, all were accommodating. I was particularly surprised at how accommodating the HRA was in both allowing me to speak with employees within the Authority, and also expressing interest in my research project. This is not to say that no challenges were encountered during the course of the empirical studies. Gaining ongoing access to RECs and REC members in Scotland, particularly the Scotland A REC, proved more challenging than I had expected. This was due to the Scientific Officer and REC Chairs acting as first-order gatekeepers, something I had not appreciated until I had largely completed the data collection. It was not unusual for the Scientific Officer or REC Manager to inform me that I could not attend a REC meeting, even if previously agreed, because other observers (including from the Scottish Government) had requested to attend the meeting and they took priority. Though this was a frustrating experience in terms of slightly delaying the period of data collection, overall, it did not impact my research findings. I was able to attend each REC several times and gain access to the individual members with whom I wanted to speak.

---

[19]   Such access challenges for empirical investigations of ethics committees are noted, for example, by Will van den Hoonaard, *The Seduction of Ethics: Transforming the Social Sciences* (University of Toronto Press 2011) 10, 39 and Robert Klitzman, *The Ethics Police? The Struggle to Make Human Research Safe* (OUP 2015) 360–61.

Appendix 2: Sample copy of HRA Ethical Review Form[20]

Health Research Authority

Ethical Review Form (Lead Reviewer/REC Member)

The HRA has an established role to promote transparency, largely through RECs and the publication of research summaries

The lead reviewer(s) should complete this form in preparation for the REC meeting. The form may also be used by other REC members. The REC Chair should use the headings as an *aide memoire* to structure the discussion at the meeting. If paper copies of this form are completed, they should be given to the REC Manager who will arrange for them to be destroyed once the minutes of the meeting have been ratified.

Meeting Date:

IRAS Project ID/ REC Reference Number:

Study Title:

Brief overview of study (optional depending on REC practice)

---

[20]   Health Research Authority, 'Guidance and Policy for REC Members' <www.hra.nhs.uk/about-us/committees-and-services/res-and-recs/research-ethics-committee-members-area/guidance-and-policy-for-rec-members/> accessed 23 October 2019. Published with permission from the Health Research Authority.

1. Social or scientific value; scientific design and conduct of the study (IRAS A6, A7-14, A57-62, A75) Evaluation of a treatment, intervention, or theory that will improve health and well-being or increase knowledge. RECs should take into account the public interest in reliable evidence affecting health and social care.

Use of accepted scientific principles and methods, including statistical techniques, to produce reliable and valid data. Is the research question important and necessary? Is the research design and proposed statistical analysis able to answer the question? Is there equipoise; are all treatment arms viable options for the research participants?

- **Public Involvement** – Is there involvement of patients, service users or the public, in the design, management, and undertaking of the research? (IRAS A14-1)

Comments/issues for discussion:

2. Recruitment arrangements and access to health information, and fair research participant selection (IRAS A16, A17-1, A17-2, A 27-29, A46, A47). Inclusion and exclusion of potential research participants. The benefits and risks of research should be distributed fairly among all social groups and classes, taking particular account of age, disability, gender, race, religion or belief and sexual orientation, as well as economic status and culture. How are research participants recruited? How does participation impact on their clinical care? Are compensation arrangements in place? Insurance (negligent/ non-negligent harm).

Comments/issues for discussion:

3. Favourable risk benefit ratio; anticipated benefits/risks for research participants (present and future) (IRAS A18-25 & part B3 if radiation, and part B5 if samples). Minimization of risks. Is there evidence of the consideration of any benefits/risk for individual research participants, past/future research participants, including whether the risk/intervention is sufficiently minimal to require no SSA? Are benefits/risk clearly identified for the research participant? Have steps been taken to minimize or eliminate the risk, hazards, discomfort, and distress and enhancement of potential benefits; risks to the research participant are proportionate to the benefits to the research participant and society? Is the balance between risk and benefit equitable?

Comments/issues for discussion:

---

4. Care and protection of research participants; respect for potential and enrolled research participants' welfare & dignity (IRAS A25, A50-53, A76, A77).
* permitting withdrawal from the research
* protecting privacy through confidentiality
* informing participants of newly discovered risks or benefits
* informing participants of results of research
* maintaining welfare of participants
* what will happen at the end of the study
* provision of appropriate indemnity and insurance

Trial Registration (IRAS A50) **Are trial registration arrangements in place?** (note, this is a condition of the favourable opinion, and is mandatory for the first four categories of study on IRAS)

Data protection & research participant's confidentiality (IRAS A36-43)
Where and how (anonymised/coded) and for how long will data be stored? What purpose will be served by the data? Who will access? Are research participants informed that access to their medical notes may be required? Arrangements made to deal with incidental disclosure?

Comments/issues for discussion:

5. Informed consent process and the adequacy and completeness of research participant information (A30 -34, A46, A49 & PIS). Provision of information to research participants about the purpose of the research, its procedures, potential risks, benefits, and alternatives, so that the individual understands this information and can make a voluntary decision whether to enrol and continue to participate. Is the language used clear and understandable to the research participant it is aimed at? Does it include all the procedures as described in the protocol? Have uncertainty and randomisation been explained to the research participant? Is consent taken as part of a process with research participants having adequate time to consider the information, and opportunity to ask questions? Is it clear to what the research participant consents or assents? Is there any inducement or coercion? Are vulnerable research participants involved? Is consent obtained to allow GPs to be informed? *(Is the Welsh version an accurate translation of the given English version? Wales only)*

IRAS A35 – What steps would be taken if a participant lost capacity during the study? Subject to ethical approval, tissue samples and data already collected may be retained in identifiable form and used in the research provided that properly informed and expressed consent for this was given *prior to the onset of incapacity.*

If the applicant states that the participant would remain in the study following the loss of capacity and would undergo further interventions and procedures (including the collection of new samples and/or personal data) this would constitute "intrusive research" for the purposes of the Mental Capacity Act 2005 in England and Wales and would require approval under section 30 of the Act. In Scotland, approval would be required under section 51 of the Adults with Incapacity (Scotland) Act 2000. In Northern Ireland, the common law requirements would apply.

Comments/issues for discussion:

---

6. Suitability of the applicant and supporting staff (investigator CV & IRAS question A47, A48) Are the applicant and supporting staff suitably qualified and do they have suitable experience relevant to the proposed research? Medical research involving human subjects must be conducted only by individuals with the appropriate scientific training and qualifications. Research on patients or healthy volunteers requires the supervision of a competent and appropriately qualified physician or other health care professional. Are the local facilities and arrangements suitable? Have community issues been considered? Have any conflicts of interest been considered?

Comments/issues for discussion:

7. Independent review (IRAS A54-56) Review of the design of the research trial, its proposed research participant population, and risk-benefit ratio by individuals unaffiliated with the research. The REC may be satisfied with credible assurances that the research has an identified sponsor and that it takes account of appropriate scientific peer review.

Comments/issues for discussion:

8. Suitability of supporting information E.g. GP letter, interview schedules, questionnaires, lone working policies etc.

Comments/issues for discussion:

9. Other general comments: E.g. missing information / typographical errors / application errors.

10. Consider and confirm the suitability of the summary of the study (IRAS A6-1). This summary will be published on the HRA website in this format together with the summary of the REC's ethical opinion.

Confirmed satisfactory

Changes requested:

Index